D0503021

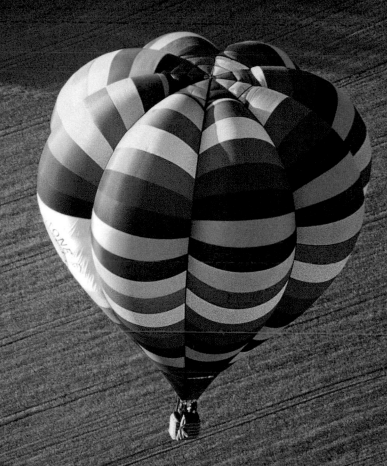

Hawkes' Eye View
BRITISH ISLES
JASON HAWKES

AA

Photographer: Jason Hawkes
Author: Mike Gerrard
Managing Editor: Isla Love
Senior Designer: Kat Mead
Picture Library Manager: Liz Allen
Image retouching: Michael Moody
Production: Stephanie Allen

Produced by AA Publishing

ISBN-10: 0-7495-5226-3
ISBN-13: 978-0-7495-5226-8

ISBN-10: 0-7495-5537-5
ISBN-13: 978-0-7495-5537-5

Published by AA Publishing (a trading name of Automobile Association
Developments Limited, whose registered office is Fanum House,
Basing View, Basingstoke RG21 4EA; registered number 1878835).

A03256

The contents of this book are believed correct at the time of printing. Nevertheless,
the publisher cannot be held responsible for any errors or omissions or for changes
in the details given in this book or for the consequences of any reliance on the
information provided by the same. This does not affect your statutory rights.

Colour separation by MRM Graphics Limited, Winslow
Printed in Dubai by Oriental Press

« **PREVIOUS**
Hot Air Ballooning, Hampshire
In 1766 when British scientist Henry Cavendish
isolated hydrogen, he suggested it could be used
to raise objects from the ground. It wasn't long
before the Montgolfier brothers sent some farm
animals into the sky, suspended under a balloon
filled with hot air. Today you can see balloons on
English summer days, floating gently in the sky to
give a new perspective on the British Isles.

Hawkes' Eye View

BRITISH ISLES

JASON HAWKES

AA

INTRODUCTION

I started out as an aerial photographer back in 1991. Having studied photography for three years and assisted various fashion and still life photographers, I happened to go flying in a microlight one weekend and caught the flying bug. A few weeks after my first flight, a couple of friends and I purchased a microlight and I spent a few months sitting in the back building up a portfolio of work.

A year later I traded in microlights for helicopters and launched my career by concentrating solely on shooting images from the air. Since then, I've hung out of microlights from 200 feet, taken photos whilst wearing oxygen masks from planes flying at 20,000 feet, spent hours alone, but for the pilot, flying over rigs in Norway in the back of a huge helicopter that could hold 24 people, flown down streets in New York below the height of surrounding buildings, travelled across the desert in Morocco in a balloon, almost lost a helicopter after inadvisably landing on a sandbank a mile out to sea, and even spent the night in a police cell under suspicion of stealing a helicopter!

I generally feel completely safe when flying but I have had a couple of flights that I thought might be my last. There was an incredibly near miss while I was shooting a book in South Carolina – even the pilot was pretty shaken up about it. As for the other aircraft, well, he didn't even see us. A year or so after that I was lucky enough to be commissioned by the British Council in Colombia to mount a travelling exhibition of my work. My wife and I were invited across and spent a few days in Medellín, where I took the opportunity of chartering a local pilot to go and take some photographs. We took off and spent the first fifteen minutes literally being tossed around the sky. The pilot sat there nonchalantly, being used to such turbulence coming down off the surrounding mountains, but I can honestly say I was terrified. After the most nerve-racking flight I have ever experienced, we eventually climbed up over the mountains into smoother air. Needless to say I didn't try that again.

All in all, I've never regretted my career choice. No two flights or jobs are the same, and I've seen countries from a perspective that few people get to experience. However, as always with these things there is a flip side. I now spend days processing out digital images, scanning, captioning and generally sitting in front of a couple of computer monitors – just like most people seem to these days. I shoot digitally using mainly Hasselblad cameras attached to gyro stabilizing mounts. This usually necessitates working with an assistant to check the images on a laptop as they are being shot.

I fly with the door of the helicopter off, harnessed to a hard point in the machine for safety and wearing headsets to talk to and direct the pilot to a suitable position to capture the right image. We fly from all types of helicopters using the larger twin-engined machines over London and heavily built up areas and smaller 4-seaters elsewhere. Heights vary from around 400 feet up to generally no more than 2,000 feet. Flying around in tight circles with the pilot banking the helicopter right over onto its side does make you feel sick after a while. You have to spend most of the time looking through the viewfinder or making notes, and on more than one occasion I've wished to be back on the ground.

Flying around the UK shooting images for books on Britain involves a fair amount of preparation. I usually have a tight shoot list in place but inevitably we vary from our course as I see interesting manmade and natural patterns that you could never be aware of from the ground. I talk to the pilot every evening when shooting, to plan the next day, and often we might stay away for a few days at a time, landing at suitable hotels along the way for the night.

Britain's weather is amazingly unpredictable and often leads to days sitting in aerodromes or quick dashes avoiding cloudbanks to get back on the ground or to refuel. On more than one occasion I have sat in the helicopter in the middle of nowhere after being grounded by bad visibility, which I suppose I should be grateful for really, as you certainly could not do that in a plane.

I hope you enjoy looking at the images in this book as much as I enjoyed flying around the country taking them. It's easy to become jaded by most of one's job, but after a flight somewhere particularly interesting, I always try and remember that being able to look down from above is a privileged view to have.

Jason Hawkes
www.jasonhawkes.com

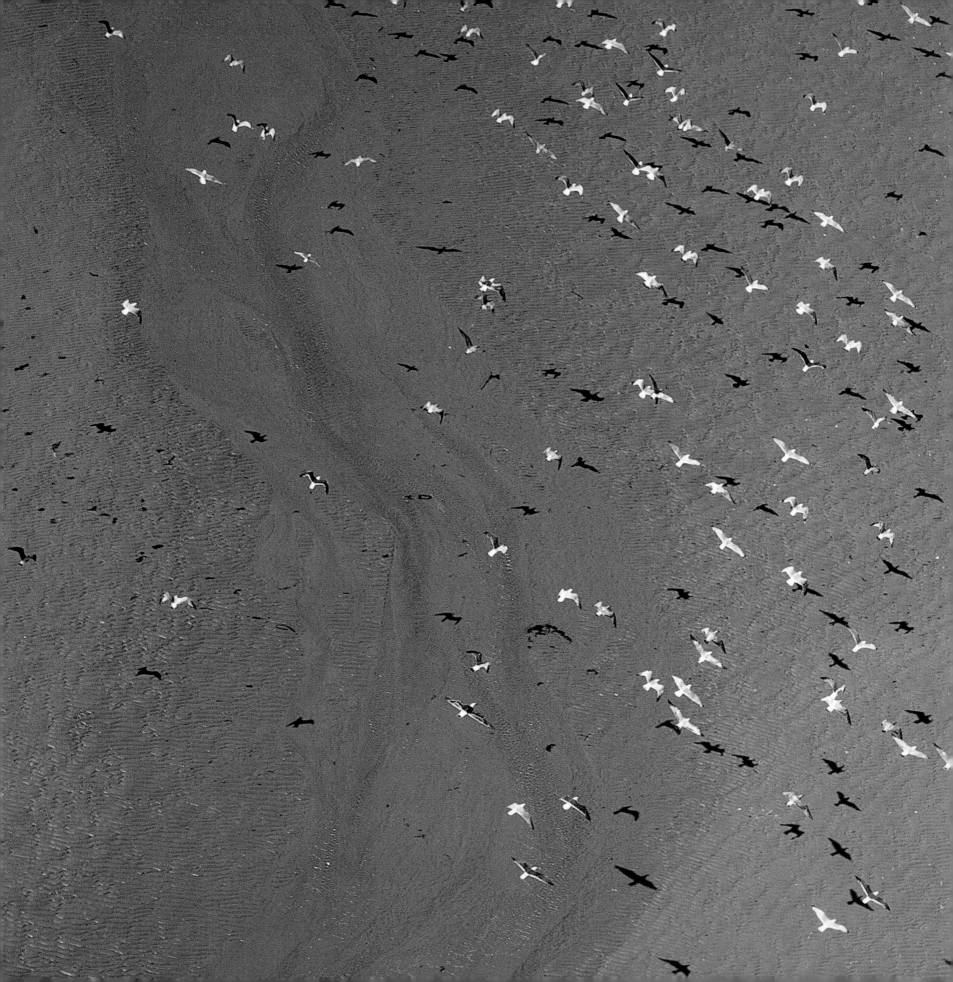

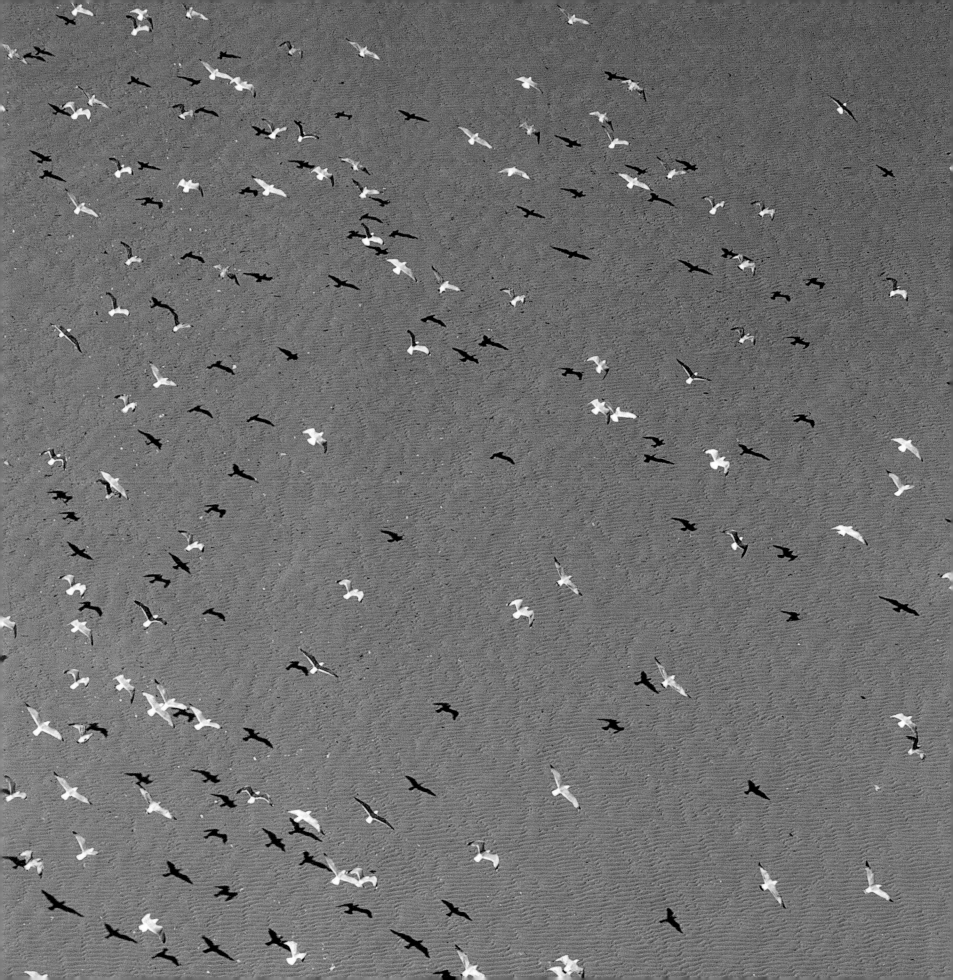

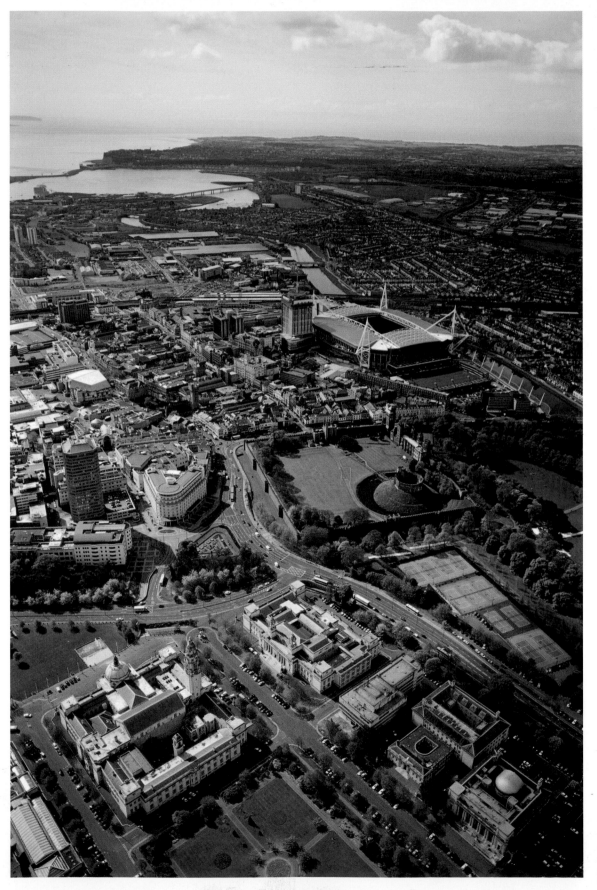

« PREVIOUS

Birds flying over the beach, Norfolk

The North Norfolk coast is one of Britain's greatest bird watching centres, a magnet for the nation's ornithologists. Tens of thousands of gulls and waders make the shore their home, a spectacular sight when they take flight and swoop over the sandy beaches.

> RIGHT

Cardiff, Glamorgan

Cardiff's Millennium Stadium now dominates the city's skyline even more than Cardiff Castle (now barely visible in front of it) once did. Past the stadium flows the River Taff, from which the nickname for a Welshman, Taffy, comes. The river once took Wales's black gold, the coal from its mines, down to Cardiff Bay from where it was shipped around the world, bringing wealth to the Welsh capital.

> OPPOSITE

A tractor cuts the grasses, Dorset

Looking like a toy, a tractor cuts the lush grass in this Dorset field. The ancient West Saxon kingdom of Wessex once stretched from Southwark in London to Land's End, but is more associated now with rural Dorset, where author Thomas Hardy lived and set novels like *Jude the Obscure*.

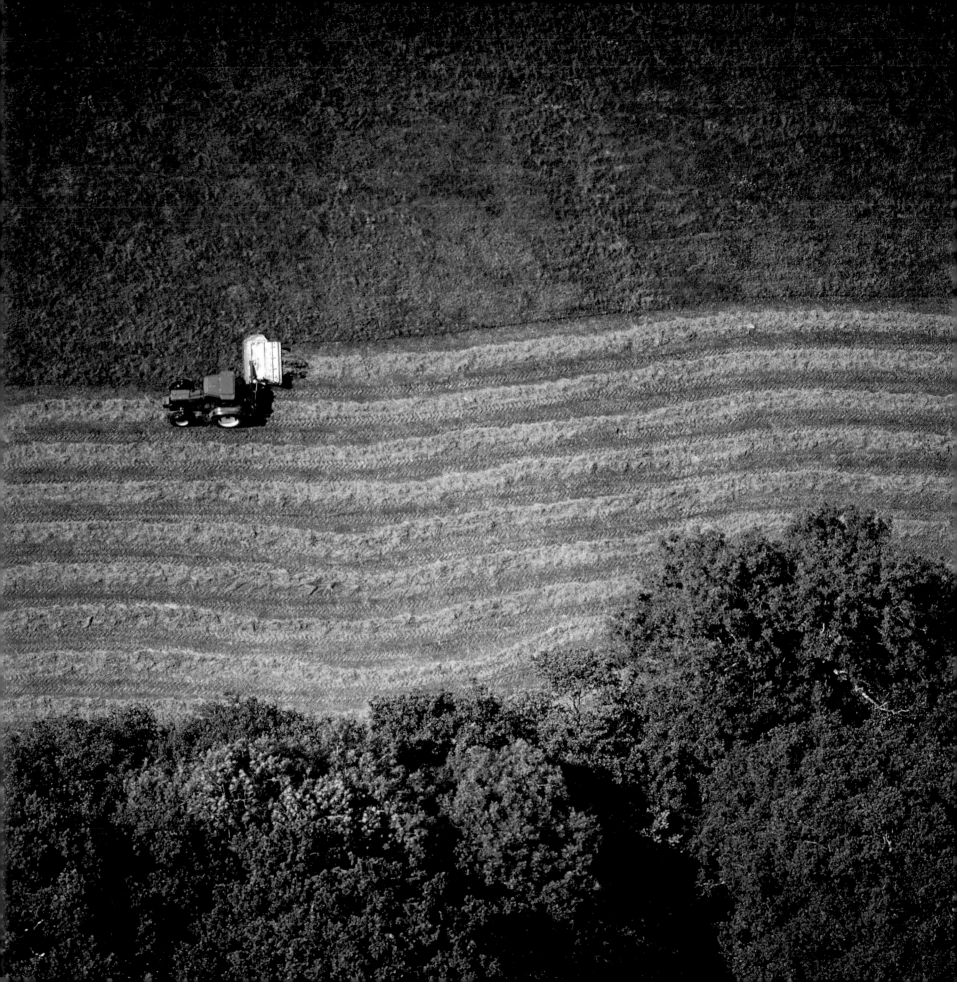

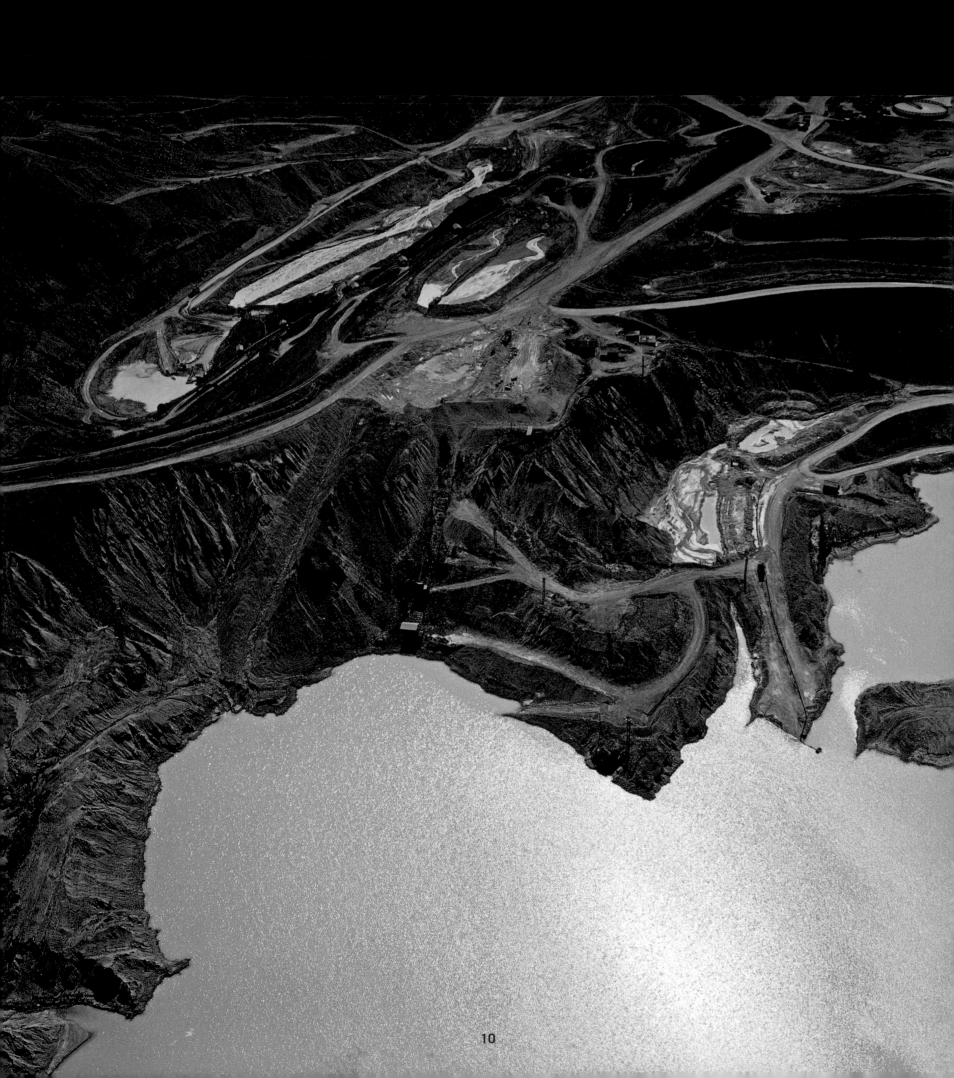

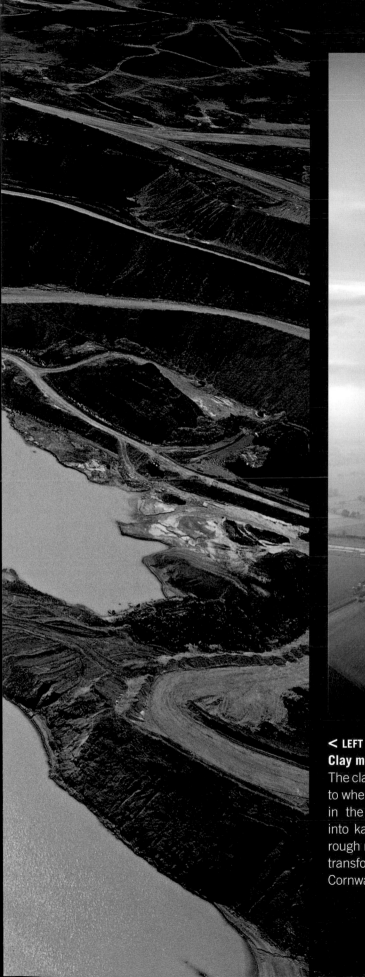

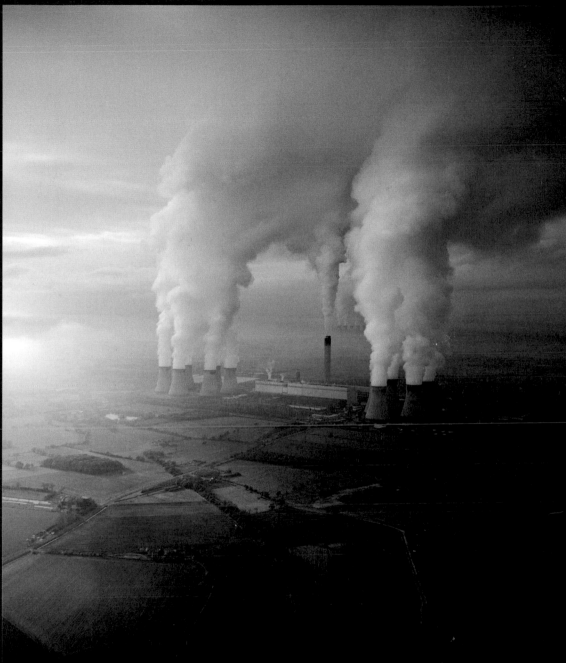

< LEFT
Clay mine, Cornwall

The clay pits of Cornwall go back 300 million years, to when the area was granite moorland. A mineral in the land, white felspar, slowly decomposed into kaolinite, a vital element in china clay. The rough reality of this clay pit contrasts well with the transformation that has taken place elsewhere in Cornwall, for example at the Eden Project.

^ ABOVE
Drax Power Station, Yorkshire

Looking like a giant throwback to the days of the Industrial Revolution, the Drax Power Station near Selby in North Yorkshire dates from the 1970s. It may not be in the running for any prizes for beauty, but it is an impressive piece of modern industrial architecture, being the largest, cleanest and most efficient coal-fired power station in Britain. This power station alone supplies about 7 percent of the UK's electricity.

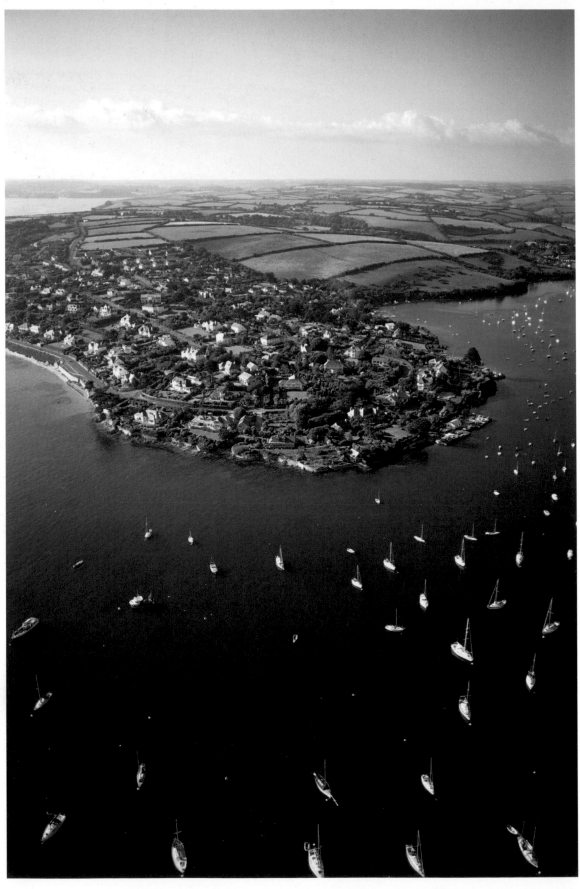

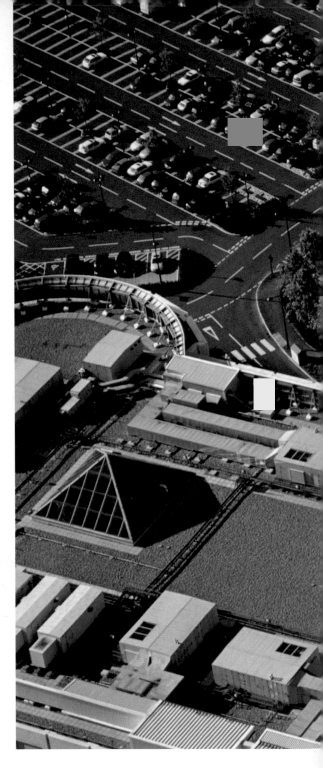

< LEFT
Carrick Roads Estuary, Cornwall
The Carrick Roads Estuary in Cornwall is part of Falmouth Harbour, the third largest natural harbour in the world. Carrick Roads was once a dry valley, until the sea levels rose with the melting waters of the Ice Age, and the valley flooded to create this picturesque little estuary.

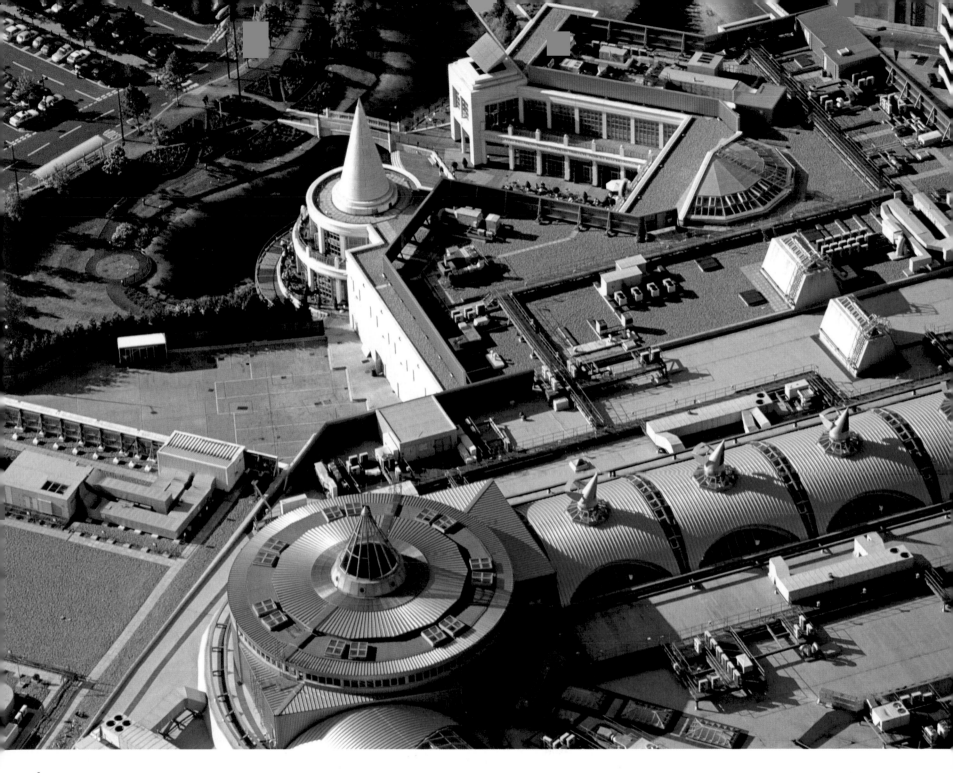

^ ABOVE

Bluewater shopping centre, Kent

Napoleon once allegedly described Britain as a nation of shopkeepers. Perhaps he was right. The Bluewater shopping centre, just off the M25 motorway in Kent, was the biggest shopping mall in Europe when it opened in 1999. This distinction was taken from it in 2004 by another English shopping centre, the MetroCentre in Gateshead.

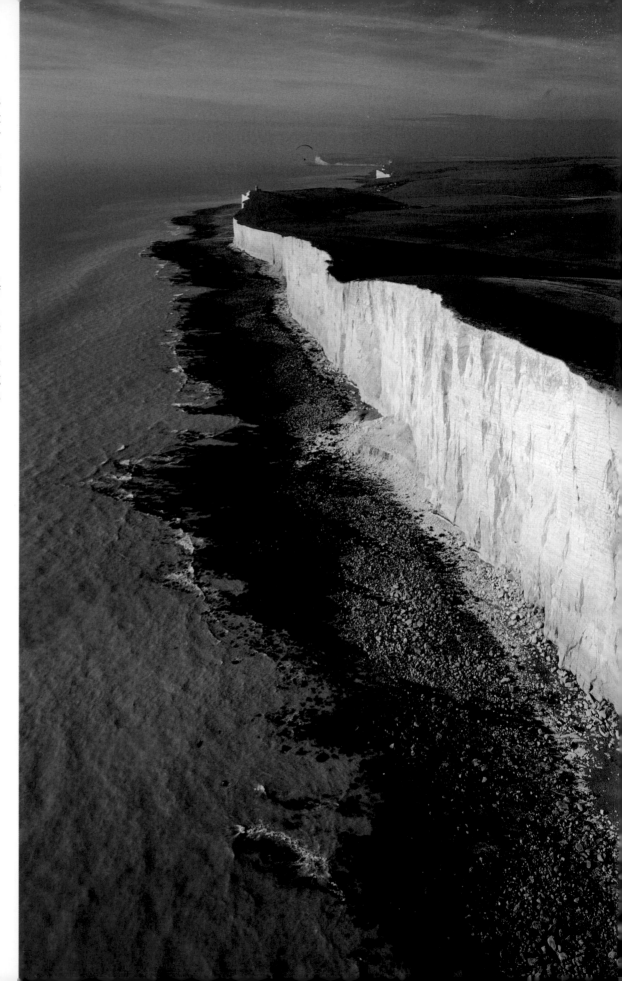

> RIGHT

Beachy Head, East Sussex

The White Cliffs of Dover may be the most famous chalk cliffs in England, but Beachy Head in East Sussex has the highest cliffs in Britain. At their peak they tower 530 feet (162m) above the sea, and their name is nothing to do with any beach below. It is a corruption of the French name Beauchef, or Beautiful Headland.

> OPPOSITE

Cambridge, Cambridgeshire

It may lack the grace of a Venetian gondola, but the English punt is just as much a part of the tourist scene in a handful of English towns, including Cambridge. These pleasure punts were not introduced to Cambridge until the early 1900s, about 40 years after they were first tried out on the River Thames. They evolved from simple fishing or cargo boats, but these days their only cargo is the visiting tourist or university student.

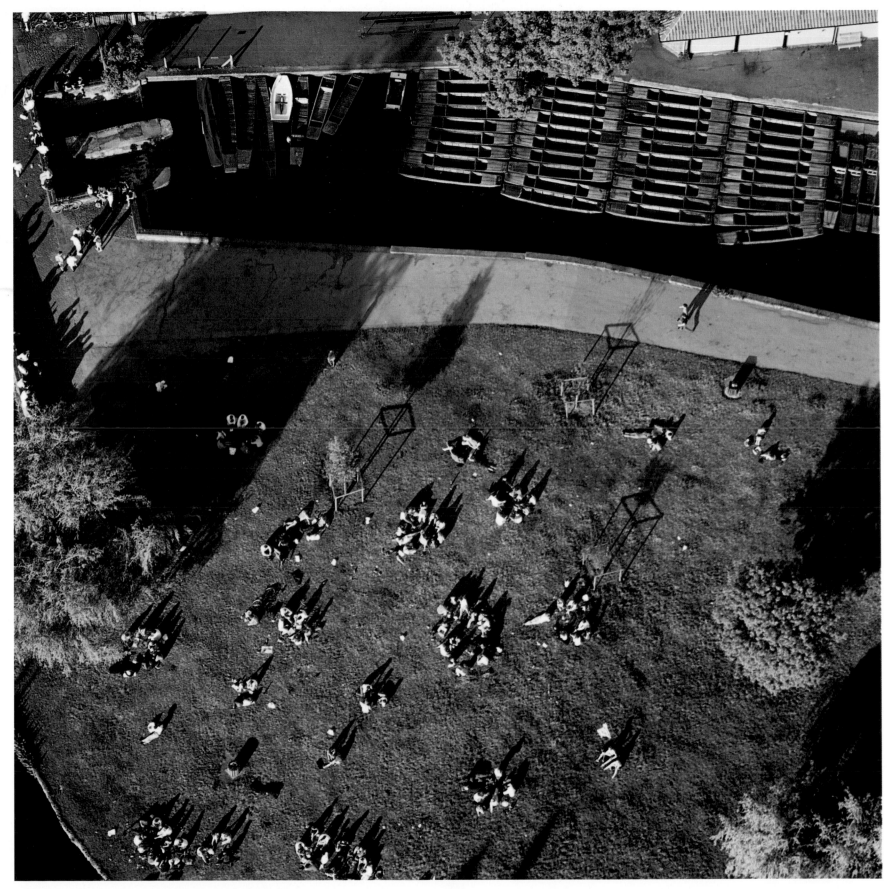

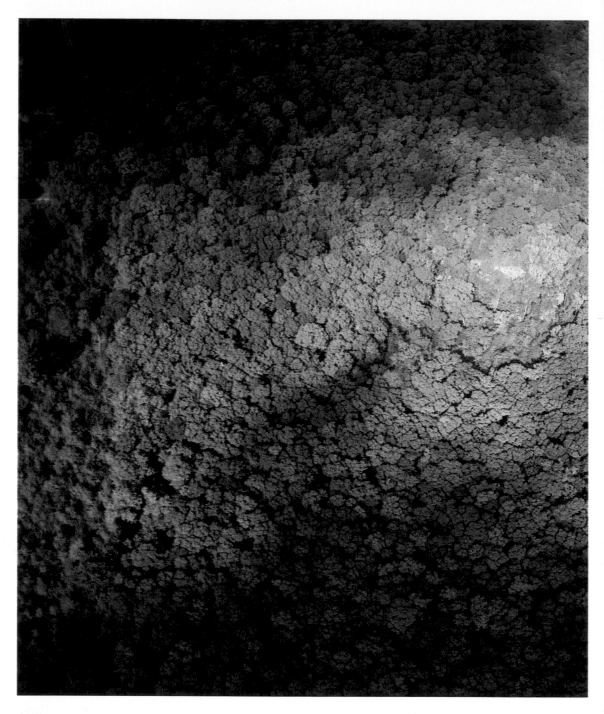

^ ABOVE
Lyme Regis, Dorset

Looking from the air a little like a giant head of broccoli, this stretch of woodland is at Lyme Regis, in Dorset. It reminds us that much of England was thick woodland like this, back when the town of Lyme was mentioned in the Domesday Book of 1086. The addition of Regis to the name came later, in 1284, when King Edward I granted the town a Royal Charter.

> RIGHT
Sand dune, Western Isles

This surreal sand dune with the ink and turquoise water rolling towards it, looks as if it could be in the South Pacific or the Indian Ocean. In fact it is in Scotland's Western Isles. In Britain the very name of the Hebrides conjures up cold and remoteness, but it is a region of dramatic beauty where windsurfers share the seas with whales and dolphins, seals and puffins.

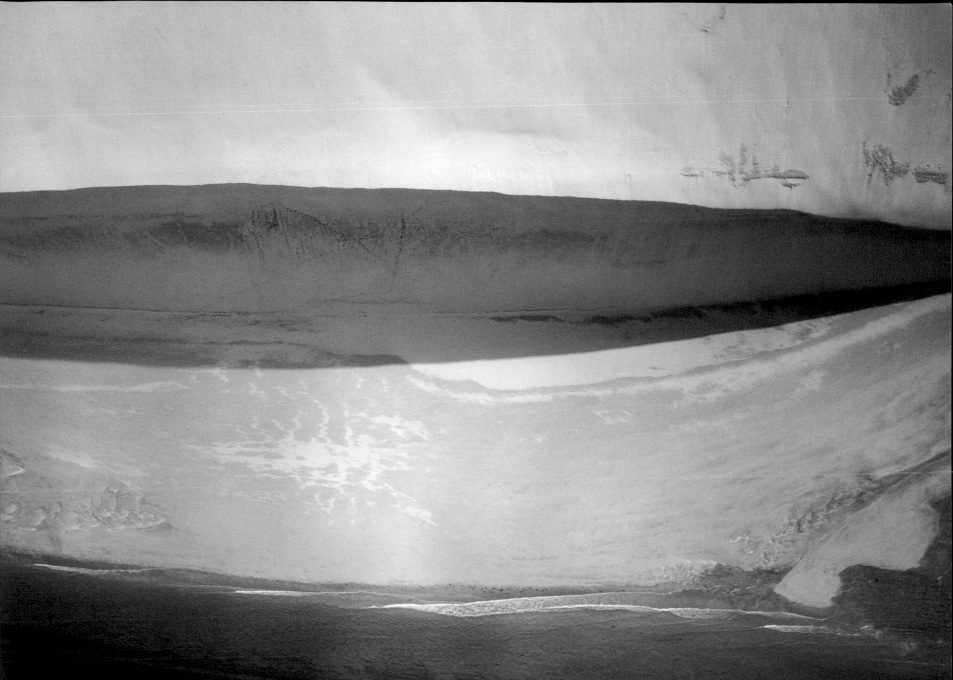

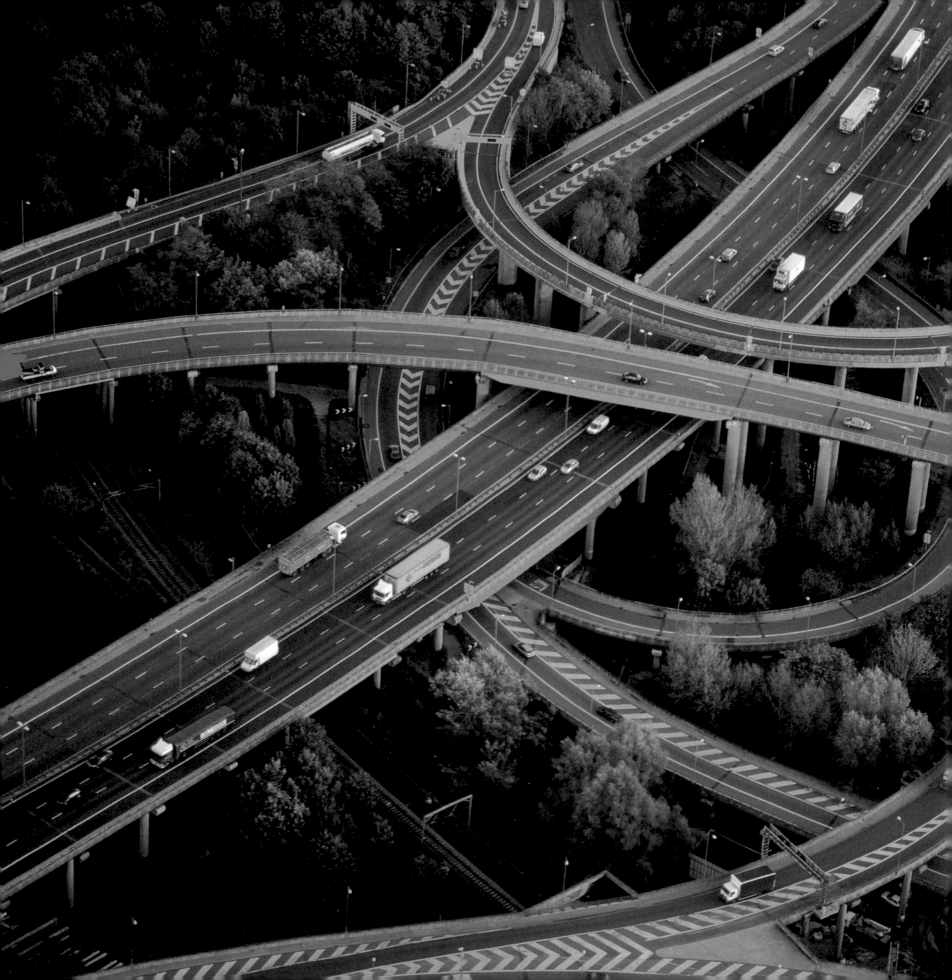

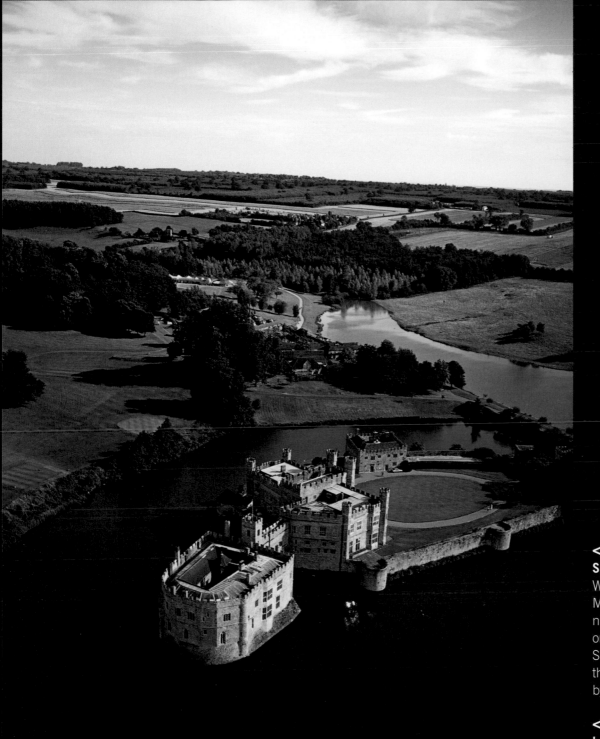

Spaghetti Junction, Birmingham

When the Gravelly Hill Interchange on the
M6 motorway opened in 1972, its immediate
nickname, Spaghetti Junction, seemed highly
original and appropriate. In fact there are many
Spaghetti Junctions throughout the world, and
the British version near Birmingham is quite tame
by comparison – tame but also rather graceful.

< LEFT
Leeds Castle, Kent

A sense of the vast history of England can be
gained from this view of Leeds Castle in Kent.
Parts of the castle go back almost 900 years, to
1119, but even then a house had stood on this
site for another 400 years before that. In the 13th
century it was the royal castle of King Edward I,
and today its doors are open to all to visit.

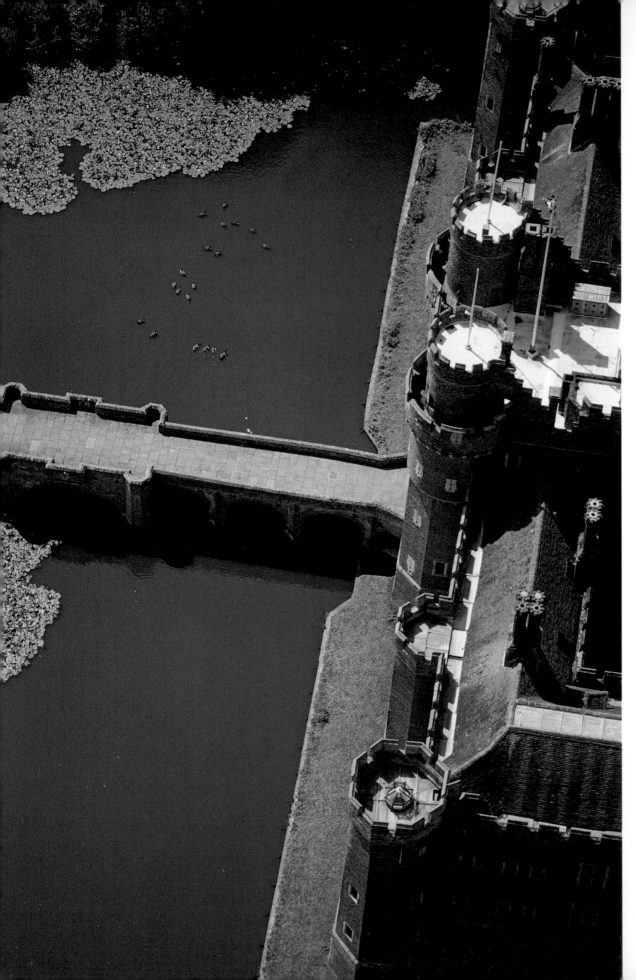

Herstmonceux Castle, East Sussex

Only 12 miles from Hastings where the famous battle took place, Herstmonceux Castle shows the links between this part of England (East Sussex) and France. The Domesday Book mentions a small settlement on this beautiful spot, and the unusual name comes from a later liaison between an Idonea de Herst and a Norman nobleman, Ingelram de Monceaux.

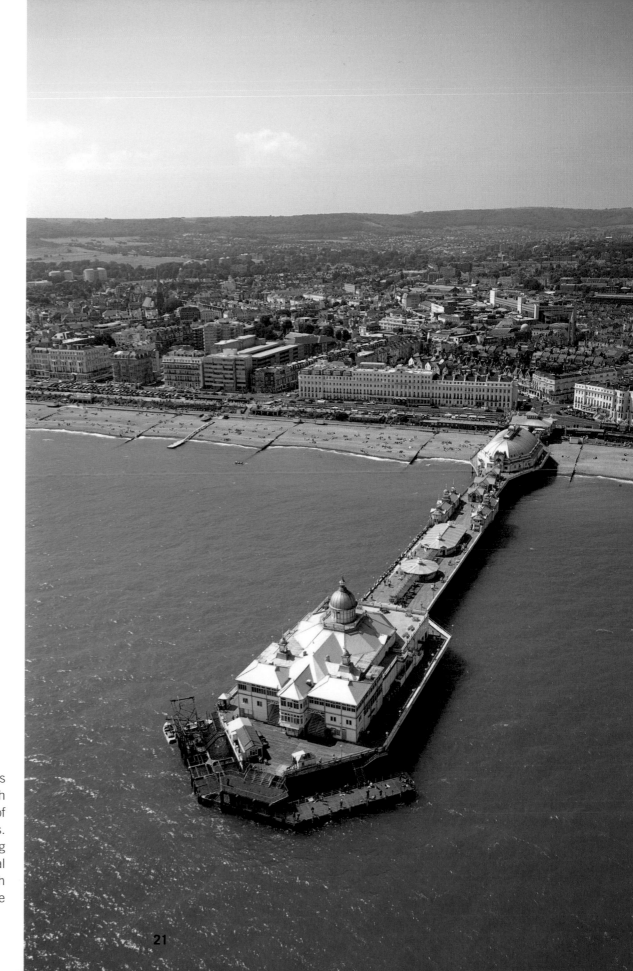

Eastbourne Pier, East Sussex

Eastbourne Pier owes its existence to later invaders of the East Sussex coast, Victorian tourists, though at the entrance to the pier, evidence was found of Eastbourne's much earlier visitors, the Romans. Today the pier is a fine example of a diminishing breed, the English pier, and noted for the annual Birdman Competition, when people launch themselves into the air in attempts to fly. No one has yet made it to France.

THE COAST

According to the CIA, no less, the British Isles has a coastline of 8,673 miles (13,877km). This means that these little islands have more coastline than Mexico, and almost as much as the People's Republic of China. Writers including Paul Theroux (in *The Kingdom by the Sea*) have walked the coastline in an attempt to get a sense of the state of the nations, and great walkers such as Alfred Wainwright and Christopher Somerville have felt compelled to tramp from coast to coast across England or down the length of Ireland, going from sea to shining sea.

The huge success of the recent BBC TV series, Coast, which has spawned books, DVDs and a magazine, shows the fascination people have with Britain's coastline, and its endless diversity. On the coast you can find nuclear power stations as well as absolute emptiness; isolated rocks where thousands of gannets gather to eat and to breed as well as brash resorts like Blackpool where thousands of people go for their annual holiday. There are docks where the world's largest cargo ships come and go, and tiny fishing villages where one man sets out to sea in his bobbing boat.

Britain's coast has symbolic importance too, as it does for any island nation, because it's the line that foreign invaders have to cross to invade the territory. Until the advent of airborne invasions, it was to the sea and not to the skies that Briton looked, for signs of trouble. Winston Churchill's famous rallying speech made to the House of Commons on June 4 1940, when there seemed a real possibility of a German invasion, included the famous phrase, 'We shall fight them on the beaches.' Churchill knew full well the military importance of defending the country's coast, but even more its symbolic importance in the minds of the people. That phrase is remembered as the focal point of the speech, in the same way that Martin Luther King's most famous speech is referred to by just one phrase: 'I have a dream.'

The coast has many other roles to play too. It's a measure of the health of the nation and of the planet. Every part of it tells a story: the state of the sea waters offshore, of the estuaries, the strength of the cliffs, the health – even the very existence of – the mudflats, which look so ordinary but which are so extraordinary. Humans see beaches as places to go and lie in the sun, but they are also vital habitats for wildlife and plants, and a key link in the food chain of our world.

Sea levels are currently rising at the rate of about 3mm a year, less than one eighth of an inch. That may seem a tiny amount but it's 24 centimetres, more than nine inches, in the course of one person's lifetime. One of the measures of our world which we thought was fixed – the sea level – is moving. For those who live in the south and east of England, this has greater significance because here the land is sinking too as the country tilts slightly, with the northern half rising. The east coast is sinking by as much as half a centimetre a year, and to use the same analogy, that's a whole metre during the average person's lifetime.

The significance of changes in the coastline can be appreciated when you realise that over half of Britain's best agricultural lands lie less than 5 metres above sea level. Rising sea levels mean rising river levels and much more flooding. Almost half of Britain's manufacturing industry is also near the coast, along with 10 percent of our nature reserves – not to mention nearly half the population.

Along with the rising sea level, coastal erosion is also a concern. Cliffs are crumbling into the sea, particularly in East Anglia and East Yorkshire. Here there have been prominent cases of houses and land falling into the sea. The area of Holderness in East Yorkshire has the dubious honour of having the fastest eroding coastline in Europe, and it contains a great deal of rich agricultural land. And imagine what a psychological, as well as a physical shock it would be to have a national symbol like the White Cliffs of Dover crumble and fall into the sea.

The White Cliffs have been a potent emblem for Britain for centuries. In the days when there was only sea travel, and Dover was the nearest major port to London, the White Cliffs were the last sight many people had of their homeland, when embarking on long and sometimes dangerous voyages. They were also, of course, the first things that returning travellers saw, a sign that they were home again at last. In addition, the White Cliffs are perfectly placed to look out across the English Channel towards the old enemy, France, as if defying them to invade. If the White Cliffs ever collapse, it will be a soul-searching moment for Britain. And it cannot be ruled out. In 1999 several thousand tonnes of chalk cliffs 70 miles to the west, at that other great promontory, Beachy Head, did fall into the sea, so Dover is not immune.

There are various causes of coastal erosion, mostly natural and unavoidable, like the battering of waves against cliffs made of soft rocks, or the waves redistributing shingle over a period of centuries, where the shingle had acted as a buttress to the cliffs behind them. Occasionally man is the architect of his own destruction, as in the now deserted village of Hallsands in Devon, where the dredging of shingle from the beach in the 1890s to provide building material for a naval dockyard near Plymouth, caused the beach level to fall and the natural sea defences to be weakened. Within only a few years damage was being reported in village houses, and even though the dredging was stopped almost immediately, fifteen years afterwards only one village house remained habitable.

Yet the coast of the British Isles holds far more pleasures than perils and has some spectacular scenery. In England, the South West Coast Path, particularly the stretch through Cornwall, has some of the country's most exhilarating walks. In Ireland there are few more genuinely breathtaking sights than the Cliffs of Moher, or the Kerry coast. In Northern Ireland there's nothing to compare with the North Antrim coast and the Giant's Causeway, a UNESCO World Heritage Site. In Wales, Pembrokeshire has Britain's only National Park that is almost totally coastal, although Scotland is in the process of creating its own coastal and marine National Park, and it isn't surprising that it is proving hard to choose from several areas of outstanding beauty around Scotland's coast.

Britain's coast, then, despite the sections occasionally slipping into the sea, still provides some of the best that Britain has to offer – the ports from which sailors and explorers set out to conquer the world, the dockyards where boats were built, some of its capital cities like Belfast, Dublin and Cardiff, and some of its most remote and rugged landscapes and seascapes. But then, there is almost 9,000 miles of it.

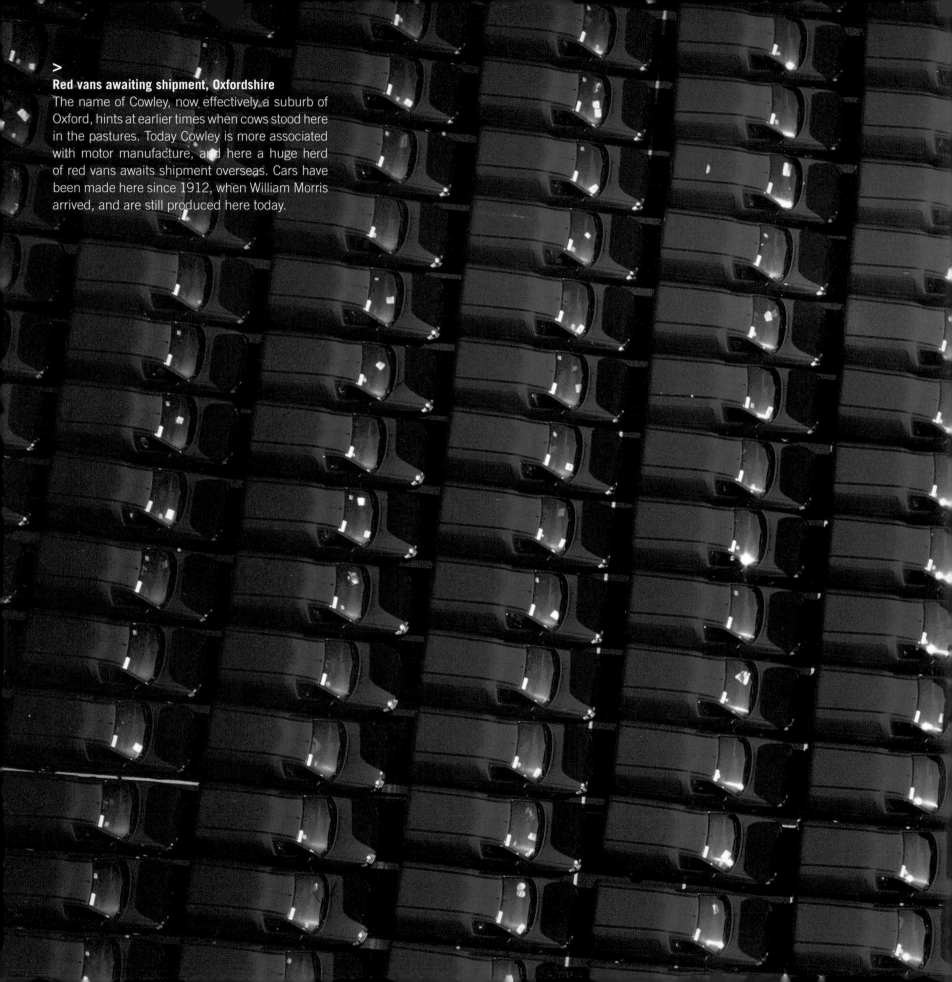

> **Red vans awaiting shipment, Oxfordshire**
The name of Cowley, now effectively a suburb of Oxford, hints at earlier times when cows stood here in the pastures. Today Cowley is more associated with motor manufacture, and here a huge herd of red vans awaits shipment overseas. Cars have been made here since 1912, when William Morris arrived, and are still produced here today.

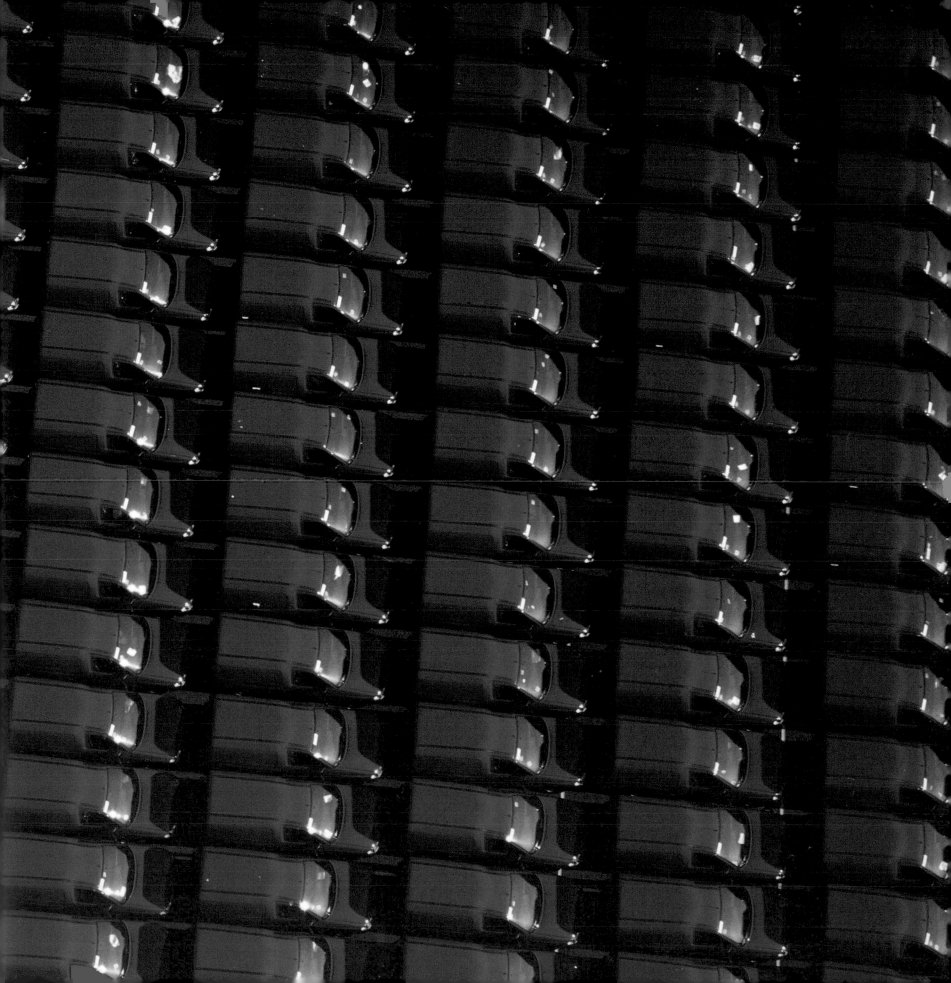

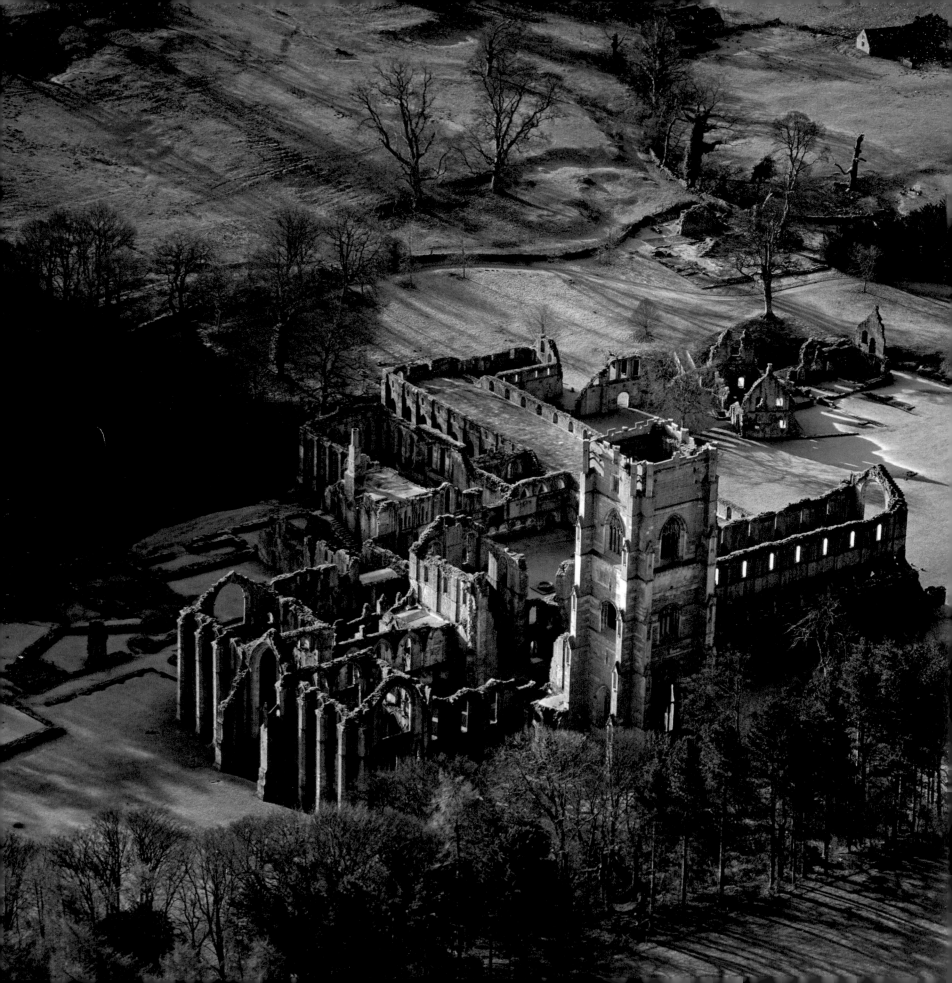

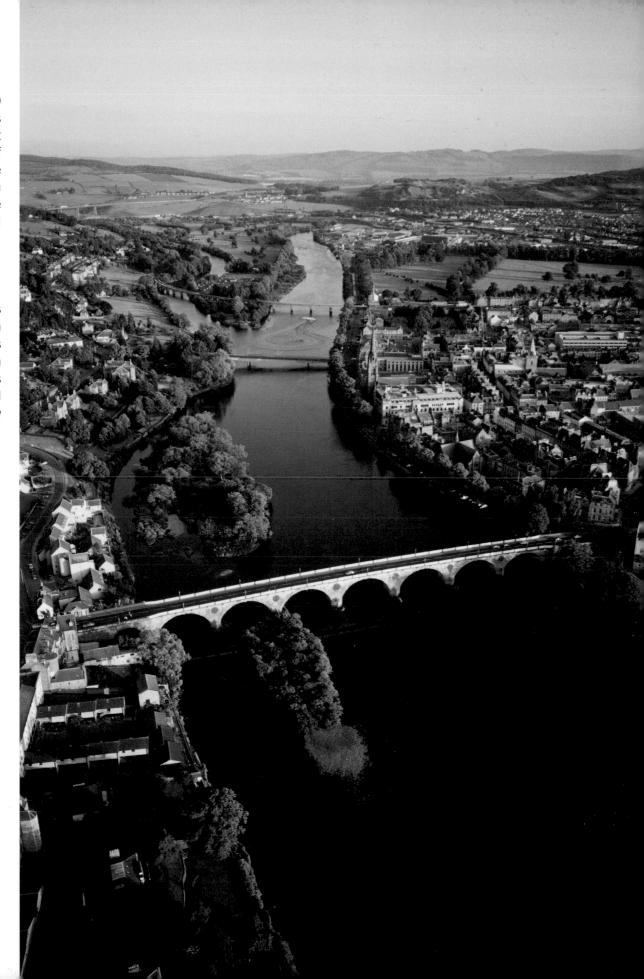

< LEFT

Fountains Abbey, Yorkshire

The magnificent Fountains Abbey is a UNESCO World Heritage Site, and one of those buildings whose history is evoked by its ruins. It is almost possible to hear the early morning chanting of the abbey's Cistercian monks, which would have drifted out over the Yorkshire countryside from the abbey from its founding in 1132 until the Dissolution of the Monasteries by King Henry VIII in 1539.

> RIGHT

Perth, Perthshire

This view shows why Scotland's Perth was always known as the Fair City, until the British government changed the definition of a city as the UK approached the Millennium and Perth no longer met the criteria. This view also shows why we need cities like Perth more than we need bureaucrats, and long may the River Tay flow gently through this still fair place.

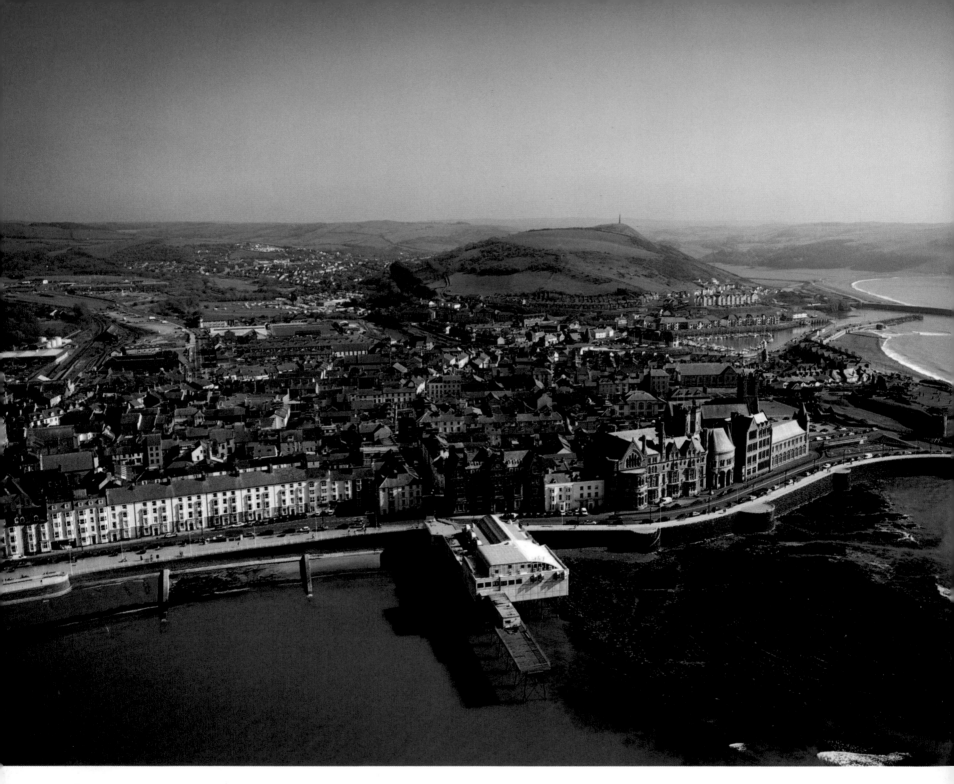

^ ABOVE

Aberystwyth, Ceredigion

Looking out over Cardigan Bay just south of the Snowdonia National Park, Aberystwyth is noted for its student population which almost doubles during term time. It is also the setting for a series of comic crime novels, including memorable titles like *Last Tango in Aberystwyth* by Malcolm Pryce.

> OPPOSITE

Chesterfield, Derbyshire

The tops of the stalls may have changed, and the buildings around, but there has been a market here in Chesterfield on this same spot, since the 1220s. With the nearby indoor Market Hall added in 1857, it makes up one of the largest markets in Britain.

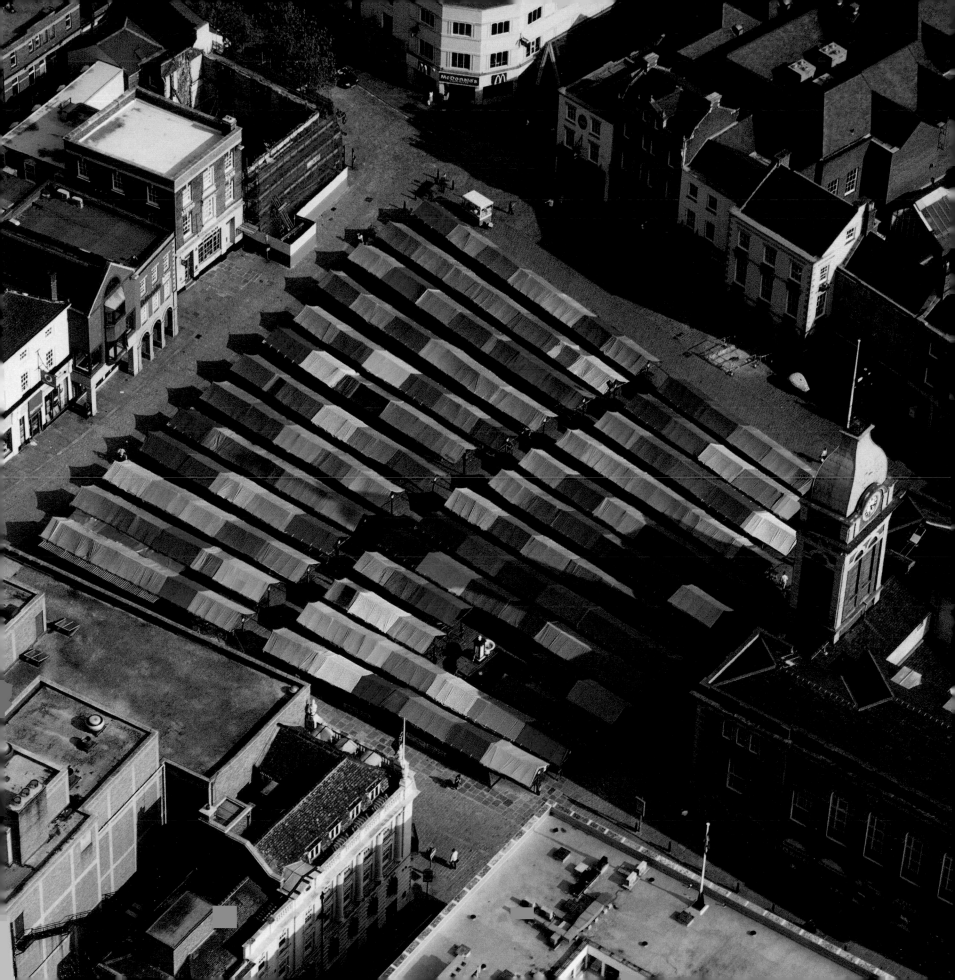

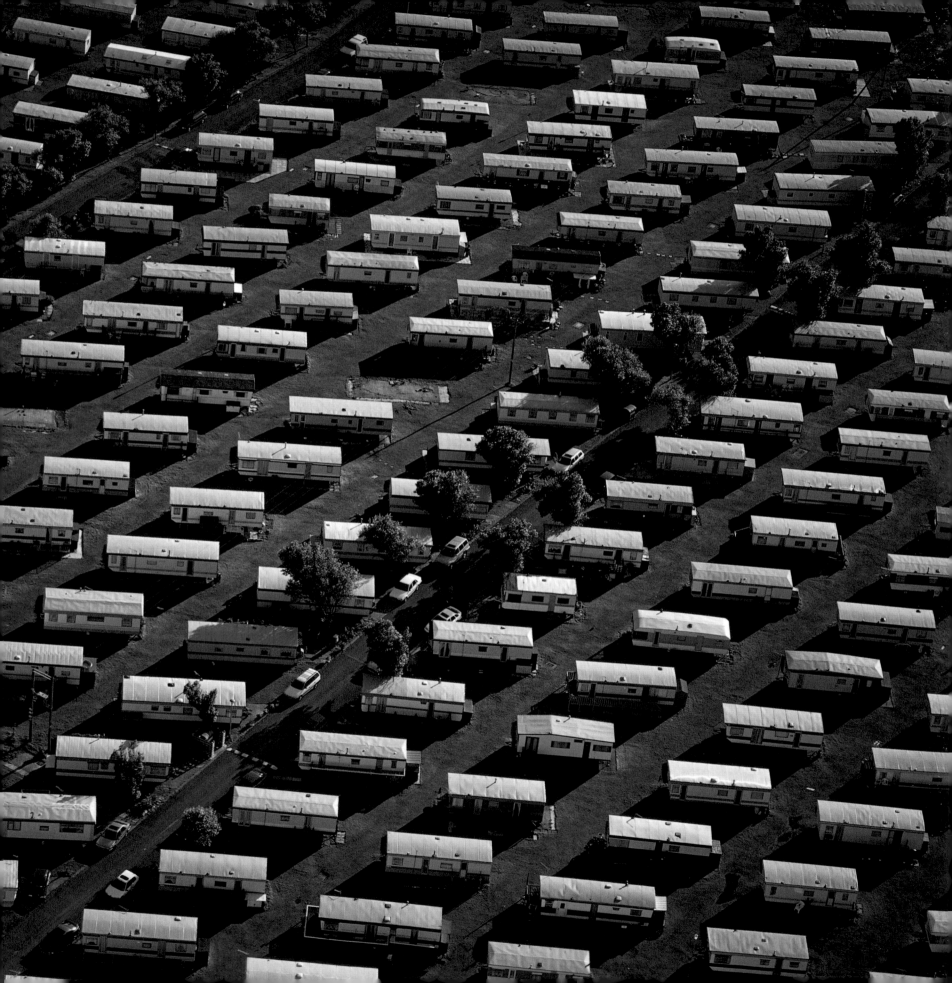

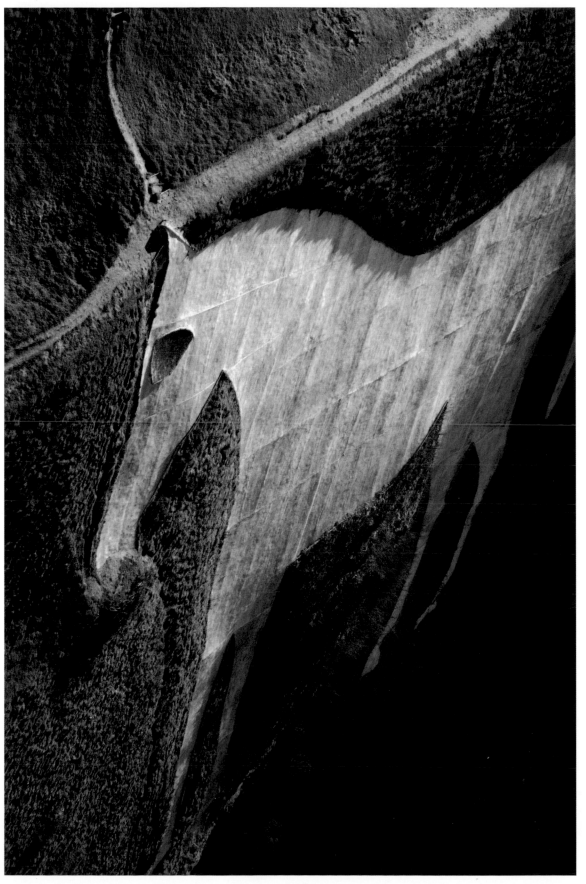

Caravan park, Denbighshire

Seeing them in rows like this at the English seaside, it's easy to forget that the word caravan was originally a Kurdish word which meant a group of people taking a journey together. The caravans would take their night's rest at stopping places called caravanserai. These caravans are going nowhere, but provide inexpensive accommodation to enable everyone to enjoy a holiday by the sea.

< LEFT
Westbury White Horse, Wiltshire

Even though the Westbury White Horse on Salisbury Plain probably only dates back to the 18th century, when there was a trend for such carvings, it still has an air of mystery about it. No-one knows for sure when it appeared. Local legends say it commemorates a battle victory by King Alfred in 878, but those legends also only appeared in the mid-18th century! One thing is certain: the Westbury White Horse is the oldest of the several white horses carved in the chalk hillsides of Wiltshire.

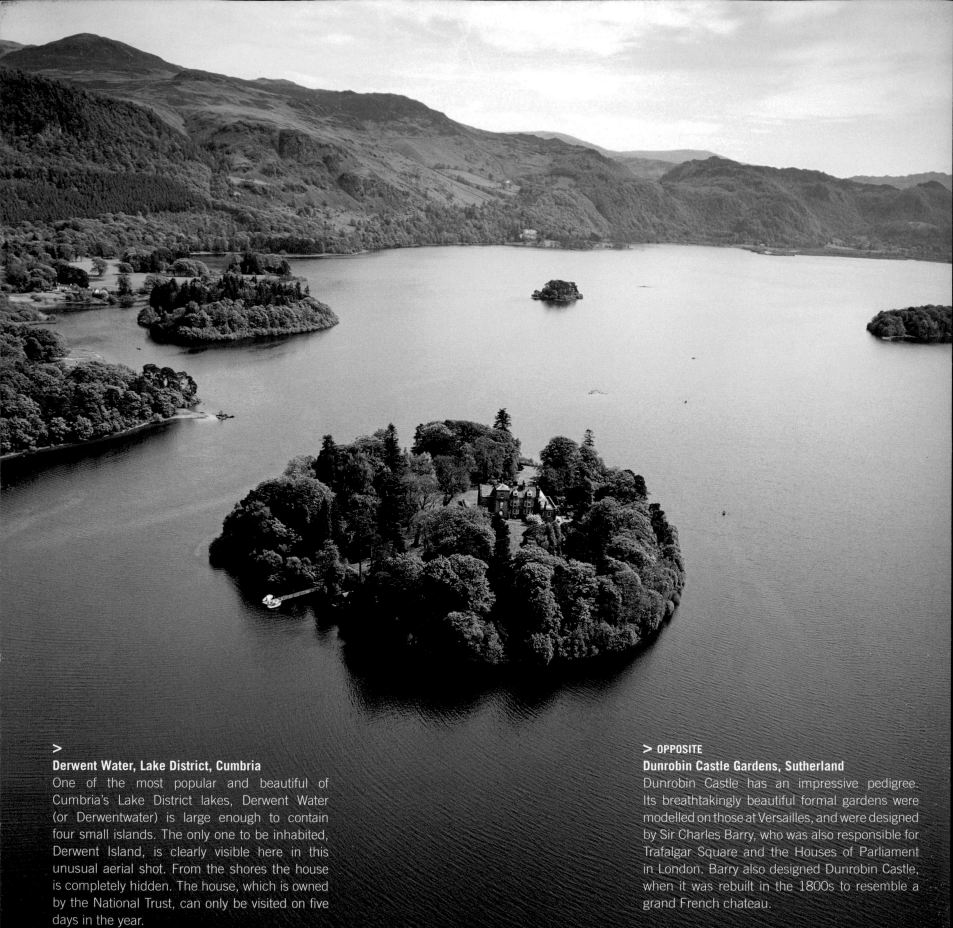

>
Derwent Water, Lake District, Cumbria

One of the most popular and beautiful of Cumbria's Lake District lakes, Derwent Water (or Derwentwater) is large enough to contain four small islands. The only one to be inhabited, Derwent Island, is clearly visible here in this unusual aerial shot. From the shores the house is completely hidden. The house, which is owned by the National Trust, can only be visited on five days in the year.

> OPPOSITE
Dunrobin Castle Gardens, Sutherland

Dunrobin Castle has an impressive pedigree. Its breathtakingly beautiful formal gardens were modelled on those at Versailles, and were designed by Sir Charles Barry, who was also responsible for Trafalgar Square and the Houses of Parliament in London. Barry also designed Dunrobin Castle, when it was rebuilt in the 1800s to resemble a grand French chateau.

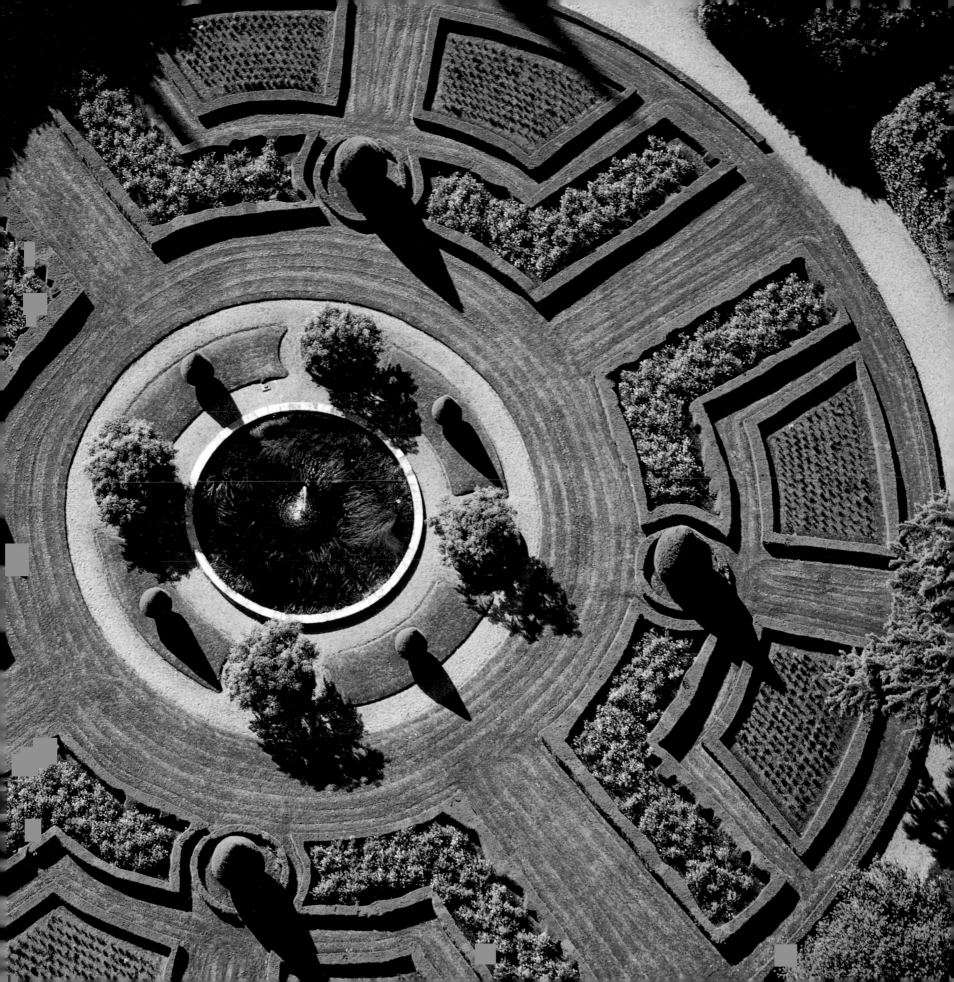

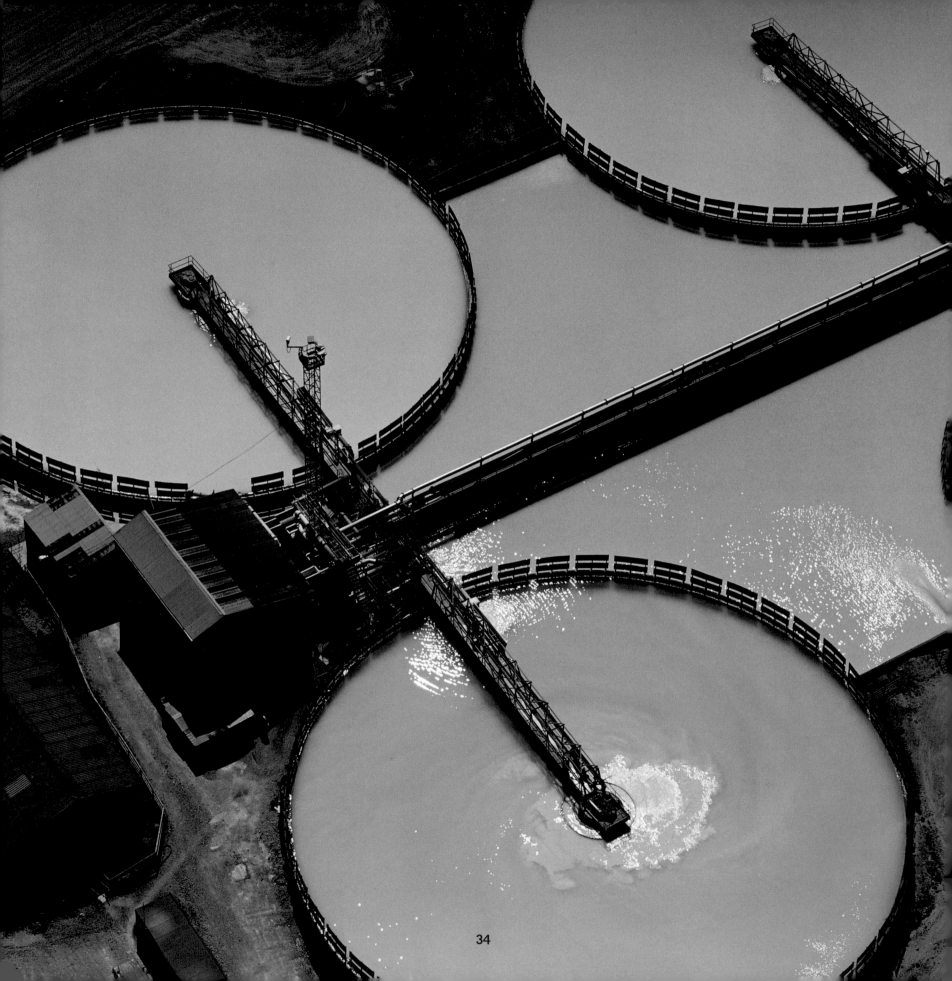

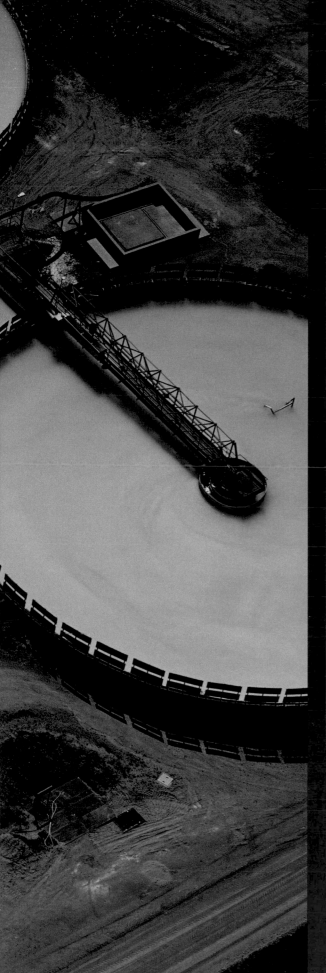

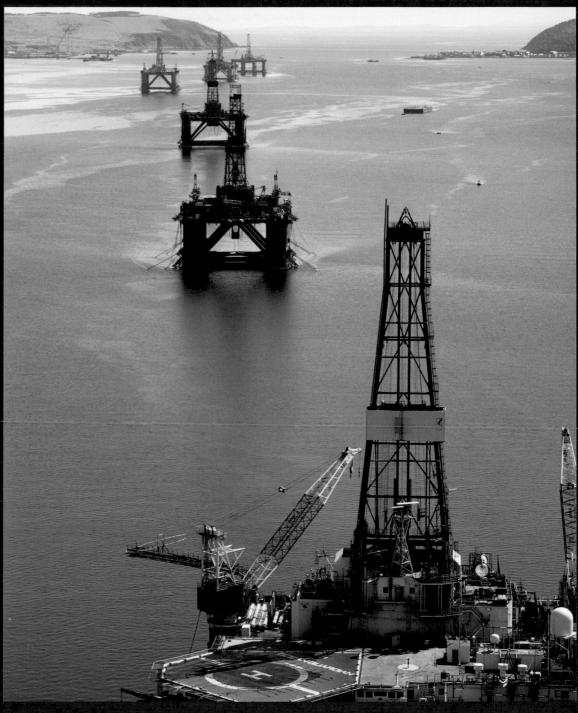

< LEFT
Blue pools at a clay pit mine, Cornwall
From Prosper Pit and Blackpool Pit to the Greensplat Pit and Tredinnick Downs Quarry, Cornwall's mining industry is as much a part of the language as of the landscape. By-products from the clay pits provide materials for road building and turquoise water, which is reminiscent of the blue of the Mediterranean Sea.

^ ABOVE
Oil rigs, Cromarty Firth
Though some might shudder at the sight of these oil rig platforms wading their way through the Cromarty Firth towards the North Sea, the oil industry here is a vital part of the British economy. Some of the largest oil rig platforms in the world are located here, and many are brought here from overseas for repair.

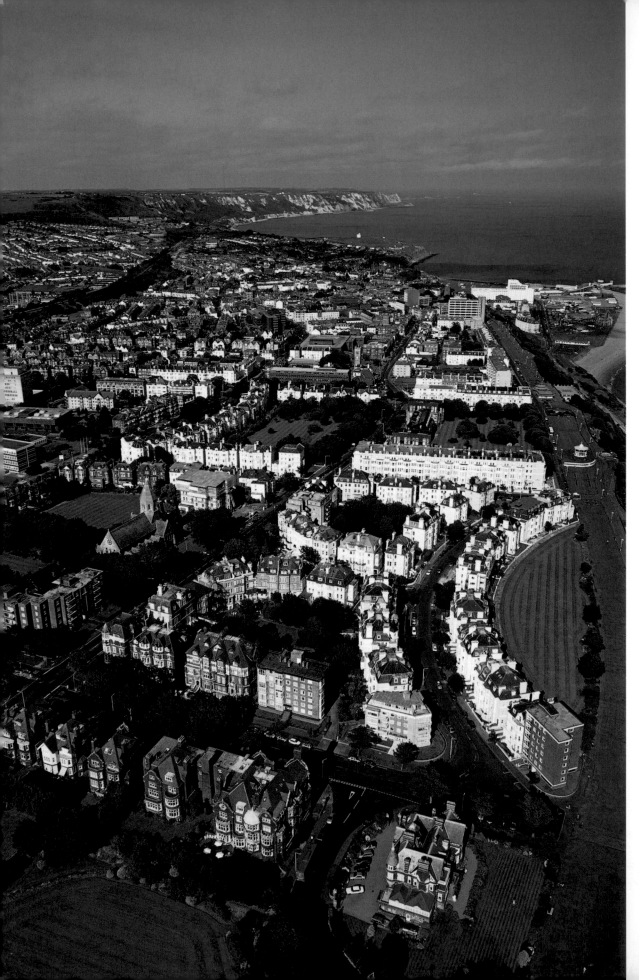

< **LEFT**

Folkestone, Kent

Imagine Folkestone in 1066, just before the Norman Conquest. It was then a gathering of a few fishermen and farmers, with nothing to worry about apart from the next catch or crop, and the occasional Viking invasion. The great change came, not with the Normans, but at the end of the 18th century, when the army arrived and established a troop station here, so convenient for crossing the English Channel to the continent. Today many more people cross the Channel from here, but by going underneath it through the Channel Tunnel, whose English end is at Folkestone.

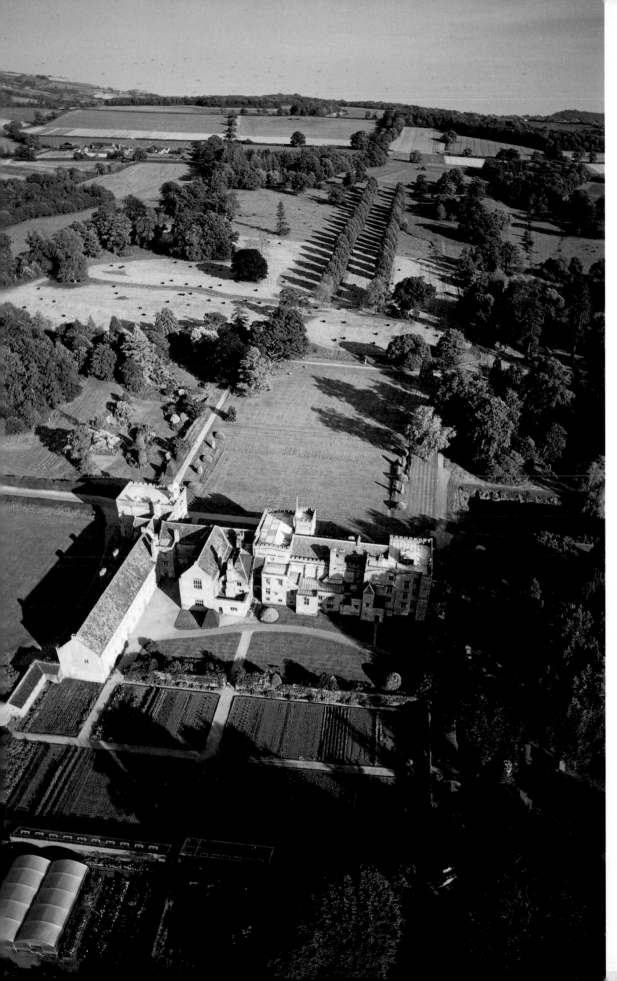

< LEFT
Forde Abbey, Somerset
For four hundred years Forde Abbey near Chard in Somerset flourished as a monastery, and this view from the air helps create a picture of what it must have been like – the monks tending their gardens and fields, surrounded by the peaceful Somerset countryside. The building at the heart of their community was first constructed in the 1140s, and has been impressively preserved to give a real glimpse into the lives of the monks who walked its cloisters.

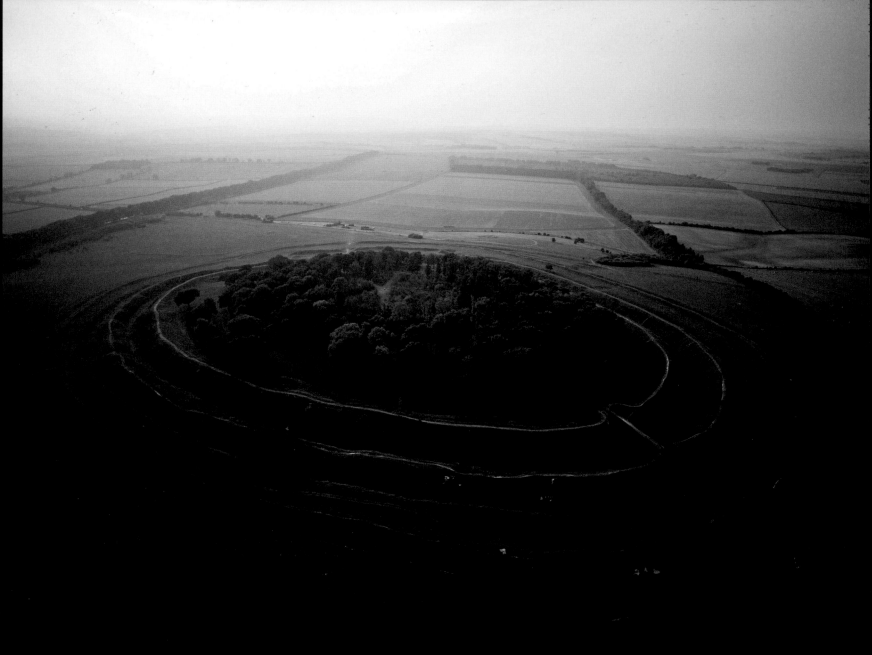

Mam Tor hill fort, Derbyshire
The hill fort at Mam Tor is the largest in Derbyshire, and the view from above gives some idea of its scale and design. Back in the Bronze Age, some 3,500 years ago, Mam Tor was built, and was still occupied when the Romans were in Britain. The whole peak is known as the shivering mountain, from the loose shale composition that still causes parts of it to crumble away today.

> OPPOSITE
Trees, Berkshire
These trees in Berkshire unwittingly hark back to the very origins of this old English county, and the derivation of its name. It is thought to be one of the oldest of English counties, first mentioned in the mid-9th century. Its name came from a forest of box trees (called boxwoods in North America) which covered much of the region, and which was called bearroc.

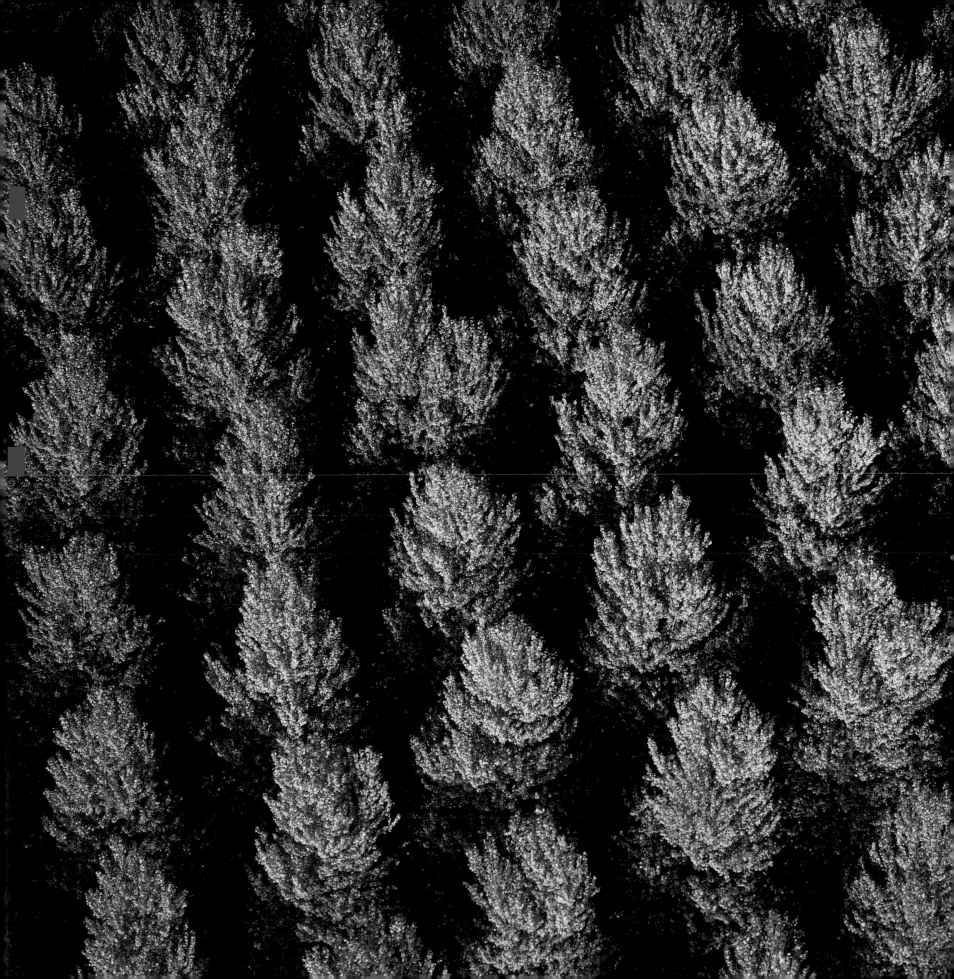

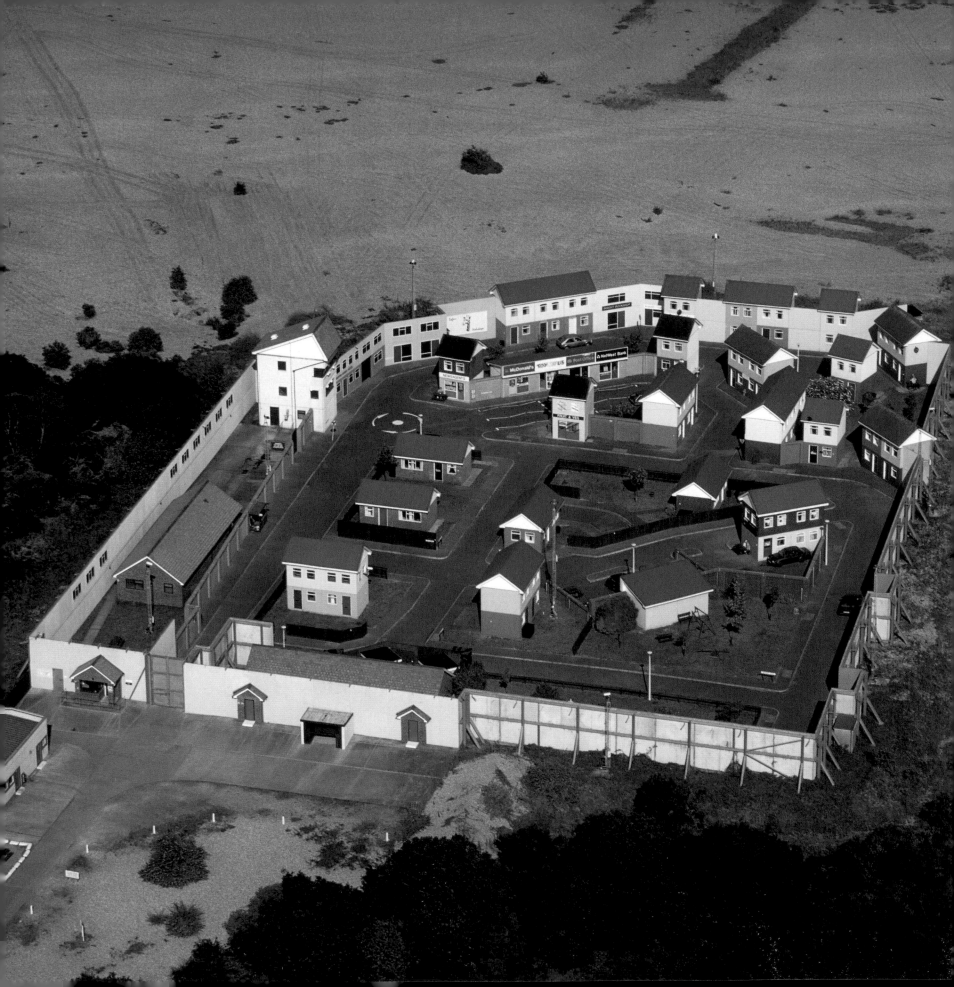

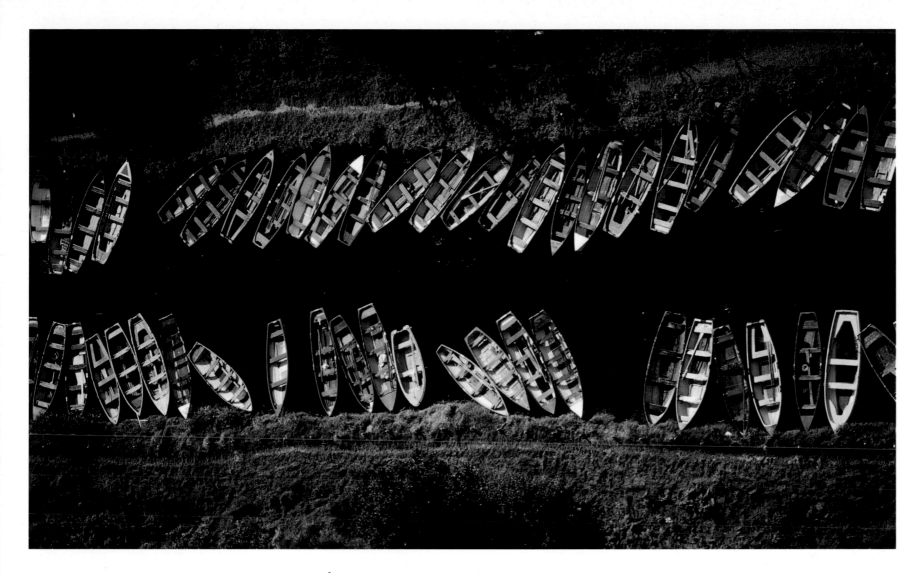

<OPPOSITE
Hythe Ranges, Kent

It was the arrival of the military at Folkestone which helped turn what had been a little fishing village into a booming port town. A few miles west of Folkestone, near the town of Hythe, are the Hythe Ranges. Set back from the sea shore, these are some of the oldest firing ranges in the country, used by the military for the firing of live ammunition for almost 200 years. Army training also takes place in 'towns' which look rather like Hollywood film sets, such as the one here.

^ ABOVE
Rowing boats, County Kerry

Kerry is one of the most scenic and popular parts of Ireland, including as it does the beautiful Dingle peninsula, the busy tourist town of Killarney and one of the most appealing drives in the British Isles, around the Ring of Kerry. With the Lakes of Killarney and three major rivers flowing through the county, rowing is a popular pastime and visitors often do what the locals do – use a rowing boat to get around.

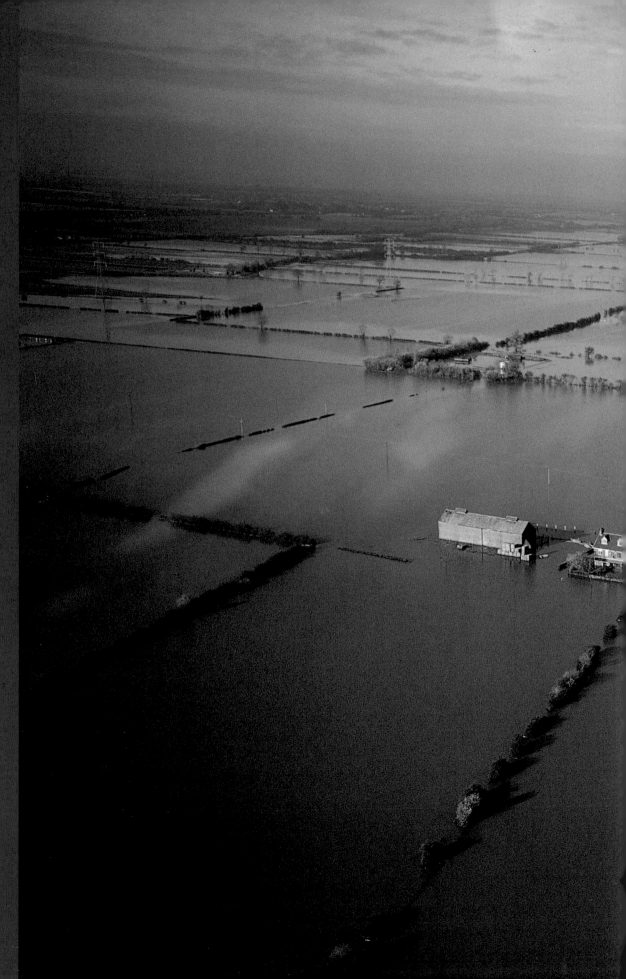

> **Flooding, River Ouse, Yorkshire**

Britain has several rivers called Ouse, as the name derives from the Celtic word for water, *usa*, and so the River Ouse is simply the River Water. It is aptly named as this photograph shows. As the Yorkshire Ouse flows through a low and wide valley, the Vale of York, where several of Yorkshire's largest rivers such as the Swale, Ure and Wharfe all meet to form the Ouse, it is prone to flooding.

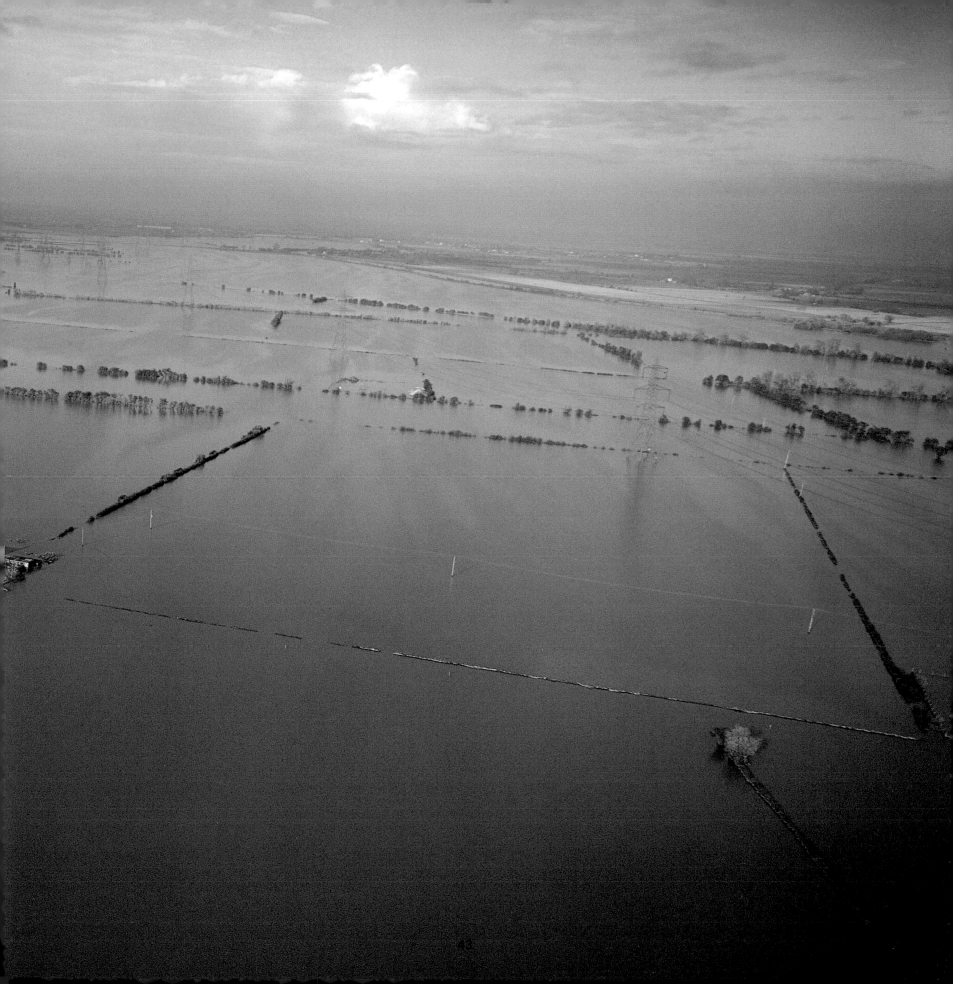

Exeter, Devon

Exeter, the county town of Devon, grew up where it did because it was the first place at which it was possible to bridge the River Exe. The place was inhabited long before the Romans arrived in the 1st century, and the extent of its considerable growth back from the river can easily be seen from the air.

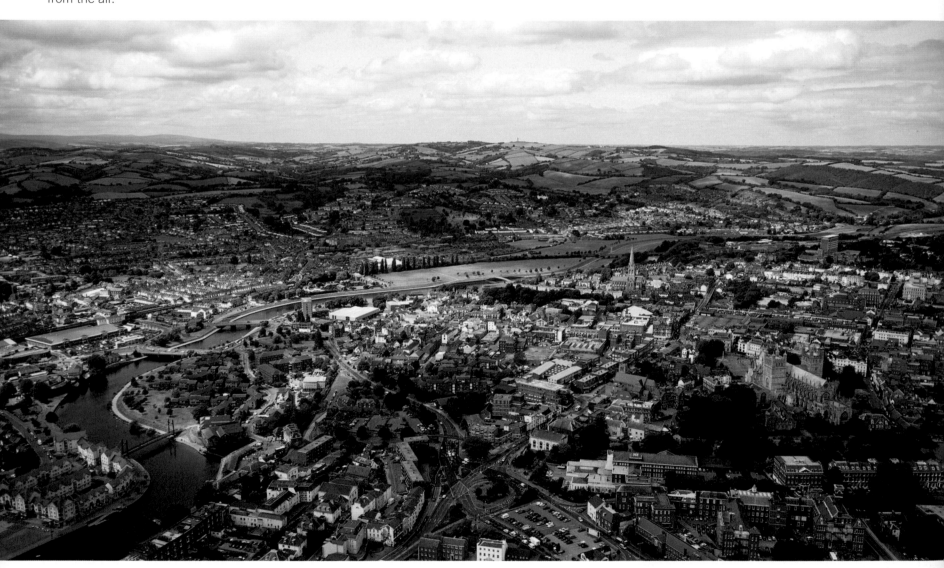

Humber Bridge, Yorkshire and Lincolnshire

Spanning the Humber Estuary to link Yorkshire with Lincolnshire was much more of a feat than spanning the River Exe (above). It didn't happen until 1981 when the Humber Bridge was opened, and at the time was the longest single-span suspension bridge in the world.

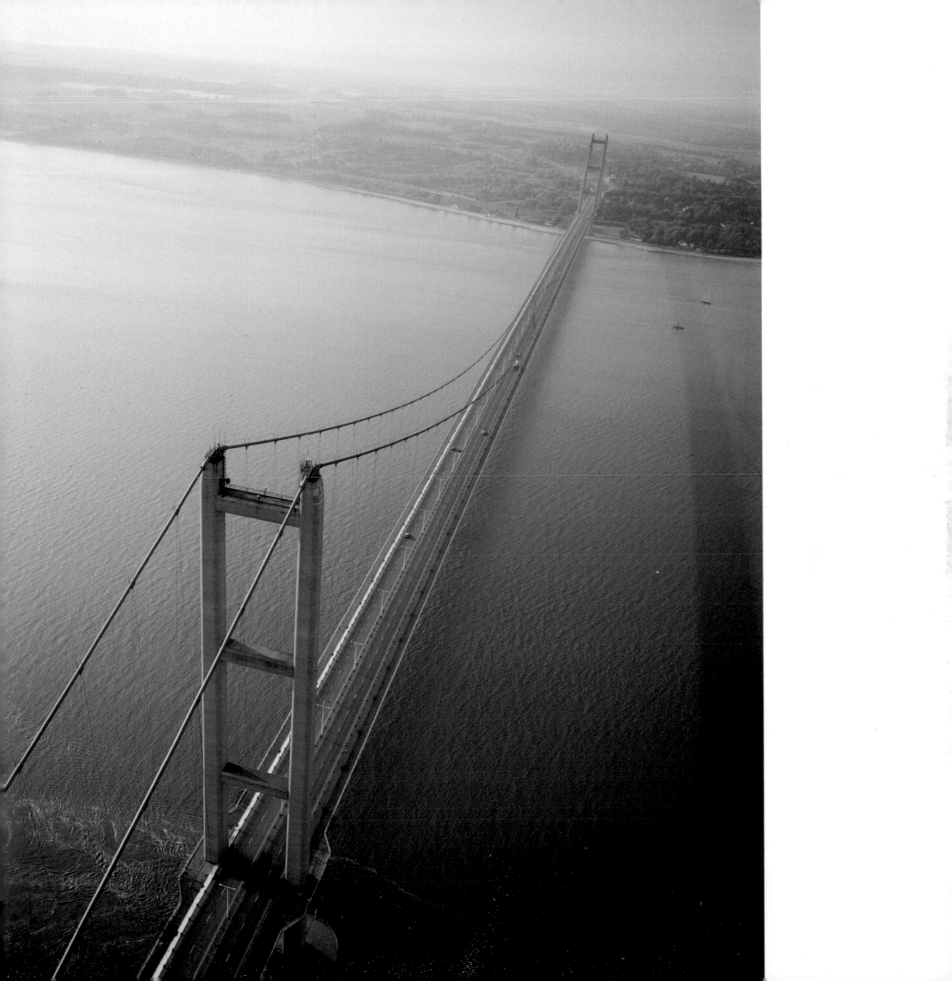

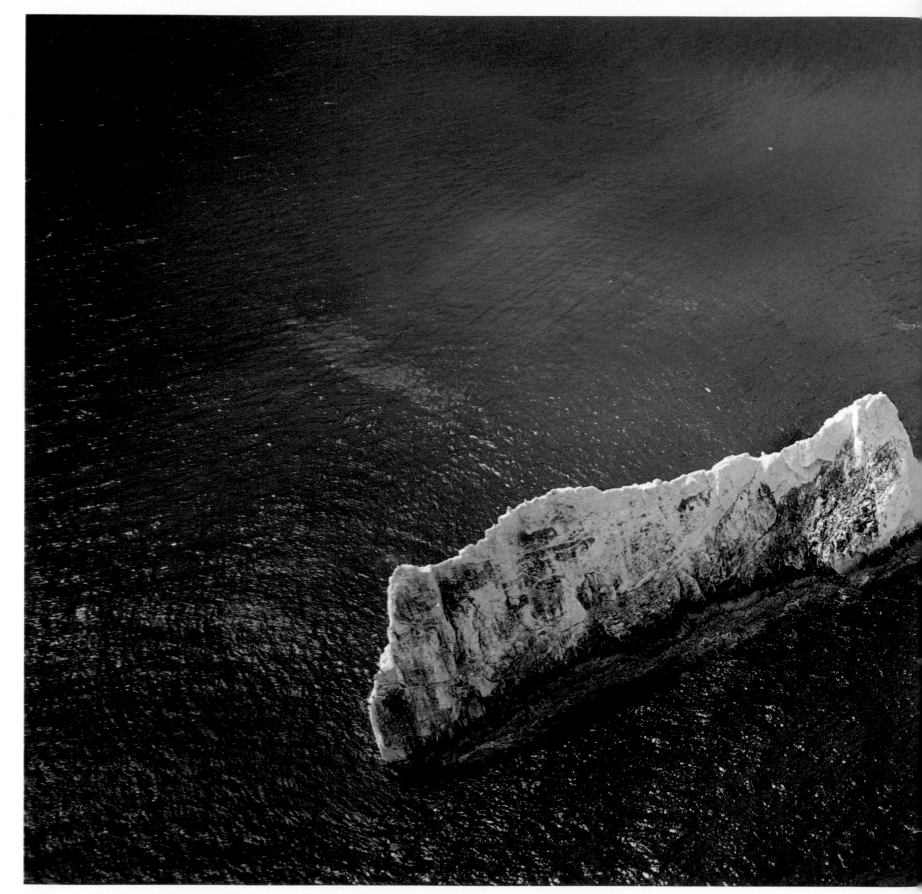

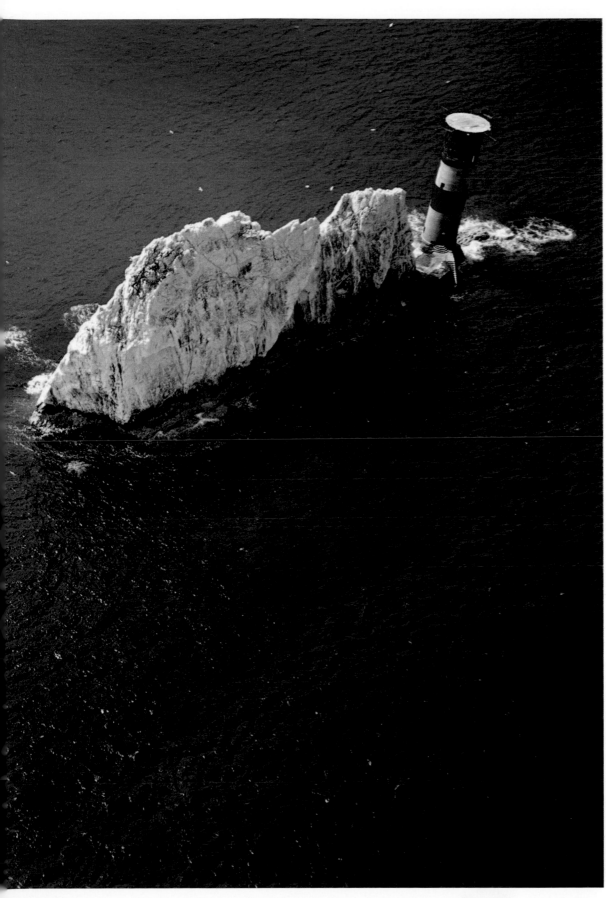

<

The Needles, Isle of Wight

The distinctive chalk stacks which rise out of the sea off the western tip of the Isle of Wight have lost the feature that gave them their name. The Needles were named for one particular needle-like stack called Lot's Wife, which collapsed into the seas during a storm in 1764. It would have appeared in the gap in the bottom left of this photograph, balancing out the Needles Lighthouse at top right, which was built in 1859.

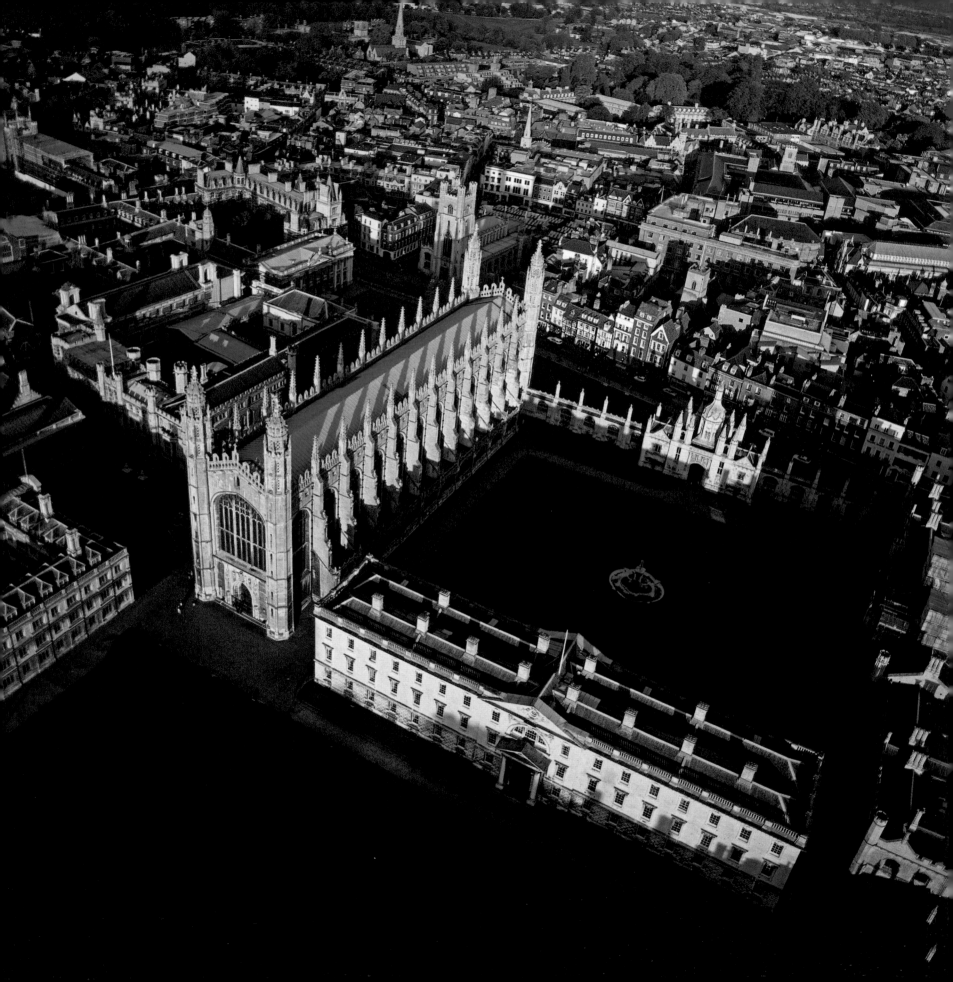

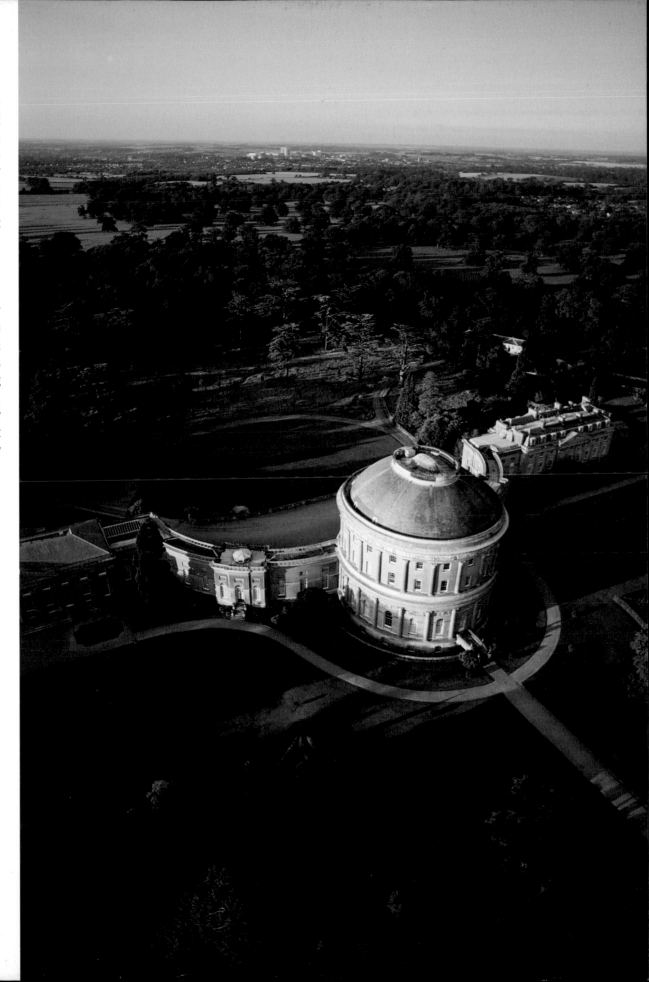

< OPPOSITE
Cambridge, Cambridgeshire

King's College has been a part of Cambridge since it was founded in 1441 by the king who gave it its name, King Henry VI. Its most impressive feature, which dominates this photo, is King's College Chapel. The King's College Chapel Choir is one of the most famous choirs in the world, and that vaulted stone roof fills with the sweet sound of their singing every Christmas Eve, a concert which is broadcast throughout Britain.

> RIGHT
Ickworth House, Suffolk

Ickworth House stands in 1,800 acres of land, near Bury St Edmunds in Suffolk. Work on the house began in 1795 on the instructions of Frederick Hervey, the eccentric 4th Earl of Bristol, who was also a bishop. He died in 1803 before the building was finished, though the exterior of the Rotunda, in the centre of this picture, was completed by then. The life-loving Earl-Bishop would no doubt be delighted to know that Ickworth House now has a flourishing vineyard.

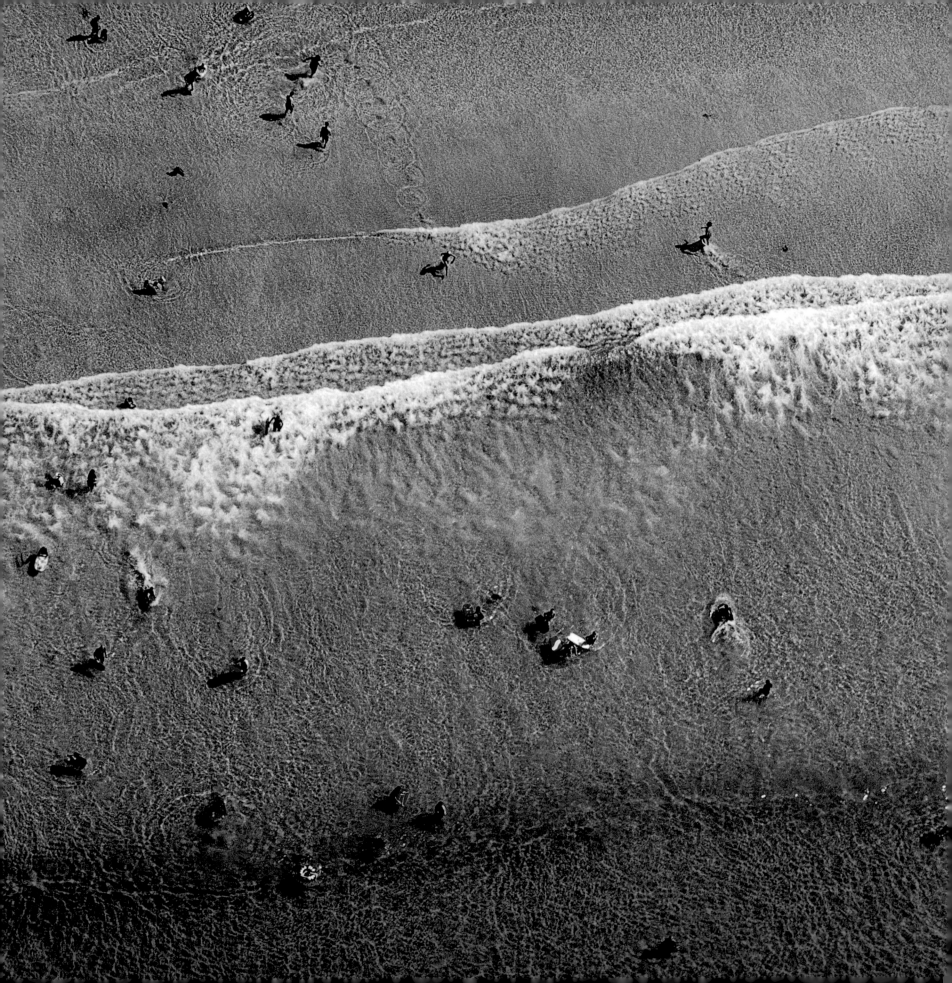

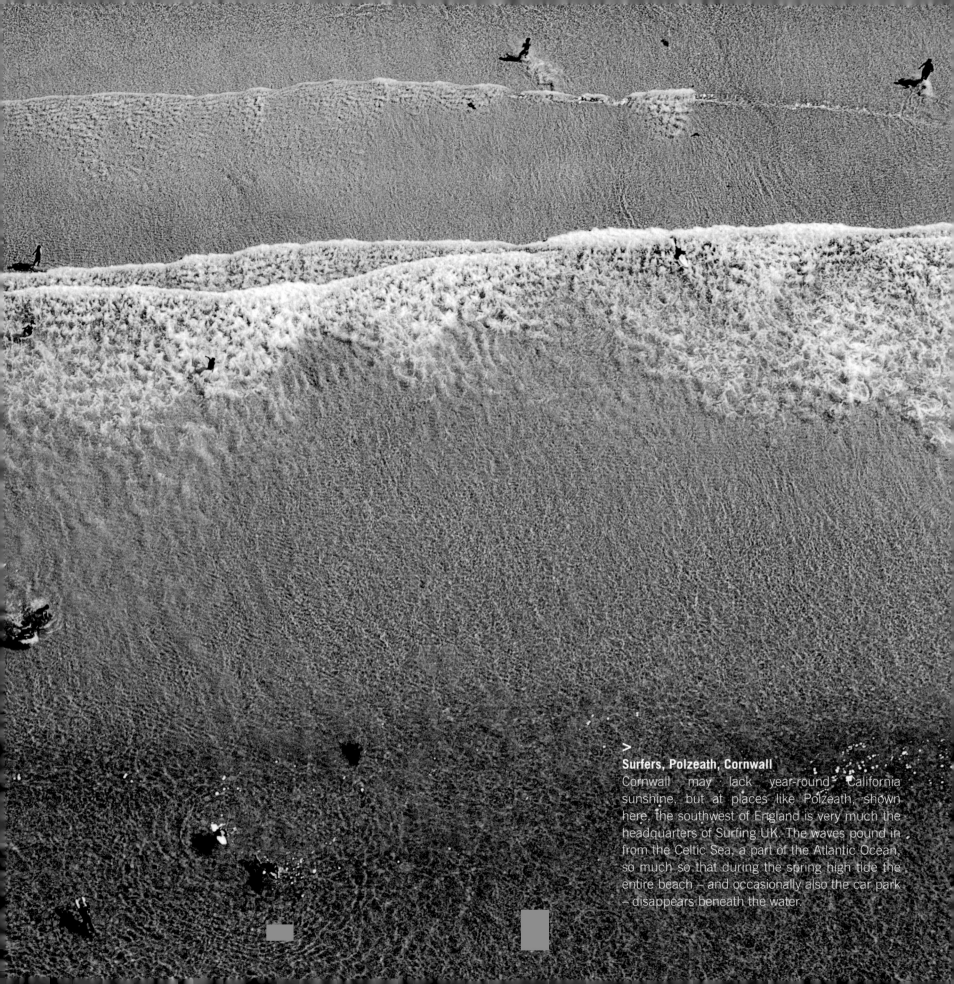

> **Surfers, Polzeath, Cornwall**
Cornwall may lack year-round California sunshine, but at places like Polzeath, shown here, the southwest of England is very much the headquarters of Surfing UK. The waves pound in from the Celtic Sea, a part of the Atlantic Ocean, so much so that during the spring high tide the entire beach – and occasionally also the car park – disappears beneath the water.

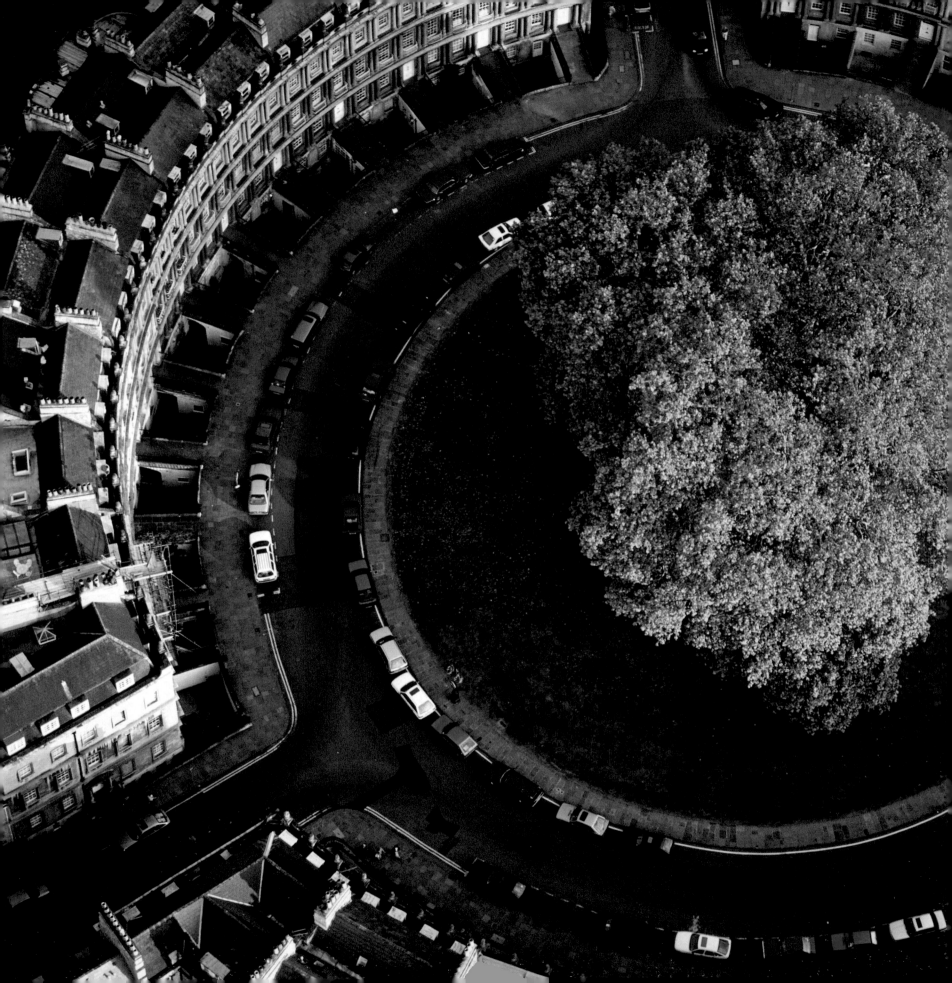

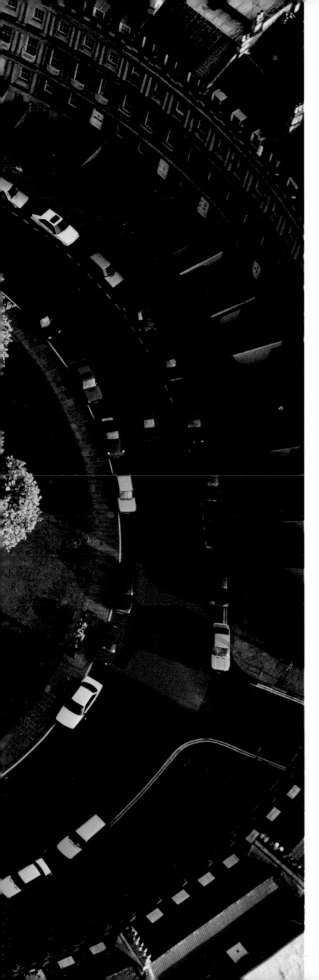

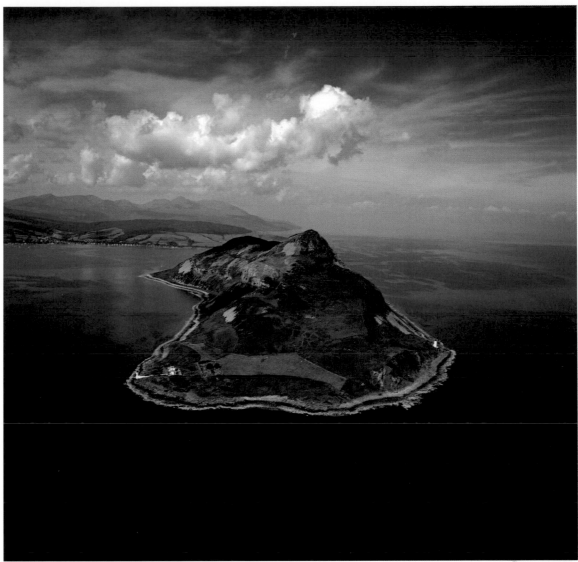

< LEFT

The Circus, Bath, Somerset

Like the equally well-known Royal Crescent, The Circus in Bath is a superb example of Georgian architecture. Work on it began in 1754 and continued for 14 years to produce this symmetrical and aesthetically pleasing result. Part of the inspiration was Rome's Colosseum, but turned inside out so that the exterior design of the Colosseum faces inward. William Pitt, Thomas Gainsborough and William Gladstone are among the more famous former residents of The Circus, whose name comes from the Latin word for a circle, *circus*.

^ ABOVE

Holy Island, off the Isle of Arran

One of several Holy Islands off the British coastline, this one off the Ayrshire coastline in the Western Isles has been noted as a healing place since at least the 6th century when a monk, Saint Molaise, lived a hermit's existence in a cave there. Later the island housed a monastery, and today it continues the tradition of religious retreat as it is now home to the Buddhist Centre for World Peace and Health. The Buddhists share the island with a community of nuns, and a Nature Reserve which protects some rare species such as Soay sheep and Eriskay ponies.

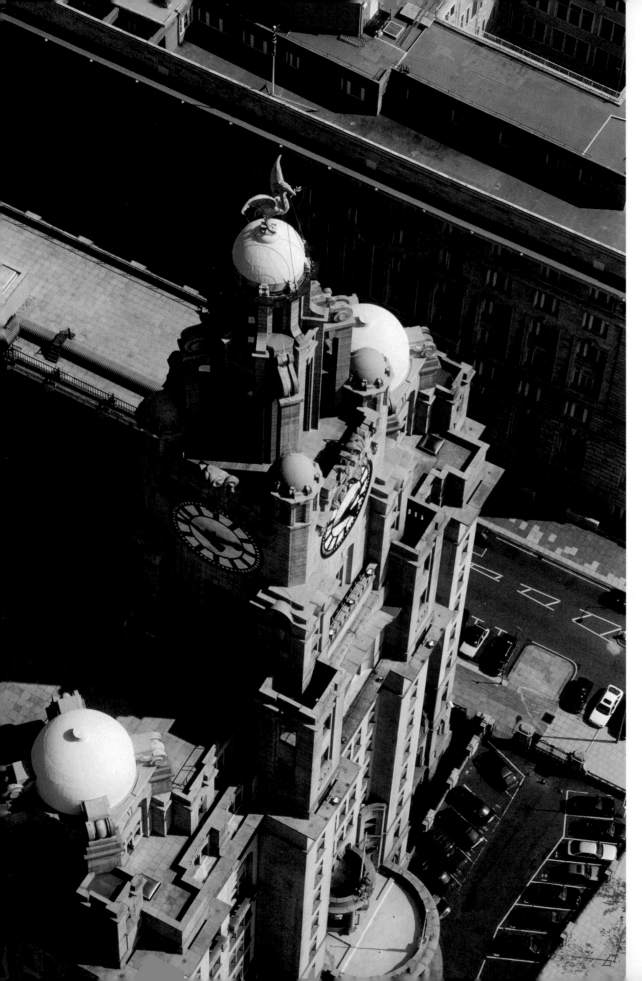

< LEFT
Liver Building, Liverpool, Merseyside
Two liver Birds sit on top of the Liver Building, down by the Liverpool waterfront. The cormorant-like bird has long been a symbol of the city, and no one is quite sure of its origins. Some say it is a mythical bird that used to haunt the River Mersey here. One of the pair is female and looks to the sea, to watch for the city's sailors returning safely home. The male of the pair looks into the city, as the sailors will want to know if the pubs are open.

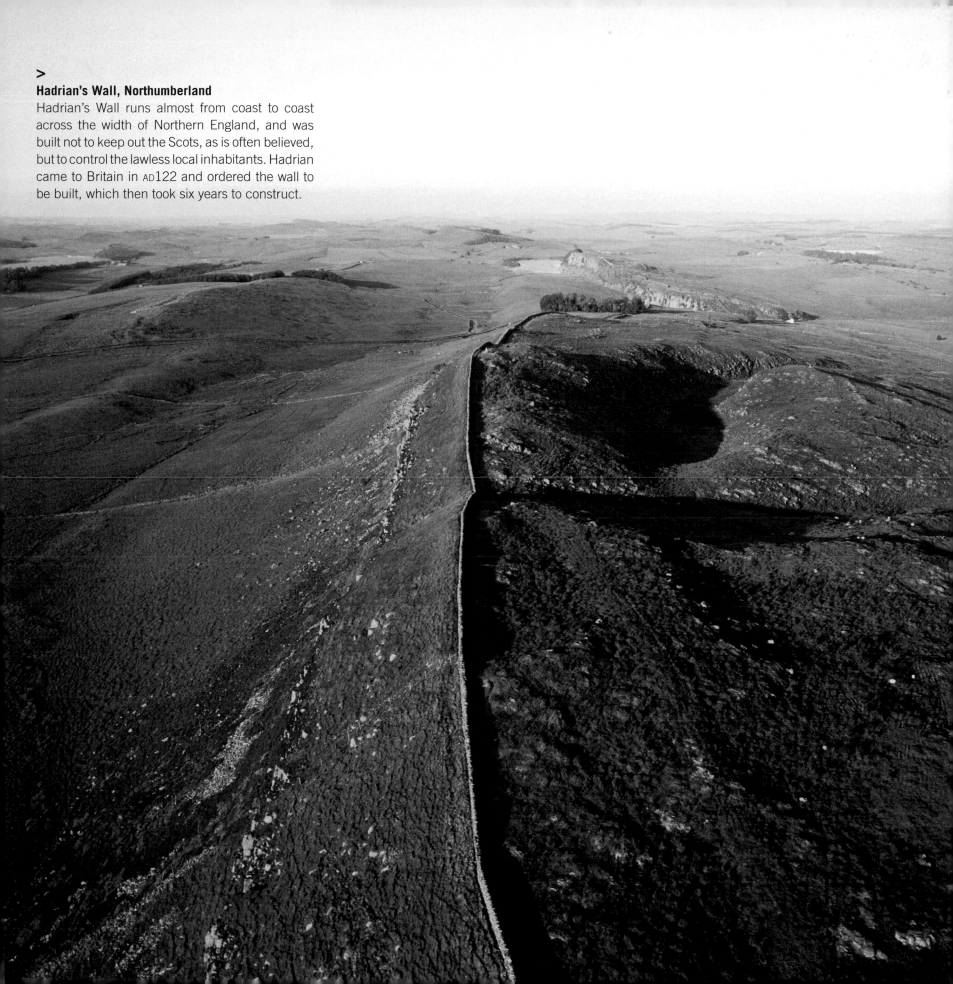

> **Hadrian's Wall, Northumberland**
Hadrian's Wall runs almost from coast to coast across the width of Northern England, and was built not to keep out the Scots, as is often believed, but to control the lawless local inhabitants. Hadrian came to Britain in AD122 and ordered the wall to be built, which then took six years to construct.

CASTLES & CATHEDRALS

For anyone interested in castles or cathedrals, the British Isles is the Promised Land. It sometimes seems hard to travel from one town to the next without encountering a magnificent cathedral or a dramatic castle, or the ruins of one or the other. Some of the finest are impressively captured with all their drama and majesty in these pages.

The two most important cathedrals in England are not in London, but at York and Canterbury. They vie with each other to claim the number one spot in the Church of England hierarchy just as much as any two rival football teams. The Archbishop of Canterbury is known as the Primate of All England, while the Archbishop of York is merely Primate of England, a linguistic distinction which means that, in terms of cathedrals, Canterbury is more important than York.

Architecturally both are hugely important. York's Great East Window, which was completed way back in 1408, is one of the largest medieval stained-glass windows in the world. Just to be in the presence of such a work of art, created by men 600 years ago, is a humbling experience. The window is almost the size of a tennis court, and cost just £58, which was paid by the Bishop of Durham.

Canterbury Cathedral is a UNESCO World Heritage Site and the Archbishops of Canterbury can be traced back to St Augustine in 597AD, who was sent to England from Rome as a missionary by Pope Gregory the Great. It has a crypt which dates back to the 11th century and is the largest in the country from that time, and a magnificent 14th-century nave which took 18 years to build. It can also claim some impressive stained glass, with one window dated to about 1176AD and others from the 12th and 13th centuries. The tradition continues with modern glass too.

Canterbury is perhaps most famous for the story of the murder of Thomas Beckett, showing that cathedrals are not simply buildings full of peace and worship. Four Archbishops of Canterbury have been murdered over the years, the first being Saint Alphege who was Archbishop of Canterbury when the city was ransacked by the invading Danes in 1011. The Archbishop was taken prisoner and held hostage for seven months. He refused to allow a ransom to be paid for his release, and so he was then murdered in London.

By contrast, the Cathedral of The Isles and Collegiate Church of the Holy Spirit on the Isle of Cumbrae tucked into the Firth of Clyde in Western Scotland has had a fairly peaceful history, and is the smallest cathedral in the British Isles. What was the largest cathedral in Scotland is now the ruined Cathedral of St Andrew in St Andrews, a town more noted these days for its golf. Legend has it that a Greek monk named St Rule brought some of Andrew's bones here to this place which became, like Canterbury, a place of great pilgrimage. Pilgrims would cross the Firth of Forth on ferries, travelling from Edinburgh up Scotland's east coast.

Gazing through the photographs in this book it's impossible not to think of the links it creates in the stories of these British Isles. It is a map of the countries, and a history and a geography, as well as a book of beautiful images. Perhaps some of the most impressive photographs in the book are of Britain's castles, almost always placed in an imposing or inspiring location. They range from ancient hill forts which date back to the first settlers, through medieval ruins to more modern creations or renovations.

Constructions like unique Cardiff Castle manage to combine history, commerce, architecture, and arts and crafts all in one building. Its history goes back at least to the first century AD, when the Romans arrived and built the first of their three forts on this site. The Normans built much of what we see today, but later the castle became a remarkable family home for the Bute family, which became hugely wealthy through the Welsh coal trade, and from the Cardiff docks. The Butes employed an extraordinary Victorian architect and designer named William Burges to transform the castle using the Gothic Revival style into a totally unique combination of grandeur, fantasy, whimsy and, most importantly, brilliant craftsmanship.

At the other end of the country a whole string of castles, as varied as the scenery, dots the landscape of North Wales. These include Caernarfon, Beaumaris, Conwy, Rhudlan, Denbigh and Flint, and down the west coast to Criccieth and Harlech. Also in this part of the country are ancient and ruined hill forts like the one at Dinas Bran. It towers high above the Dee Valley, totally safe from the floods that affected – and still affect – the lives of the ordinary citizens way down below. These hill forts – Tre'r Ceiri in Caernarfonshire is another – remind us of the history of the land we travel through – or, in these pages, above.

That very real sense of history is also evident in other great cities, like Edinburgh and Dublin. The monumental rock on top of which Edinburgh Castle stands has known inhabitants since at least 900BC, and seen much turmoil in its time. As the White Cliffs of Dover came to be a symbol, not just of England but of English security, so too does Edinburgh Castle symbolise a great deal for the Scottish people. It became a royal fortress in the 12th century, was taken by the English in the late 13th century after a 3-day siege, and was retaken by the Scots a few years later when they stormed the rock during the night. It then went back and forth

some more, once even acting as the base for Oliver Cromwell and his Parliamentary Army. Little wonder that such places become important symbols of nationhood.

Likewise the castle in Ireland's capital city, Dublin, reminds us that the countries which make up these fairly small British islands have been fighting each other for centuries, when they haven't been fighting with the invading Romans, Vikings and Normans. Ireland had already been invaded by the Vikings and then the Normans, when the English came and defeated the Normans, only to claim Ireland for themselves and to remain there for the next 750 years. It wasn't until Irish Independence at the end of 1921 that Dublin Castle could be reclaimed for Ireland. It was on 16 January 1922 when the rebel Irish leader Michael Collins received the official handover of the castle in the Great Courtyard.

Invasions, internal strife, murders and assassinations, works of art and eccentricities – the cathedrals and castles of the British Isles have seen all of these things and more. Places of warfare and of worship, sometimes both at the same time. But always special places, with special appeal for people visiting Britain's shores.

> RIGHT
Emley Moor Mast, Yorkshire

The Emley Moor Mast sends out its signals for TV and radio stations across about 10,000 square kilometres of Yorkshire. At 1,084 feet high (330.4m) it is the tallest free-standing structure in the British Isles. The current tower is made of concrete and replaces an earlier steel mast which collapsed in high winds in March 1969.

> OPPOSITE
Landfill site, Berkshire

Berkshire, one of the oldest English counties, is faced like everywhere else with one of the world's newest problems: how to dispose of the rubbish created by an ever-increasing population. Hopefully landfill sites like this, where the rubbish is ultimately buried below ground, will be needed less as recycling schemes continue to grow.

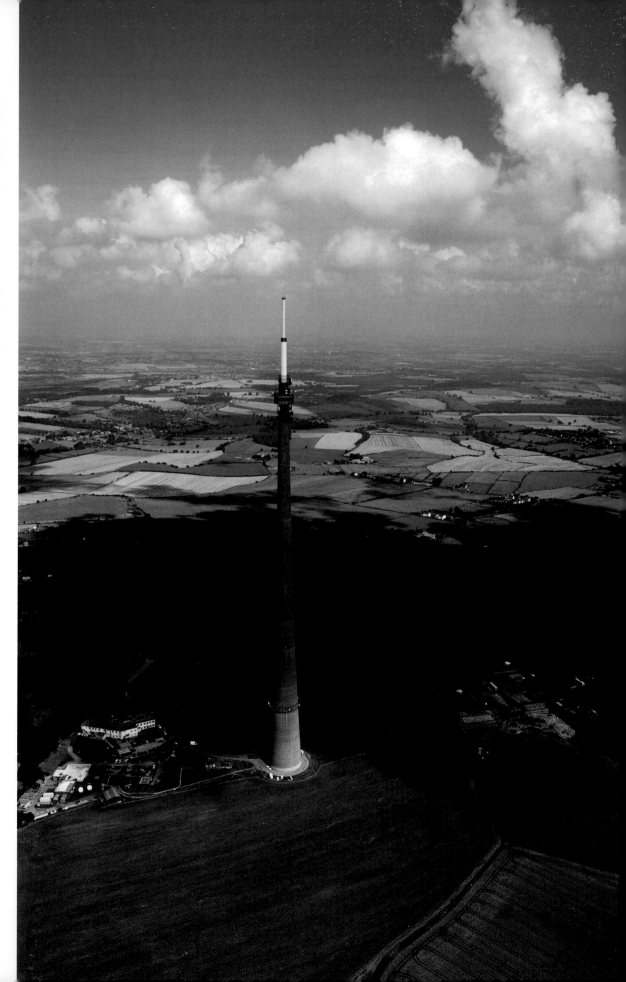

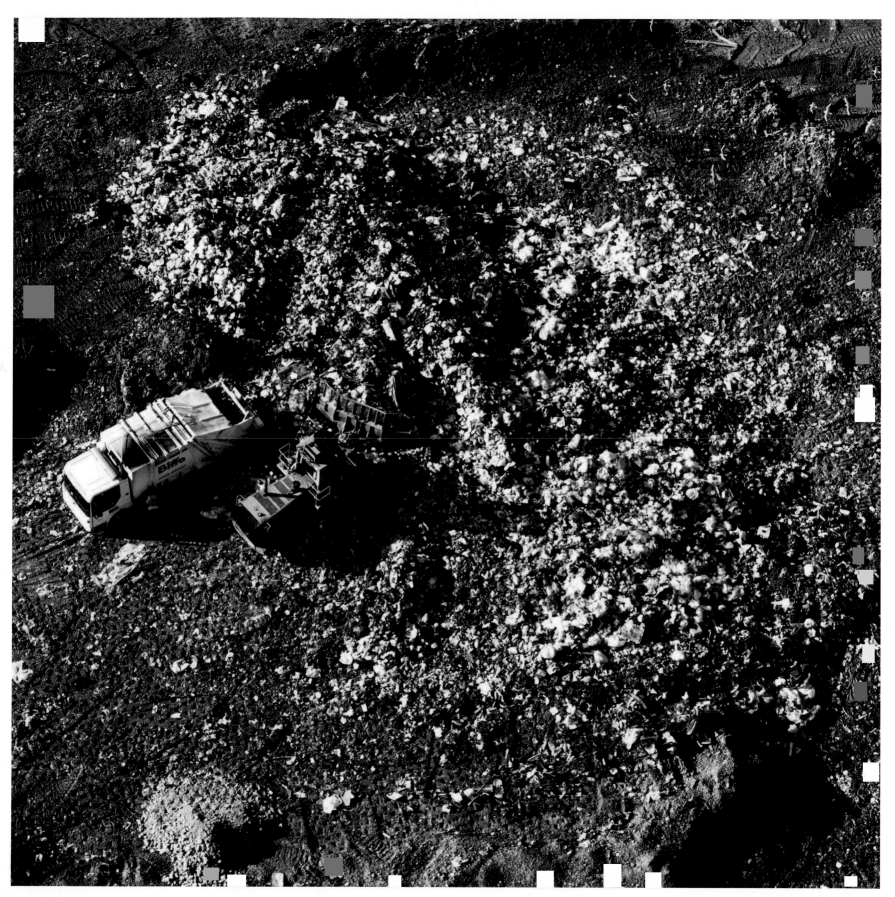

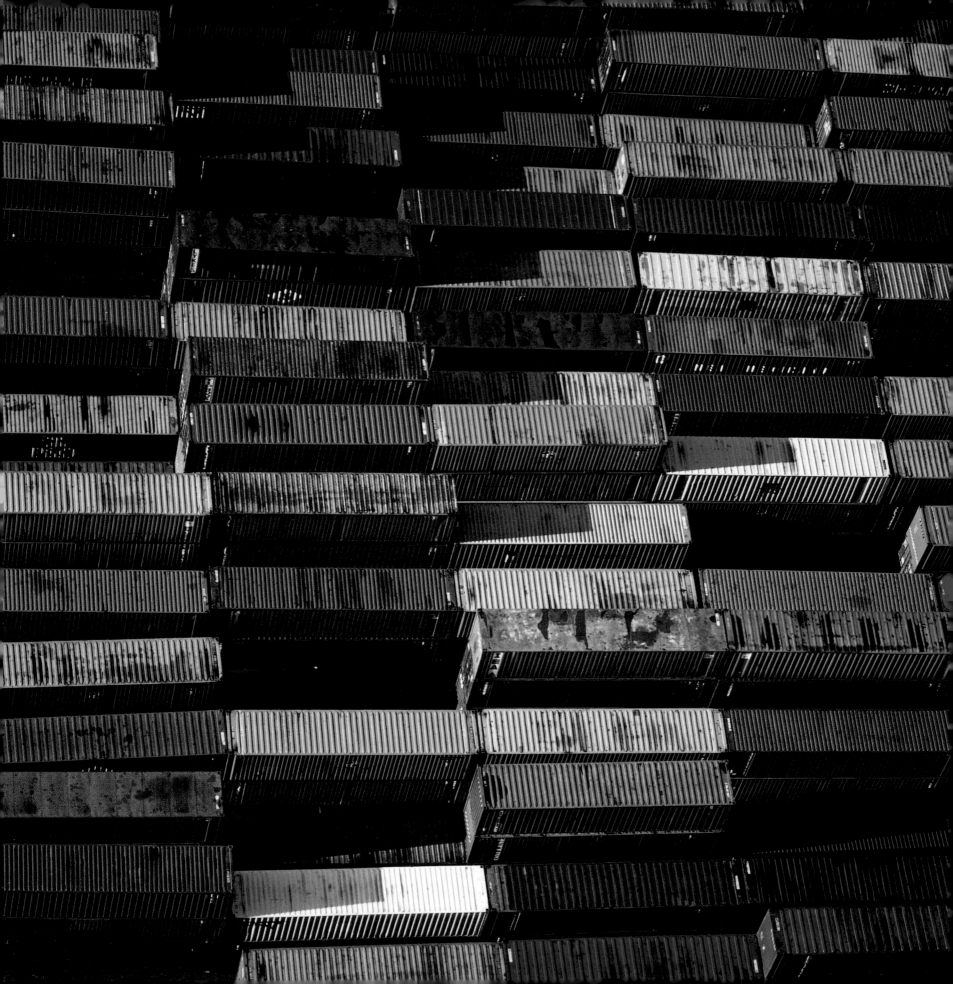

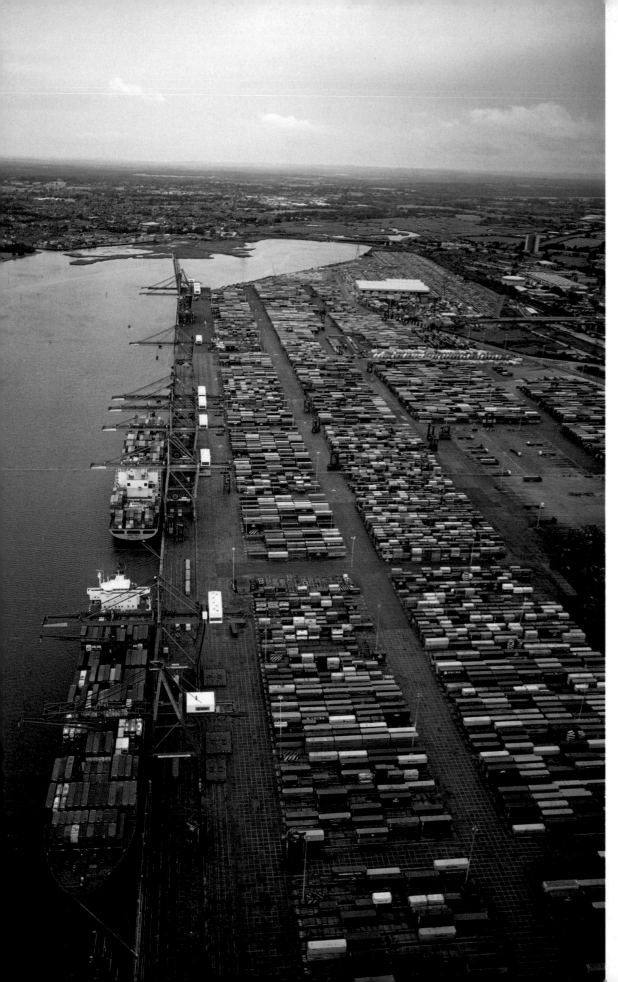

< LEFT
Southampton Port, Hampshire
Container transport has changed the face of Britain's docks and ports, and many such places – like Southampton here – now look like works of modern art. It was an important port for the Romans, servicing their nearby large towns of Winchester and Salisbury, and it is fascinating to imagine what a Roman sailor would make of the size of the port today.

< OPPOSITE
Containers at the Dublin docks
The Dublin docks were once in the city centre, and the name has remained there as most visitors will only encounter Docklands as an area being regenerated along the River Liffey. The real docks where much of the nation's imports and exports pass through are now way out of the city, well away from visitors' eyes, though they do have a certain grand majesty about them.

^ ABOVE
Fishing, Bewl Water
At Bewl Water on the Kent and Sussex border, two fishermen enjoy the peace. Fishing is one of the most popular pastimes in Britain, whether here on this man-made reservoir or on the wild salmon rivers of Scotland, Wales and Ireland.

> OPPOSITE
Solitary fisherman, Bracklesham Bay, West Sussex
A lone fisherman makes the most of the solitude of Bracklesham Bay in West Sussex. Today the tides are bringing in the fish, though on other days when the winds are right the bay's blue waters will be filled with windsurfers, surfers and kitesurfers.

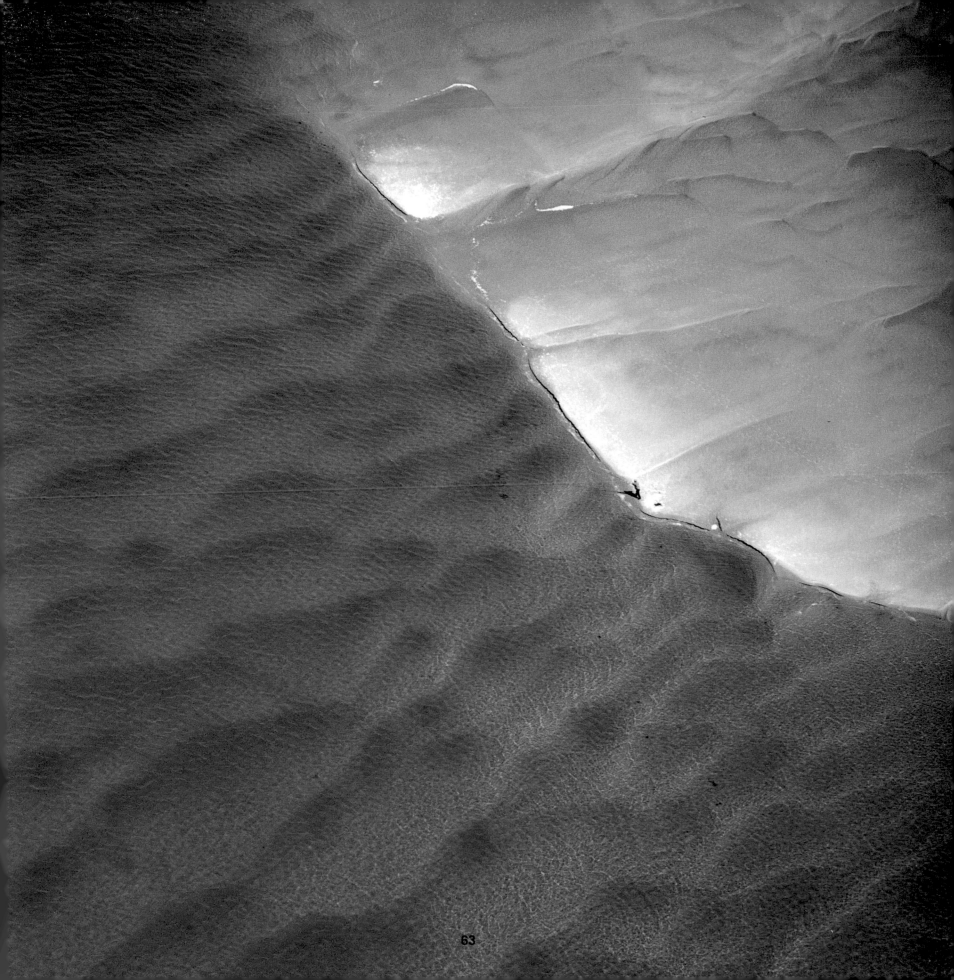

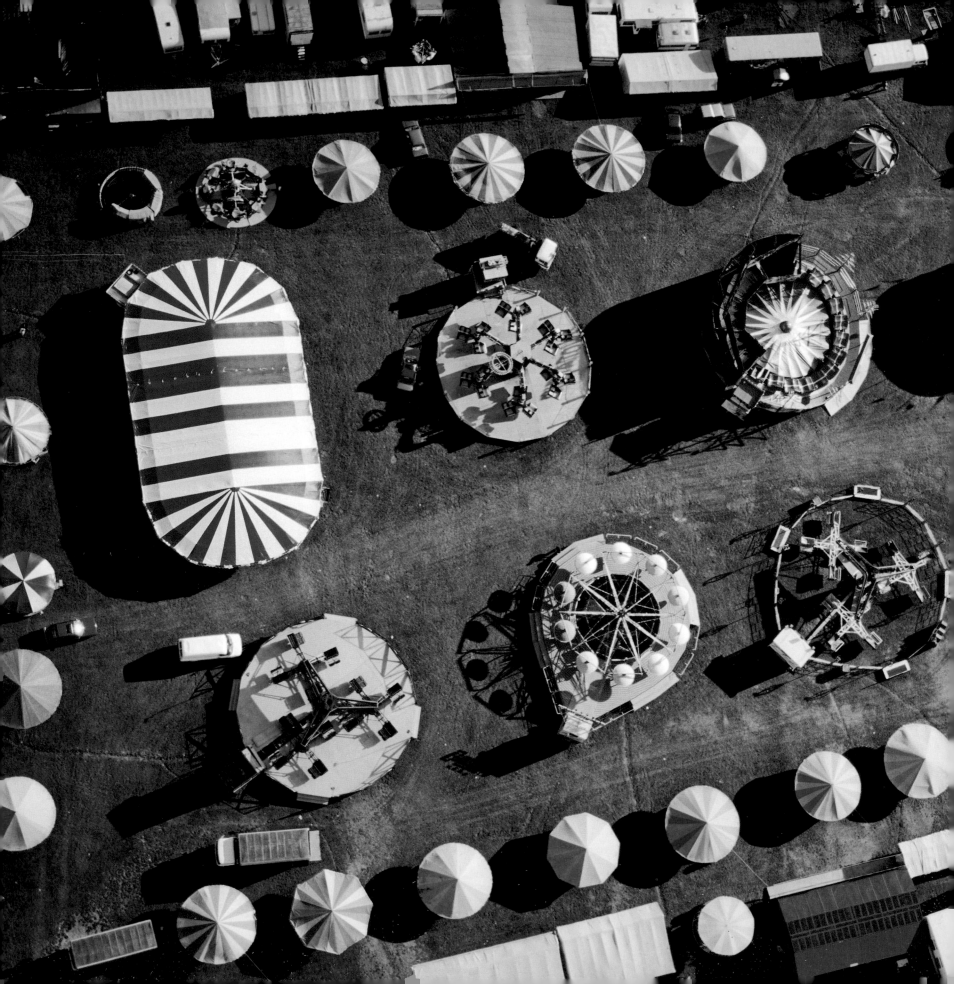

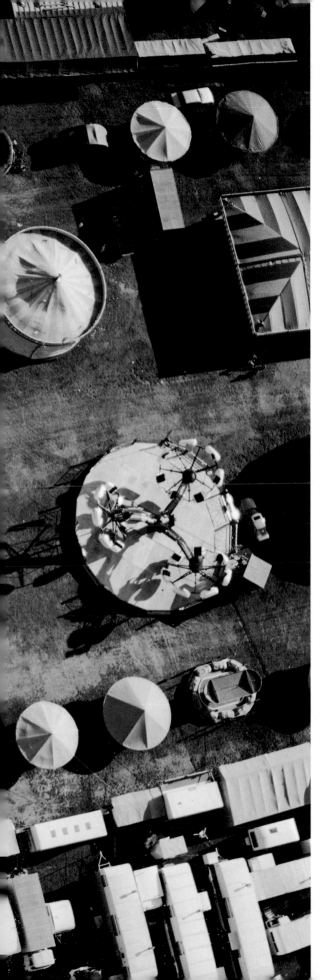

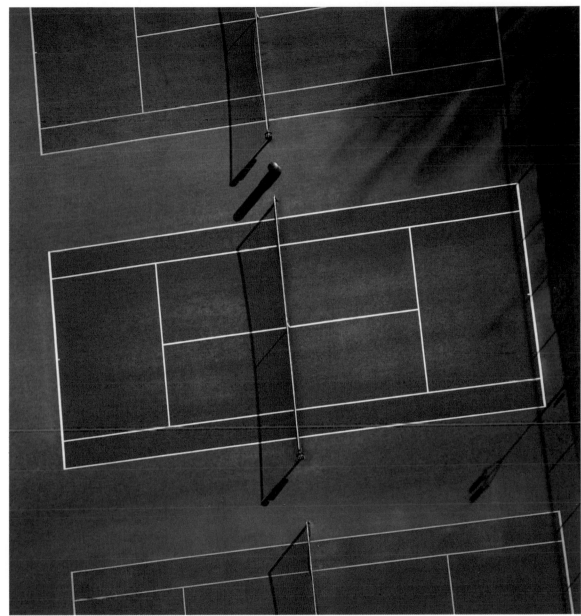

< LEFT
Blackheath funfair, London

Funfairs in Britain, like this one in London's Blackheath, developed from the strolling players and minstrels of medieval times. The players would travel the land, earning a living by bringing entertainment to those who didn't travel very far. Despite the fact that people today can tour the world themselves, and are hardly starved of entertainment, the funfairs still bring some brash diversions wherever they go.

^ ABOVE
Tennis courts, Essex

Ball games have been played by all nations throughout history, though the roots of modern tennis are thought to go back to the ancient Greeks. It was Britain which brought a formality to the game, though, in the 19th century when lawn tennis as we know it was developed. These courts in Essex are a visual reminder of the game's rules and precision.

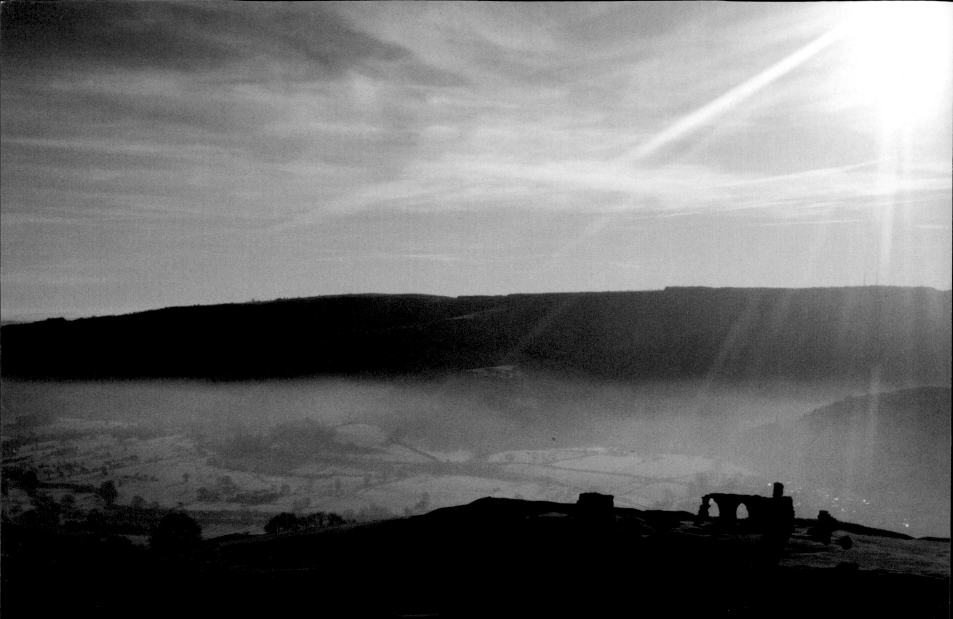

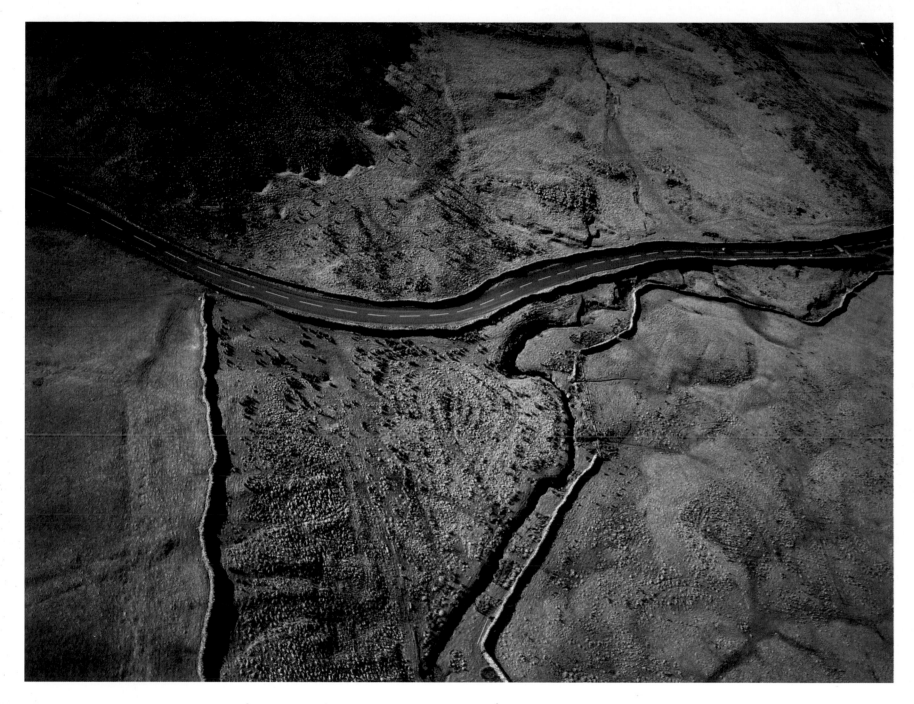

Dinas Bran hill fort, Denbighshire
Dinas Bran is stunningly situated high above the valley of the River Dee in Denbighshire, North Wales. History seeps out of this shot, as if the viewer had time-travelled back to the Iron Age, when the hill fort was built. The only modern intrusion is the sight of the ruins of Castell Dinas Bran, a 13th-century castle which also took advantage of the dramatic location.

ʌ ABOVE
The road near Malham Tarn, Yorkshire
A simple man-made road cuts through the limestone landscape around Malham in the Yorkshire Dales. Drystone walls to mark the field boundaries are the only other mark that man has made on a landscape famous for its lakes, waterfalls and the remarkable limestone cliffs of Malham Cove. The countryside here has been carved out by glaciers, not by mankind.

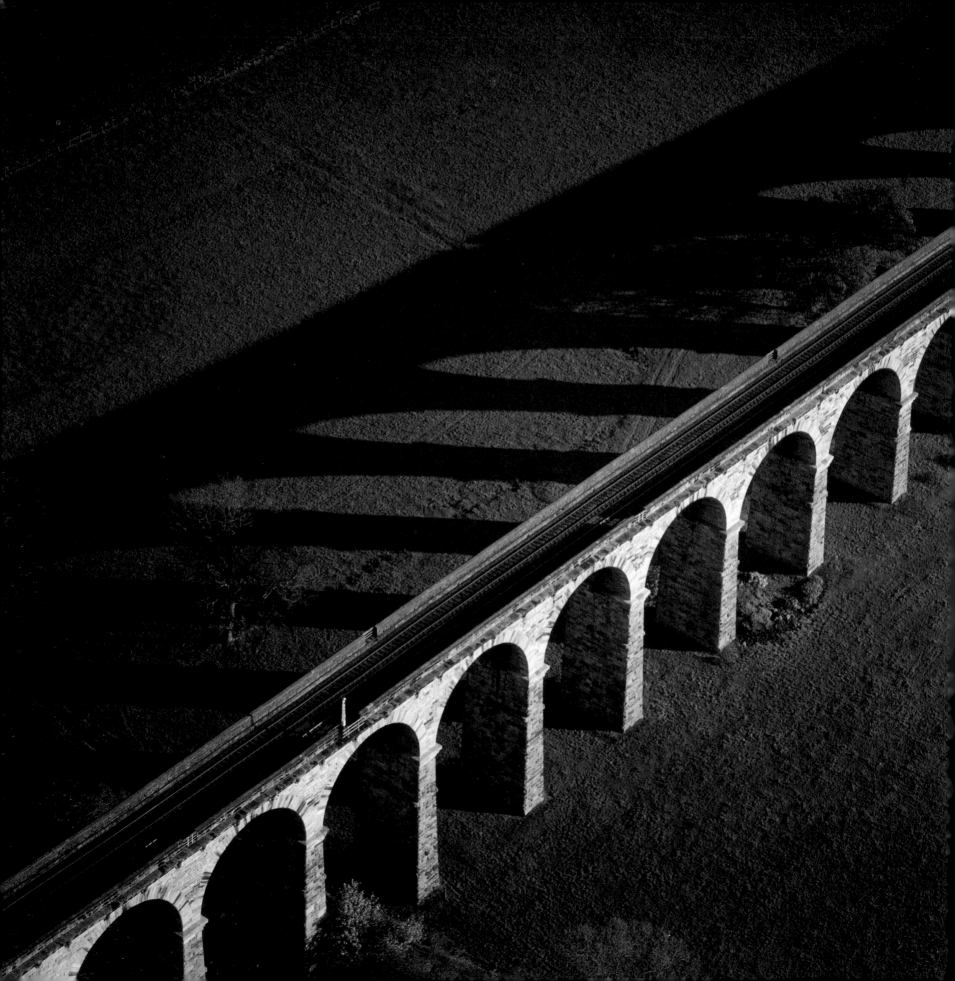

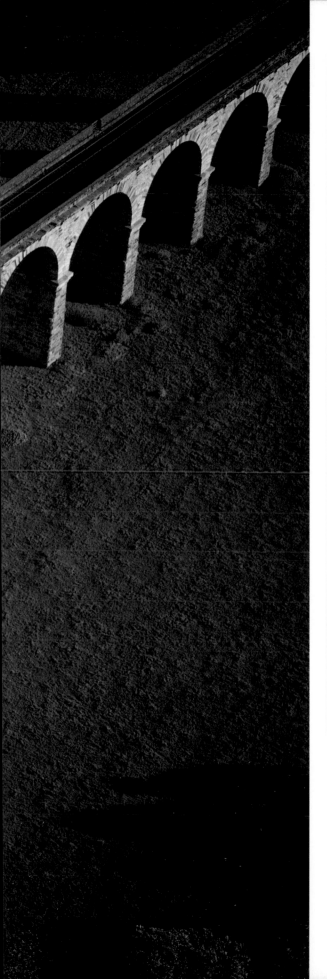

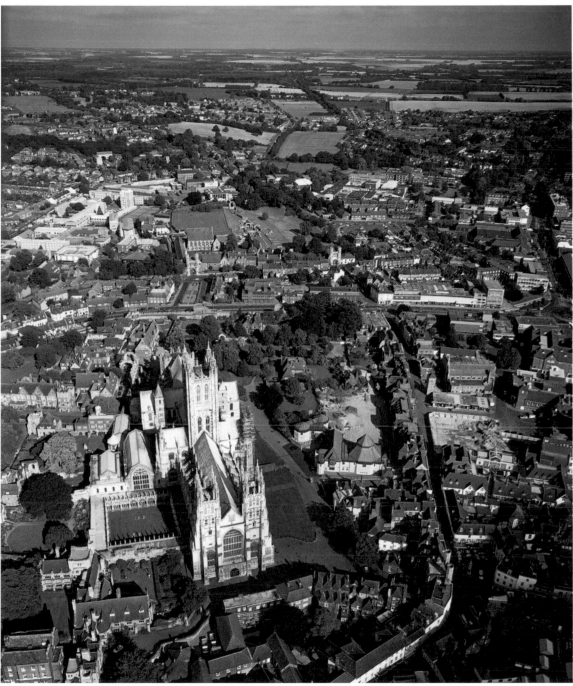

< LEFT
Railway viaduct, Yorkshire
The Romans brought us viaducts and the Victorians brought us the first real modern railways. The two together produced breathtaking feats of engineering, for which some men gave their lives in the rush to connect communities and increase trade and prosperity. In Yorkshire in particular, viaducts that have stood for over 100 years still grace the landscape.

^ ABOVE
Canterbury, Kent
Canterbury Cathedral is as much a place of pilgrimage today, for worshippers and tourists alike, as it was 600 years ago when Geoffrey Chaucer wrote his *Canterbury Tales*. These told the various stories of a group of pilgrims travelling from London's Southwark to Canterbury, to visit the shrine of St Thomas Beckett, murdered in the cathedral in 1170.

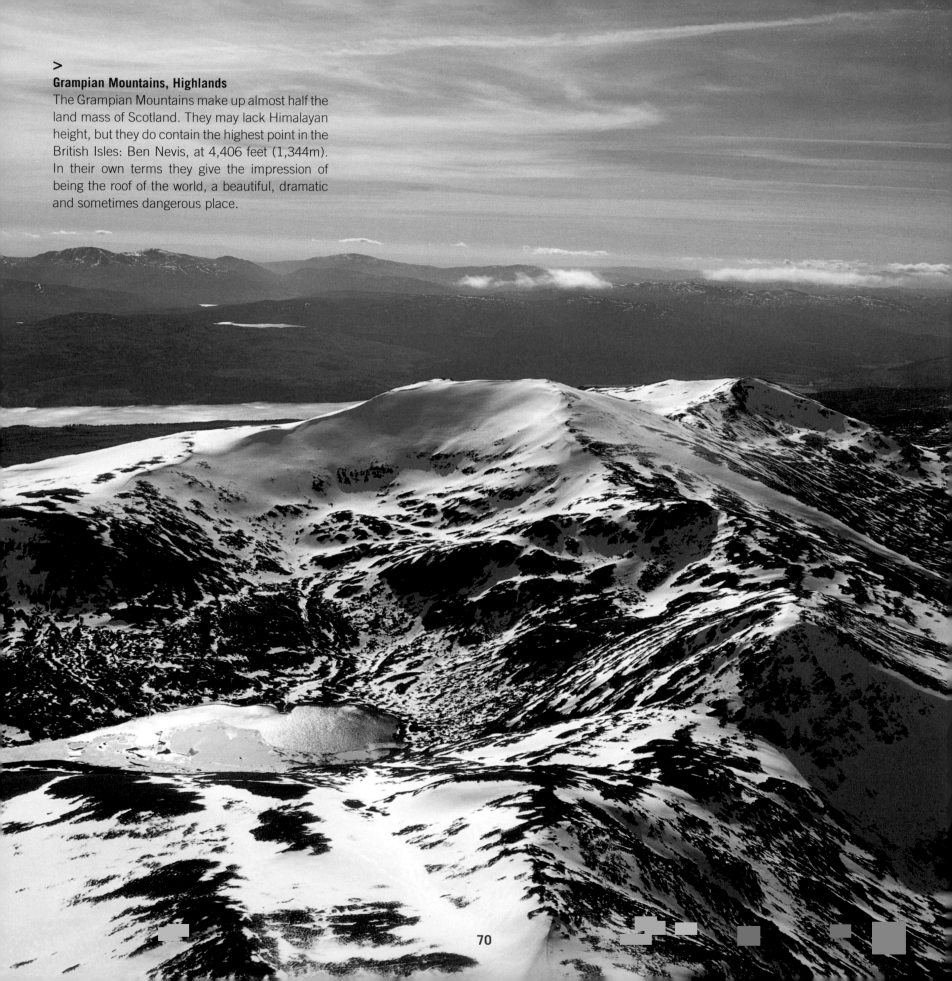

>

Grampian Mountains, Highlands
The Grampian Mountains make up almost half the land mass of Scotland. They may lack Himalayan height, but they do contain the highest point in the British Isles: Ben Nevis, at 4,406 feet (1,344m). In their own terms they give the impression of being the roof of the world, a beautiful, dramatic and sometimes dangerous place.

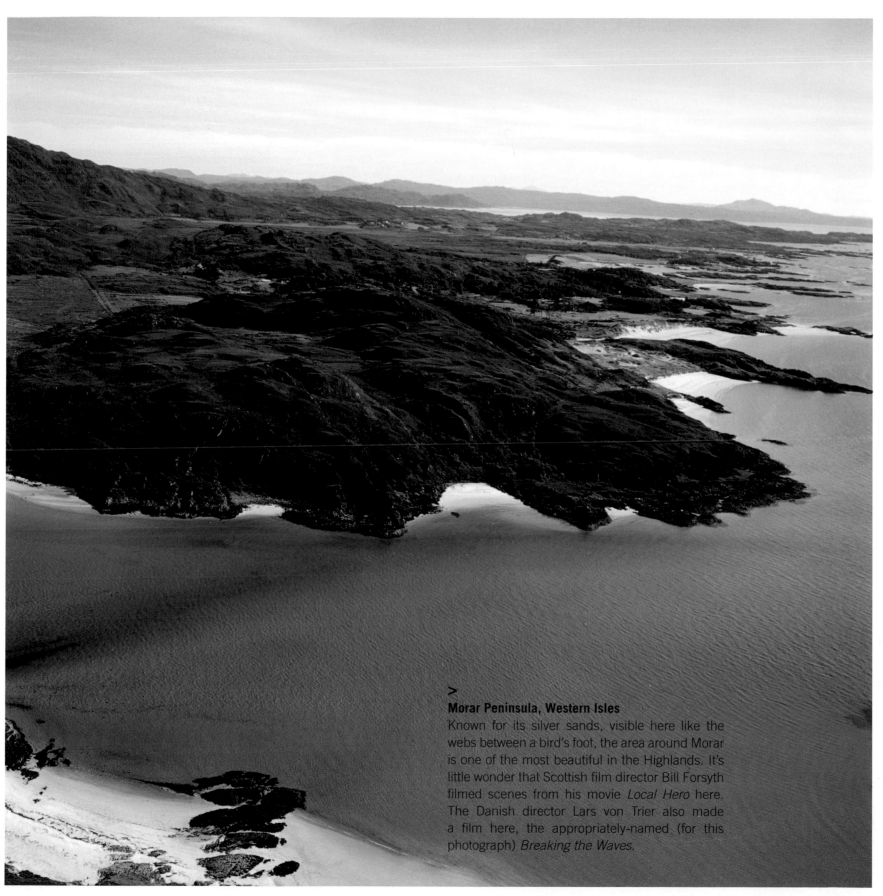

>
Morar Peninsula, Western Isles
Known for its silver sands, visible here like the webs between a bird's foot, the area around Morar is one of the most beautiful in the Highlands. It's little wonder that Scottish film director Bill Forsyth filmed scenes from his movie *Local Hero* here. The Danish director Lars von Trier also made a film here, the appropriately-named (for this photograph) *Breaking the Waves*.

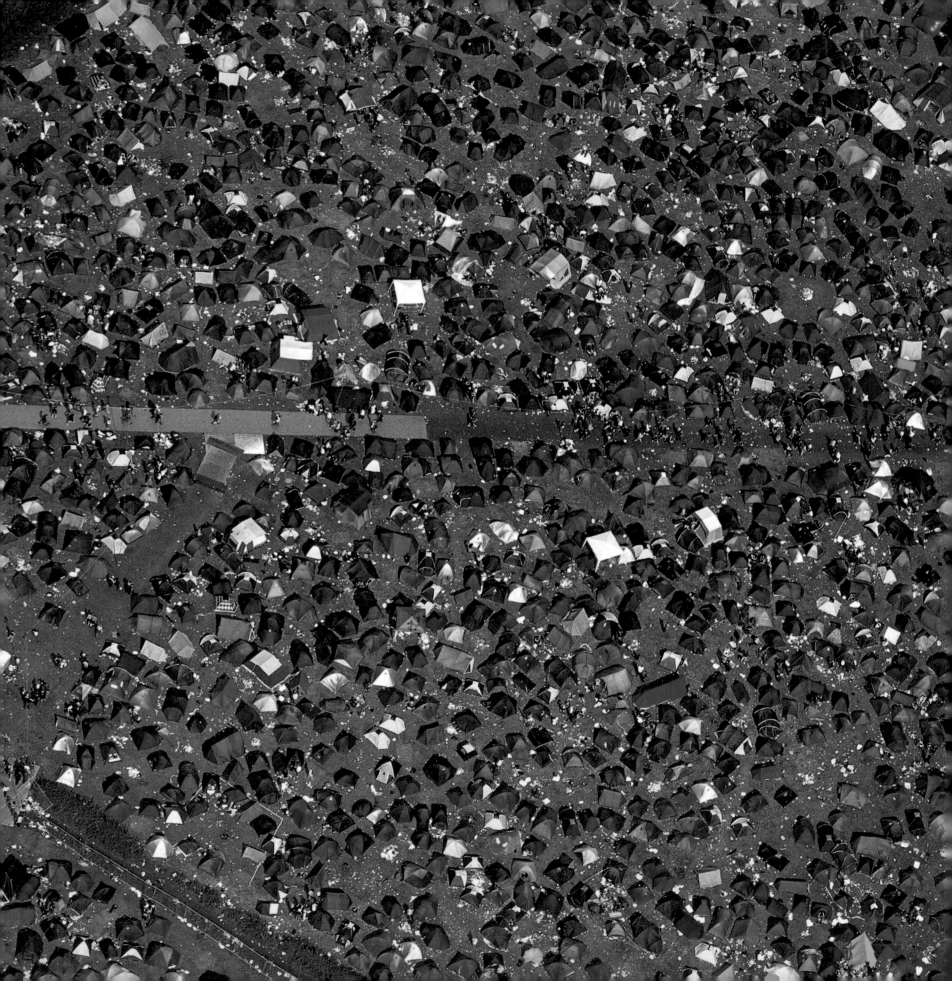

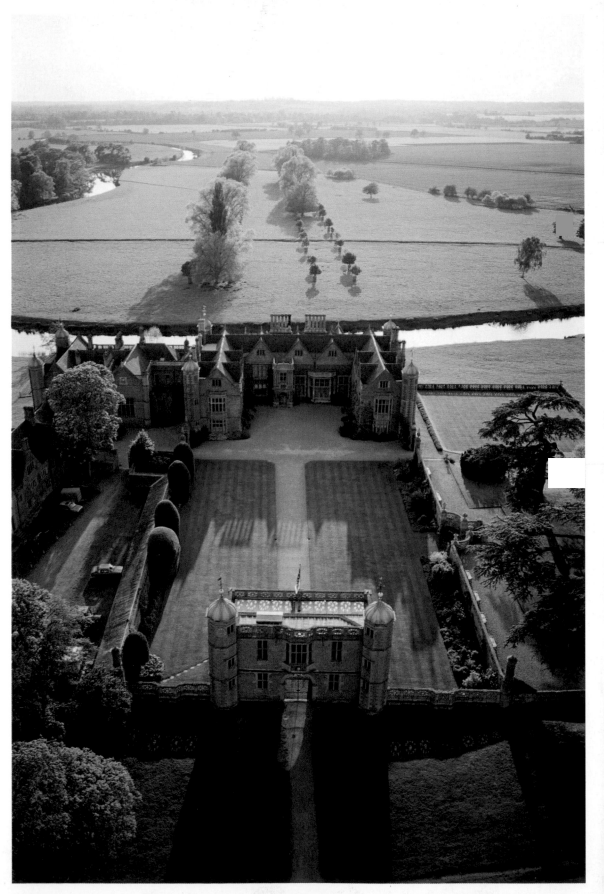

« PREVIOUS
Reading Festival, Berkshire
During the British Summer Bank Holiday weekend at the end of August, tents bloom like flowers in the fields around Little John's Farm in Reading in Berkshire, for the Reading Festival. Looking from the air like a kaleidoscope of glass or beads, the event has been held in Reading since 1971.

> RIGHT
Charlecote Park, Warwickshire
History walks almost every inch of the British Isles. Here in Warwickshire, Charlecote Park has been in the hands of the same family for 700 years, and Shakespeare is rumoured to have once been caught poaching on this estate, which stands on the banks of the River Avon, less than five miles from the busy centre of Stratford.

> OPPOSITE
Eurotunnel terminal, Kent
The Eurotunnel, or Channel Tunnel opened in 1994 and is the longest undersea tunnel in the world. This terminal at the Folkestone end guides vehicles onto one of the 25 shuttle trains that travel back and forth, linking Kent with Coquelles in the Pas-de-Calais. Around 200 million passengers have now made the journey.

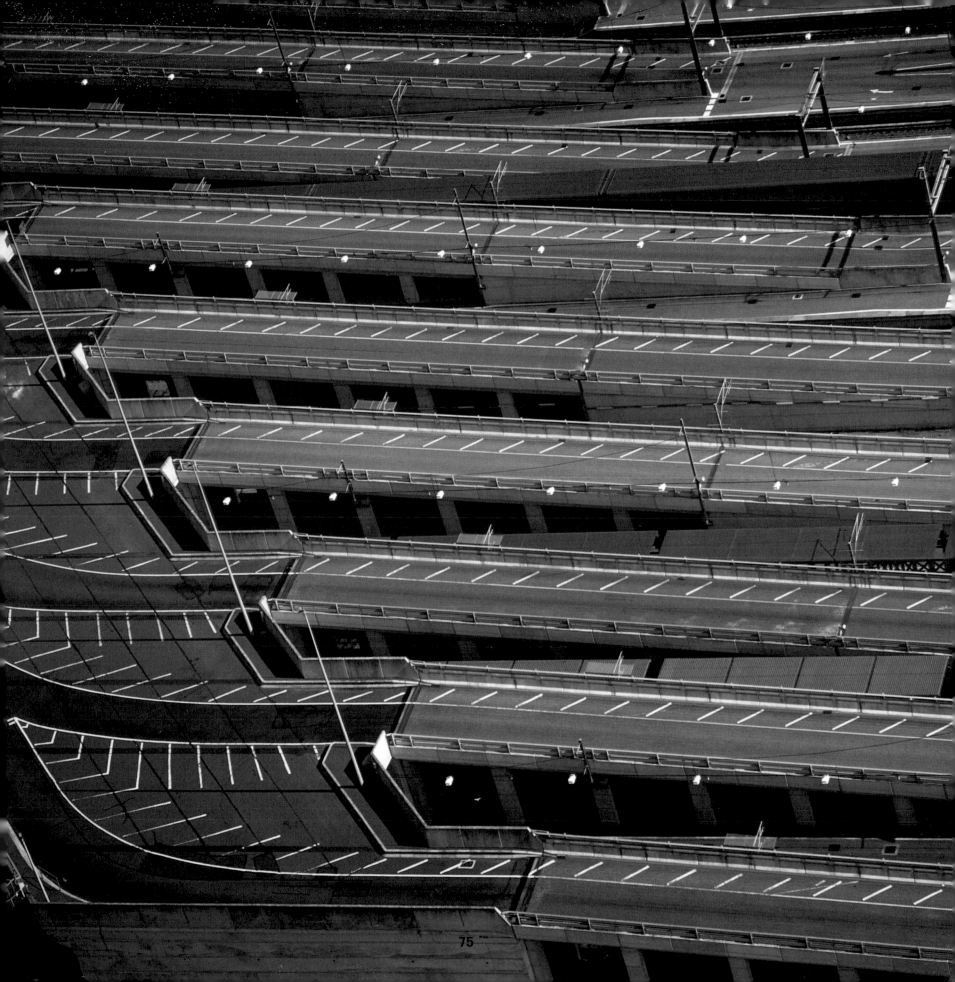

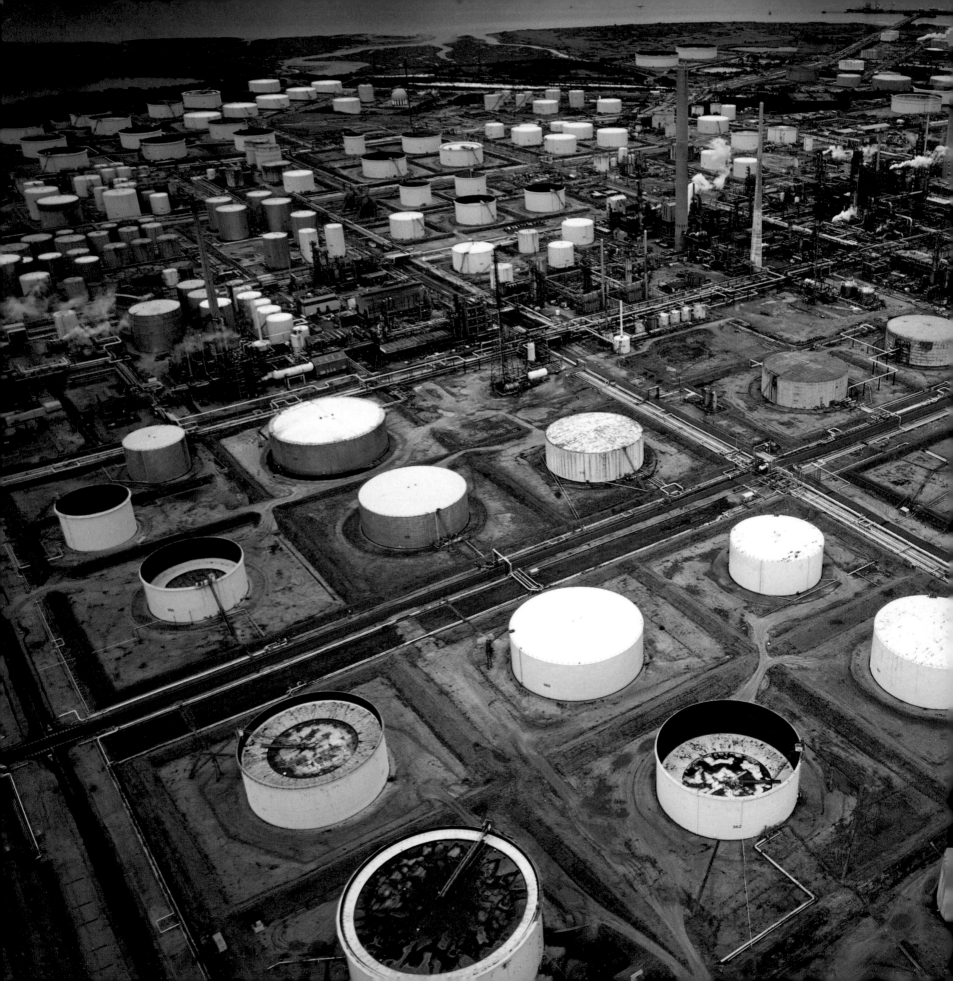

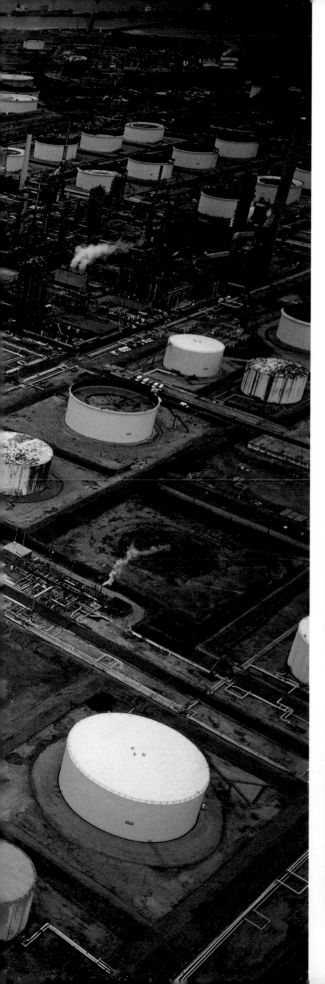

< LEFT
Fawley Oil Refinery, Hampshire
At Fawley on the Hampshire coast there were once Stone Age settlers, and later the Romans came here. There was a church here as long ago as the 10th century. Today it is known more for the Fawley Power Station and, shown here, the Fawley Oil Refinery, the largest in the British Isles.

V BELOW
Severn Bridge, Gloucestershire & Monmouthshire
The magnificent suspension bridge that spans the River Severn links England with England. The bridge leaves England in Gloucestershire but arrives first on the Beachley Peninsula, visible here at the far end of the bridge, which is still in England. Beyond there the bridge becomes the Beachley Viaduct before arriving in Monmouthshire. The later Second Severn Crossing, slightly further south, does actually link England with Wales.

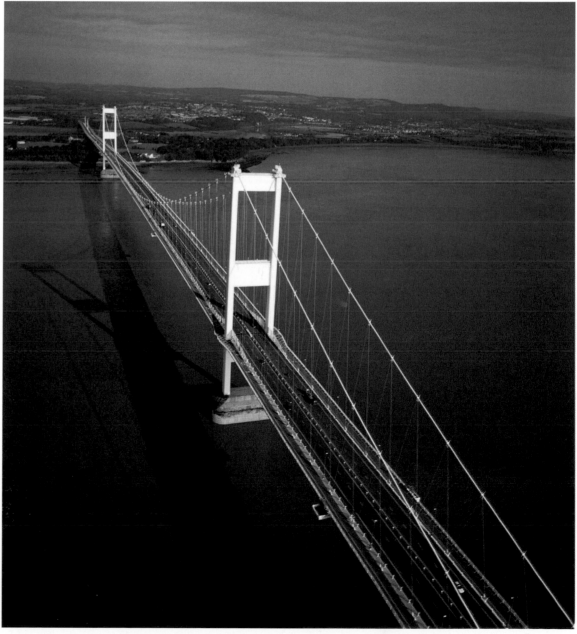

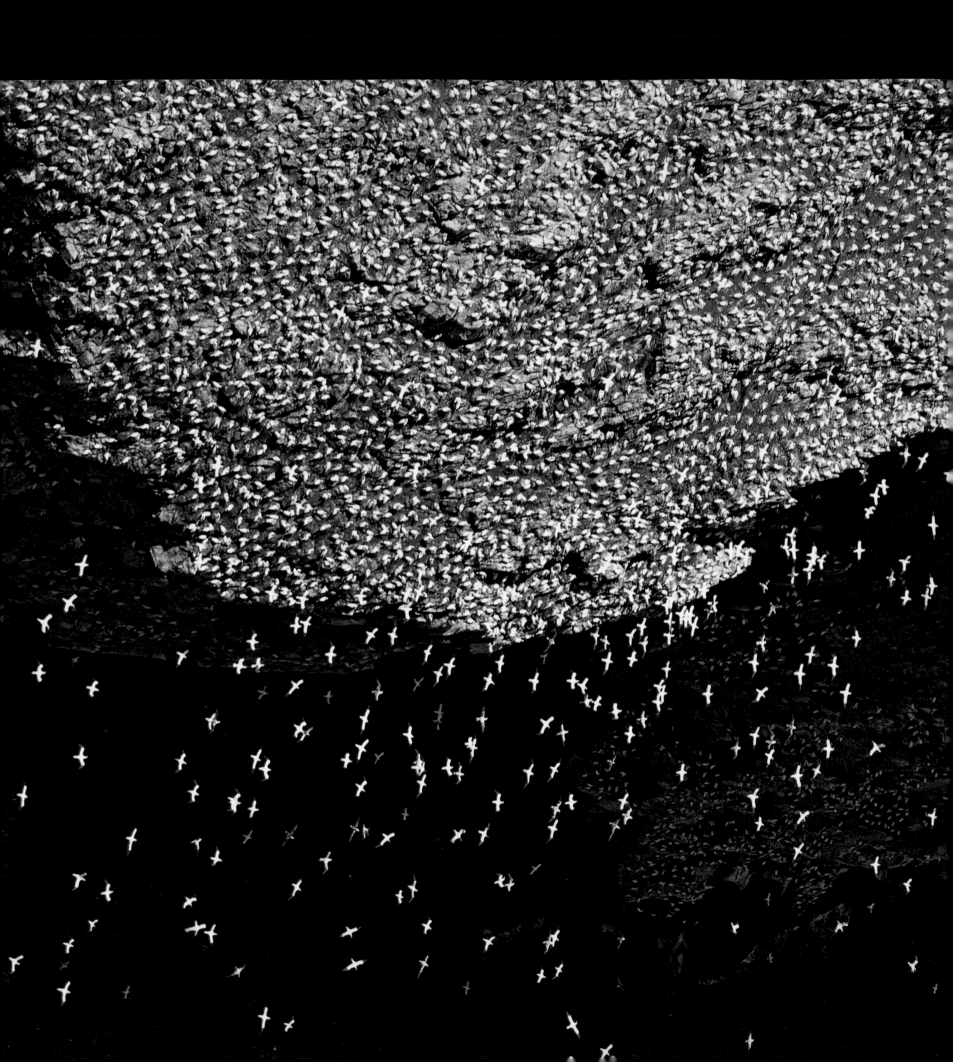

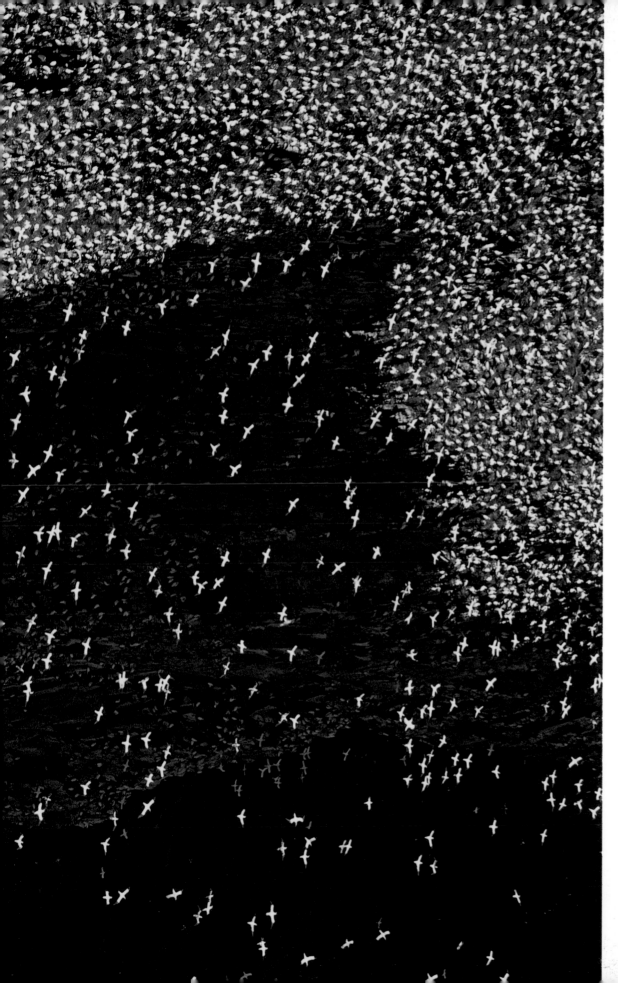

Bass Rock, Firth of Forth

The usual view of the Bass Rock, an island in the Firth of Forth, shows it from sea level towering over 100 metres into the air. This unusual acrial view captures instead the mass of bird activity that takes place on the rock and in the seas around. Almost 100,000 gannets are thought to inhabit the rock, about 10 percent of the North Atlantic gannet population. The scientific name of the northern gannet, *morus bassanus*, incorporates the name of Bass Rock because it was the place where the birds were first extensively studied.

> **RIGHT**
London
As the sun goes down at the end of the day, it bathes London's buildings in a rose-pink glow. From the 17th-century St Paul's Cathedral in the foreground, past the late 19th-century Tower Bridge and down the slinky River Thames to the 20th-century towers at Canary Wharf glistening in the distance, the city's great history spreads out visually before us.

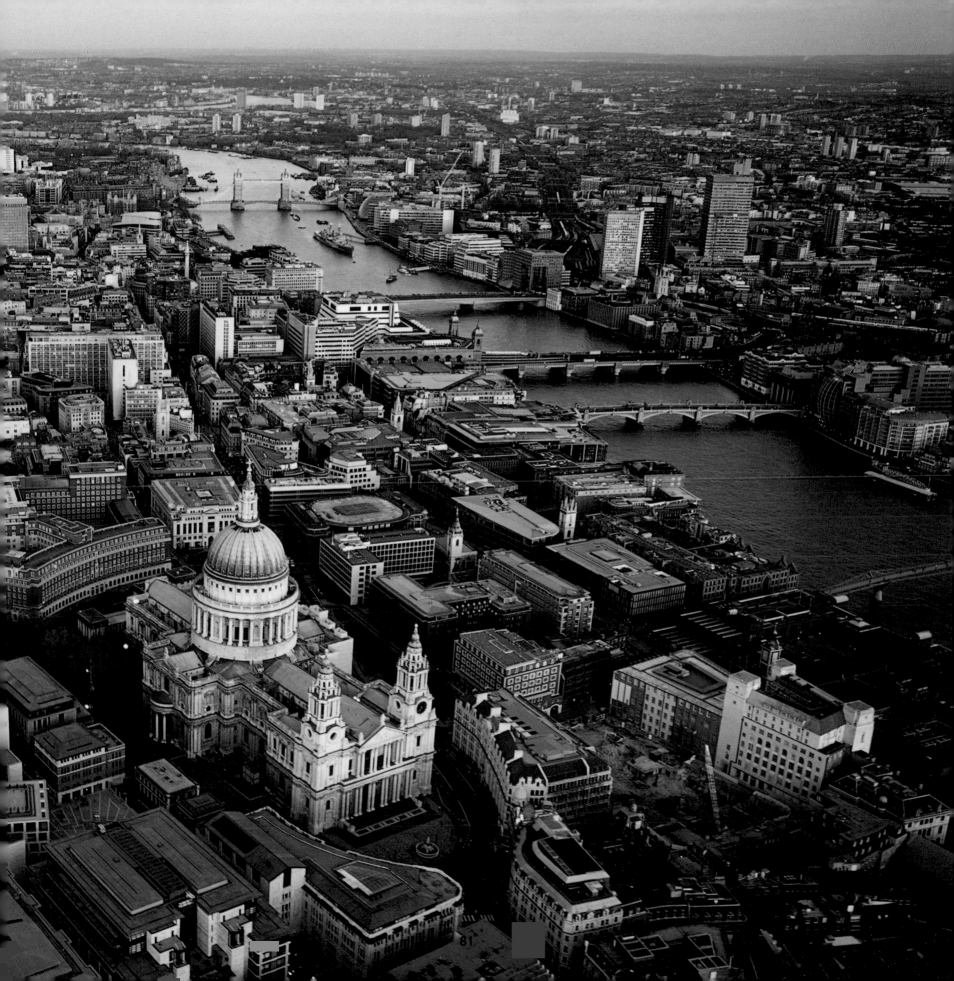

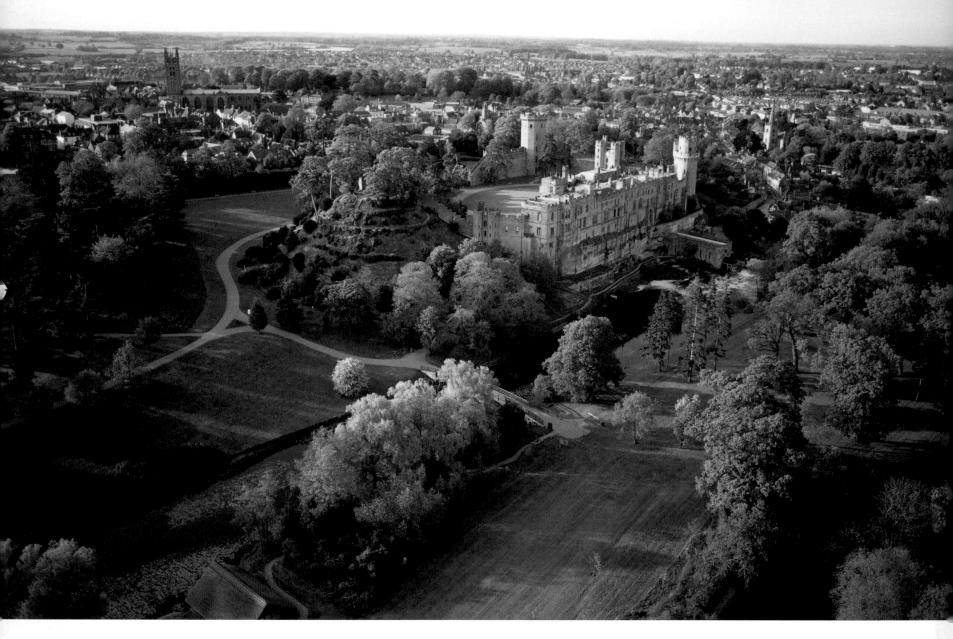

^ ABOVE

Warwick Castle, Warwickshire

In a commanding position above the River Avon, Warwick Castle still stands, one of the best-preserved castles in the country. Parts of the castle grounds date from the early 10th century, when it is said that the daughter of King Alfred the Great, Ethefleda, commanded that a castle be built on this spot.

>
Poppy field, Norfolk
North Norfolk has been known as Poppyland since 1883, when the writer Clement Scott gave it this nickname in an article he wrote in the Daily Telegraph. This view from the air shows why it's no exaggeration, but the Common Poppy has only been Norfolk's county flower since 2002, when Plantlife International organised a competition and asked people to vote for their choice.

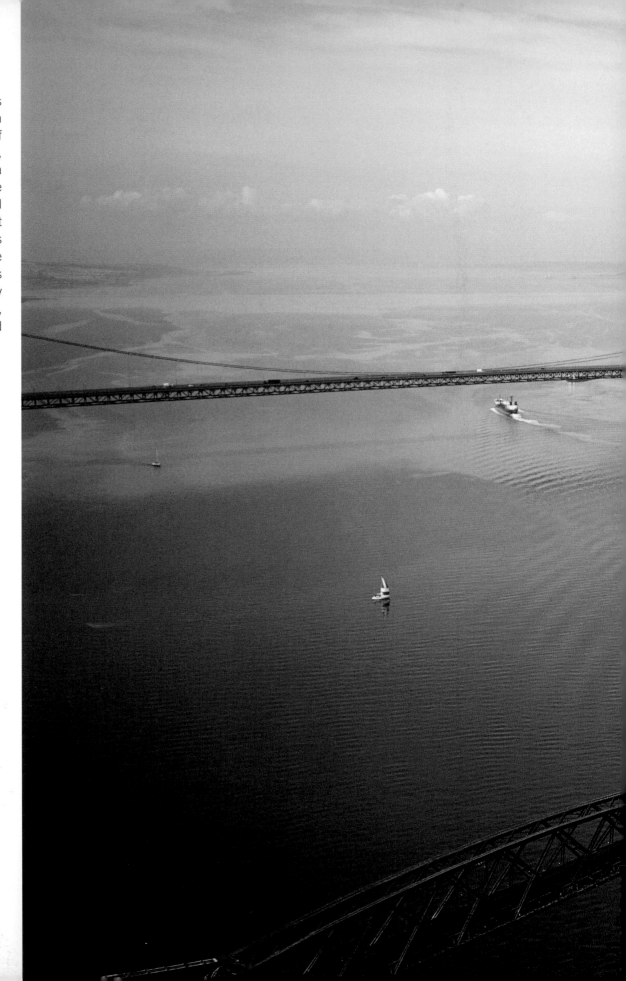

> **RIGHT**

The Forth Bridge, Edinburgh

In the foreground the Forth Bridge takes trains across the Firth of Forth, linking Edinburgh with Fife. It was completed in 1890 after seven years of work, and has even entered the English language, where painting the Forth Bridge has become a symbol for a task that never ends. In the distance is the more modern grace of the Forth Road Bridge. It was opened in 1964 making it somewhat easier for cars, cyclists and pedestrians to cross the Firth. The first ferry service here began in the 11th century, taking pilgrims north to St Andrews and Dunfermline Abbey. The ferry was begun by Margaret, the Queen Consort of King Malcolm III, which is why the towns at either end are called North Queensferry and South Queensferry.

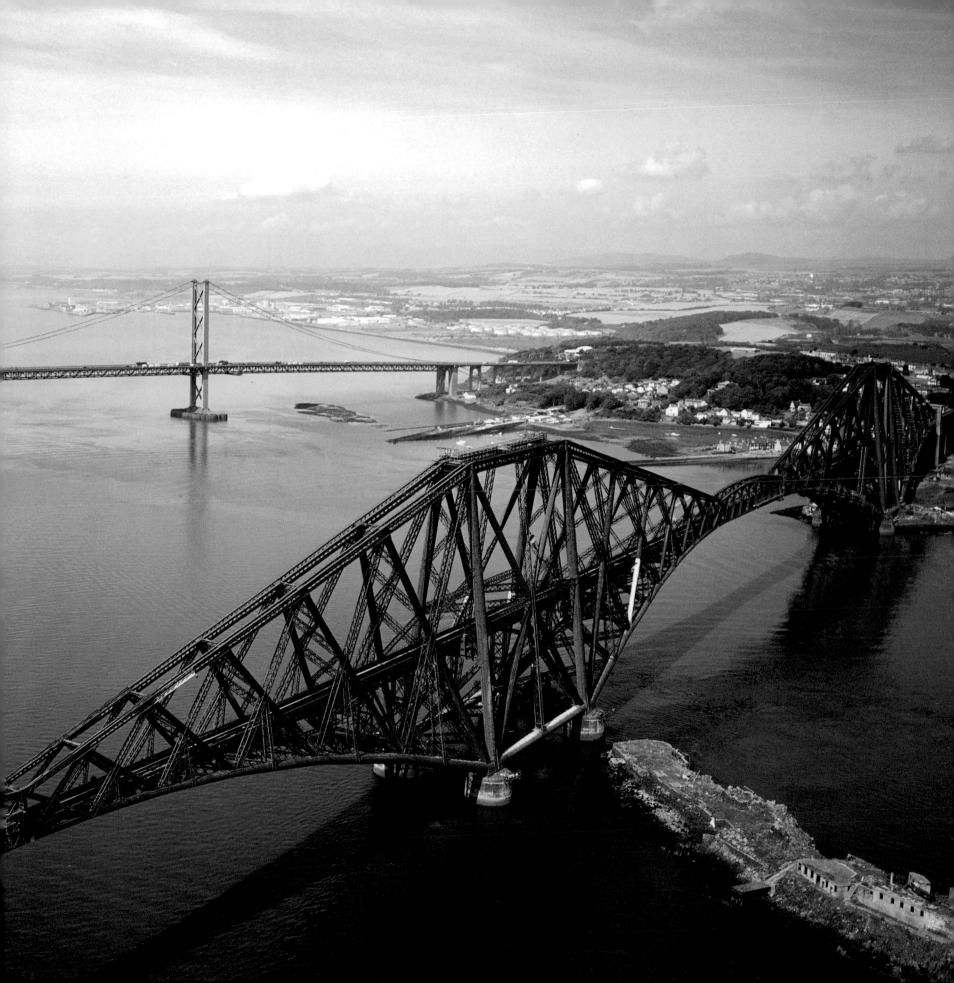

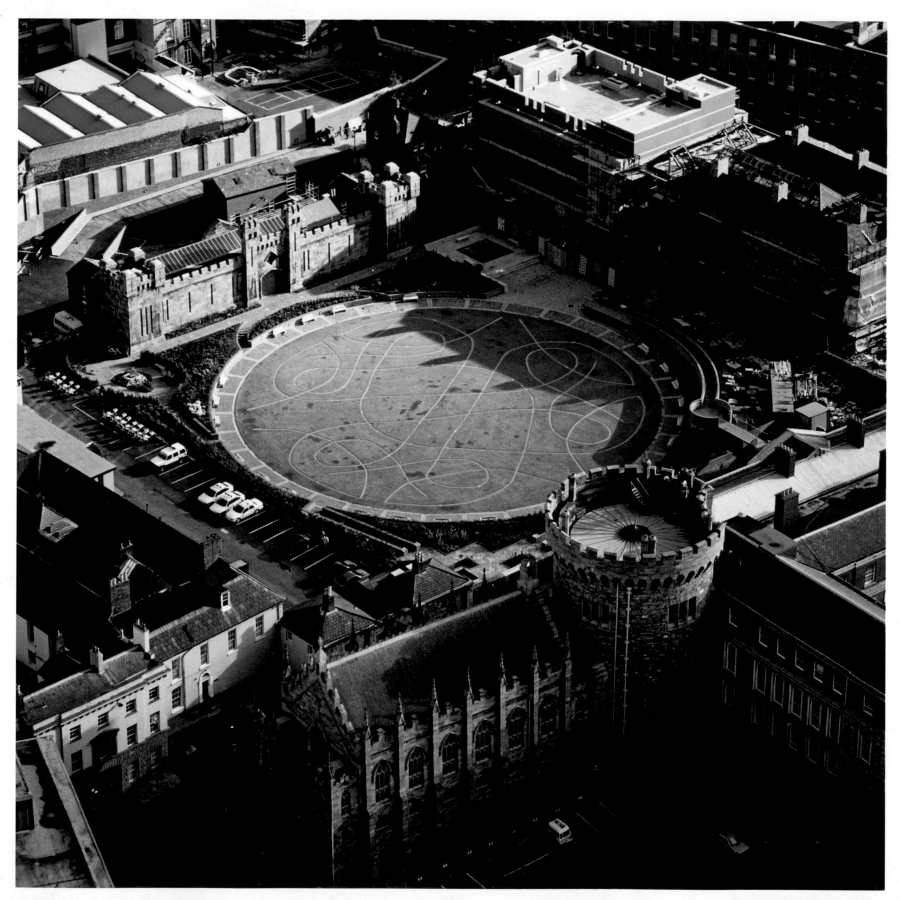

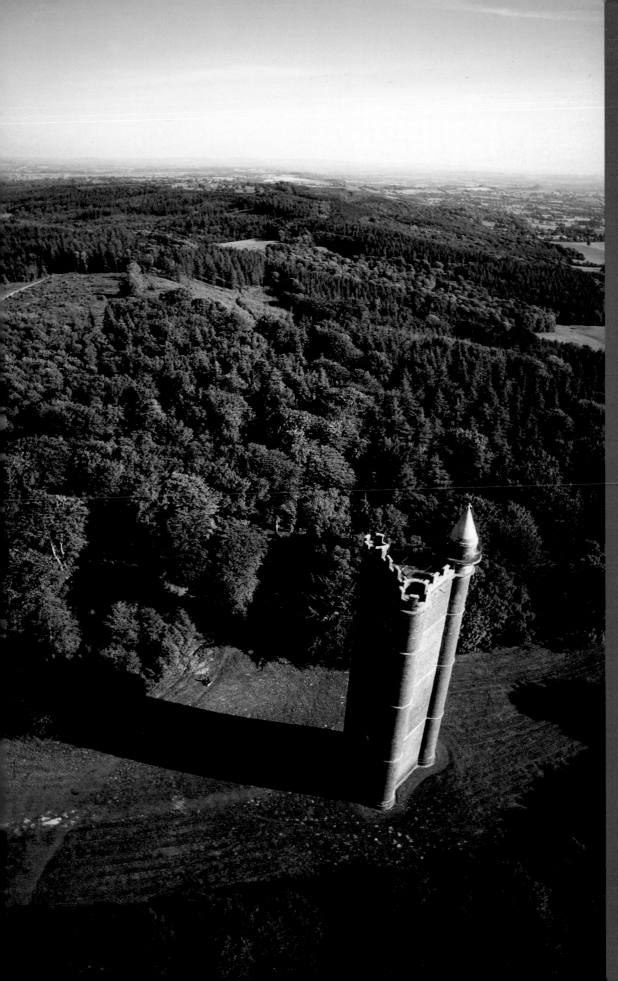

< OPPOSITE
Dublin Castle, Dublin

Layers and layers of history could be peeled away from the area round Dublin Castle, back to the very Black Pool or Dubh Linn which gave the city its name and which stood in the castle grounds. Come forward to the 10th century and picture a Danish Viking fortress standing here, and then a Norman castle made from earth and wood. In the 18th century most of the present building was constructed, and it remained a seat of government until 1922, when Ireland gained its independence from Great Britain. Since then it has served various purposes, including a courthouse, and today as well as being a tourist attraction, it is used for conferences, meetings of the European Council and other international bodies, and for the inauguration of Irish Presidents.

< LEFT
King Alfred's Tower, Wiltshire

This view from above brings out the soaring nature of King Alfred's Tower, rather than the more usual imposing impression given from the ground. It's possible to climb to the top and look out from 160 feet (49m) up in the air across the three counties of Wiltshire, Somerset and Dorset. The tower was built in 1772 for several reasons, including as a belated celebration of the accession of King George III in 1760, and in 1763 the successful conclusion of the Seven Years' War against France. The name of the tower, though, came from the belief that it is close to the spot where King Alfred rallied his troops prior to an important victory against the would-be Danish invaders.

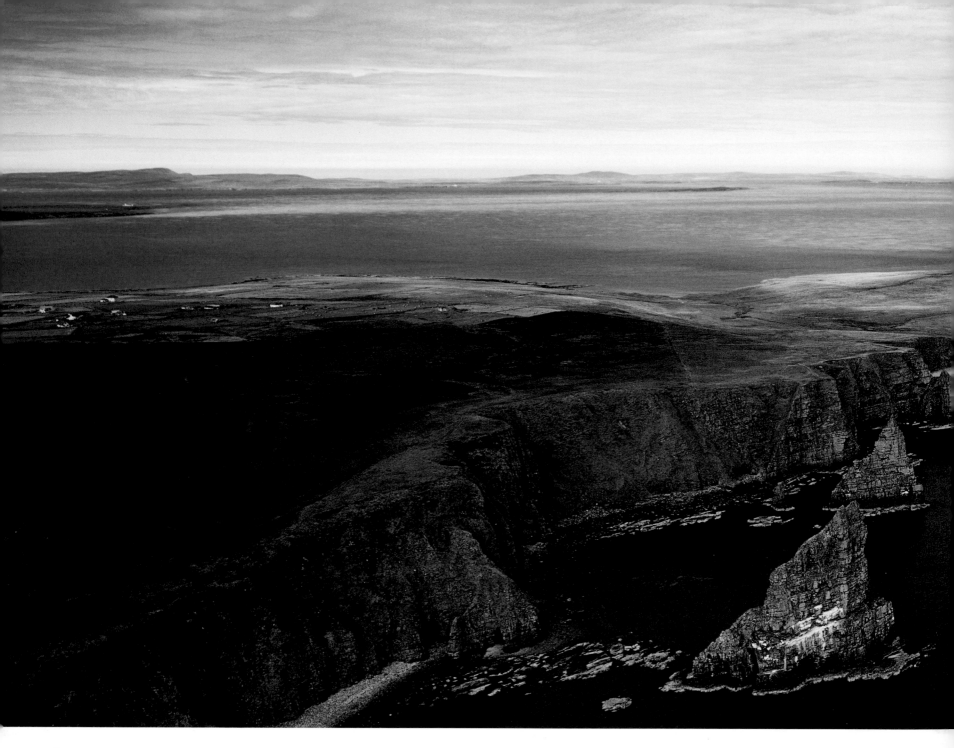

^ ABOVE

Duncansby Head, Highlands

Duncansby Head isn't quite the most northerly part of the Scottish mainland, but it's close. Right by John O'Groats, the mainland's northernmost settlement, Duncansby is noted for its red sandstone cliffs some 250 feet (70m) high, as well as the caves, sea arches and stacks carved by the wind and other elements.

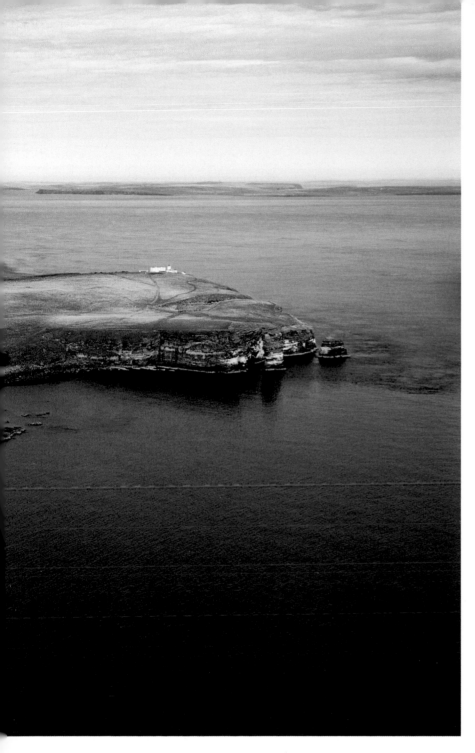

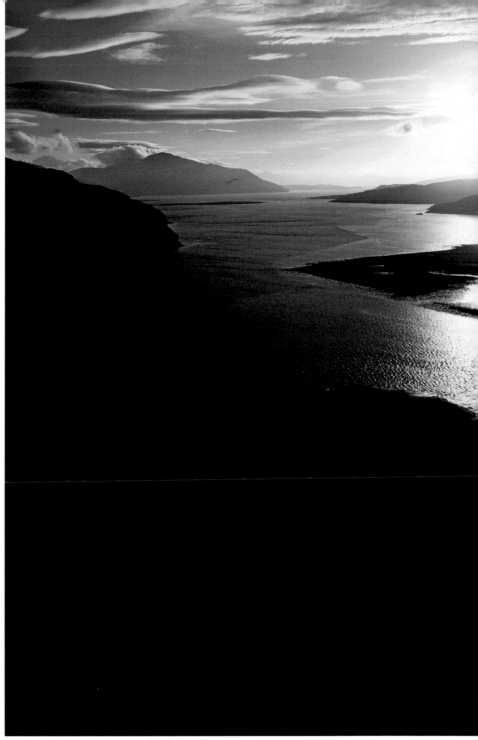

^ **ABOVE**

Eilean Donan Castle, Western Highlands

In the Western Highlands of Scotland stands Loch Duich, a sea loch, and from the shore a footbridge leads out to a tiny island, Eilean Donan. There on Eilean Donan stands what has been called the most romantic castle in Scotland. Looking at this sunset photograph, it's difficult to disagree.

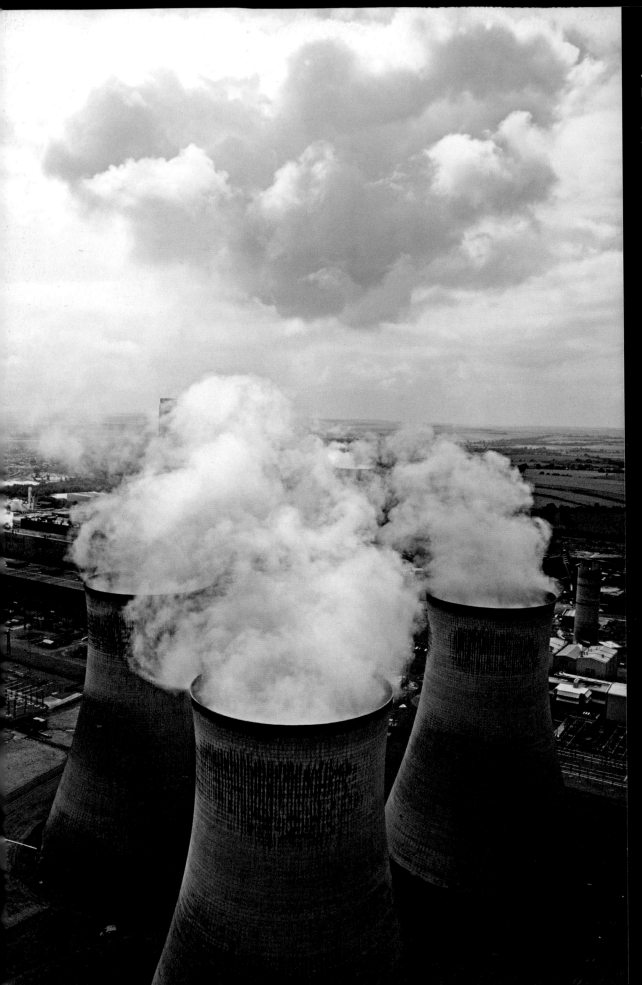

< LEFT
Didcot power station, Oxfordshire
Rising out of the Berkshire Plains, Didcot has not one, but two power stations. Although they do a vital job, they have been targeted by protestors as being among the most polluting in the country. Readers of *Country Life* magazine also voted them as one of the worst eyesores in Britain. They are certainly a powerful depiction of modern industrial Britain, reminiscent of Dante's Inferno.

> OPPOSITE
Leeds, Yorkshire
A certain sense of power and confidence oozes from this photo of Leeds, Yorkshire's main city. A sense of scale emerges, too, of the way in which the city has spread and sprawled as it expanded during the Industrial Revolution from its days as a small rural market town. It is still one of the fastest growing cities in Britain, and growing in style too, with new restaurants, shops and nightlife all making for a vibrant Yorkshire city.

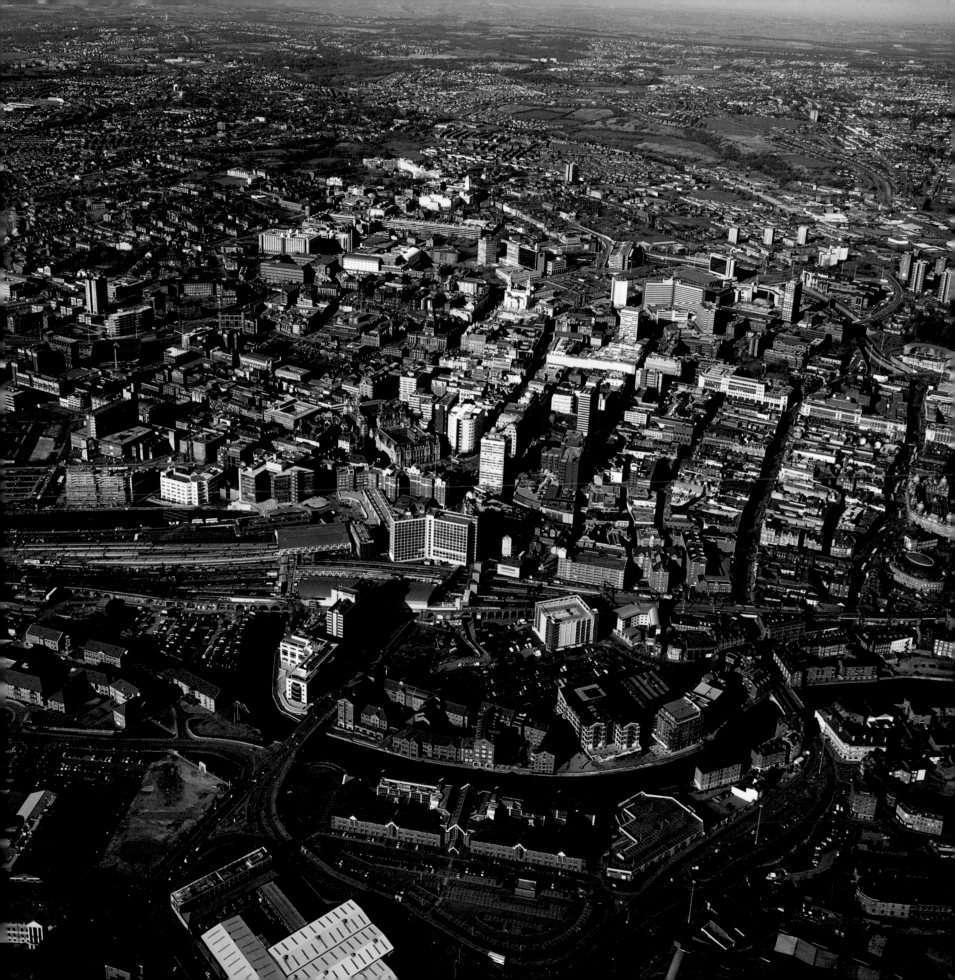

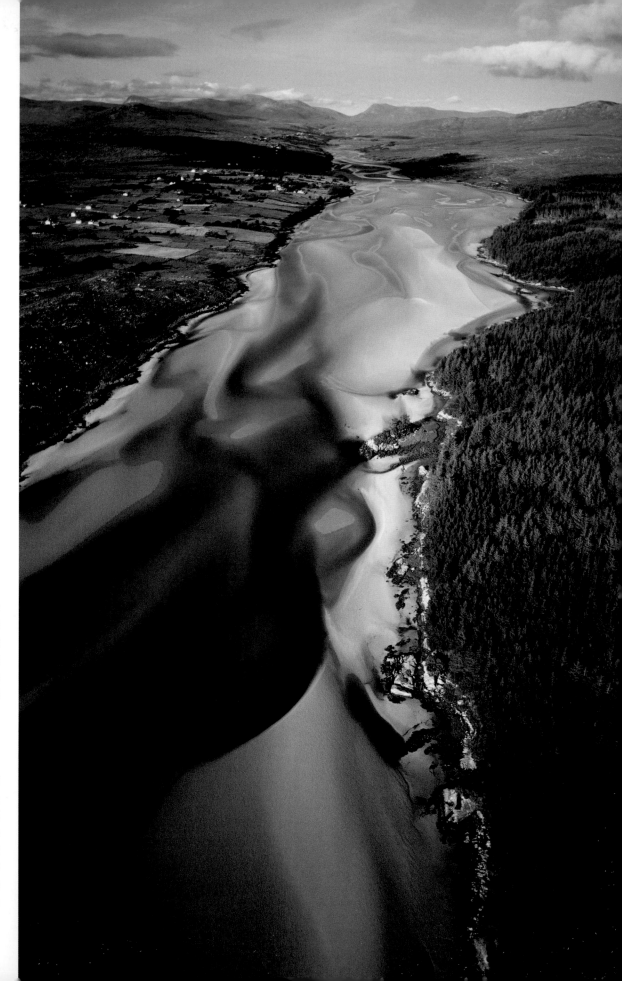

> **RIGHT**

Gweebarra Bay Estuary, Donegal

As the Gweebarra River makes its way from Lough Barra to Gweebarra Bay in County Donegal, the light, currents and reflections here make it look like a river of molten steel or lava. It is in fact a beautifully clean and healthy river, its 25-mile length filled in season with salmon and trout and with fishermen testing their skills.

> **OPPOSITE**

Mew Island lighthouse, County Down

The three Copeland Islands lie off the coast of County Down in Northern Ireland, to the north of Donaghadee. The lighthouse originally stood on Copeland Island, and was built from stone quarried by convicts, but after complaints about a lack of visible light from the lighthouse, a new one was put up on Mew Island. Not a single life has been lost since the lighthouse was opened in the 1880s.

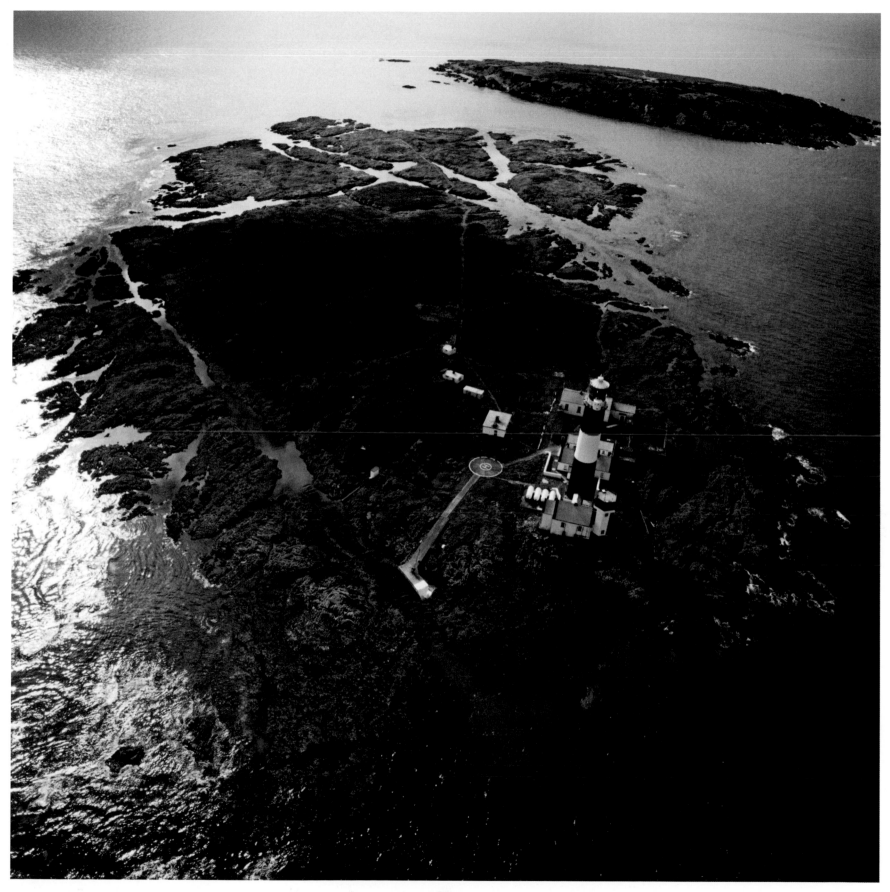

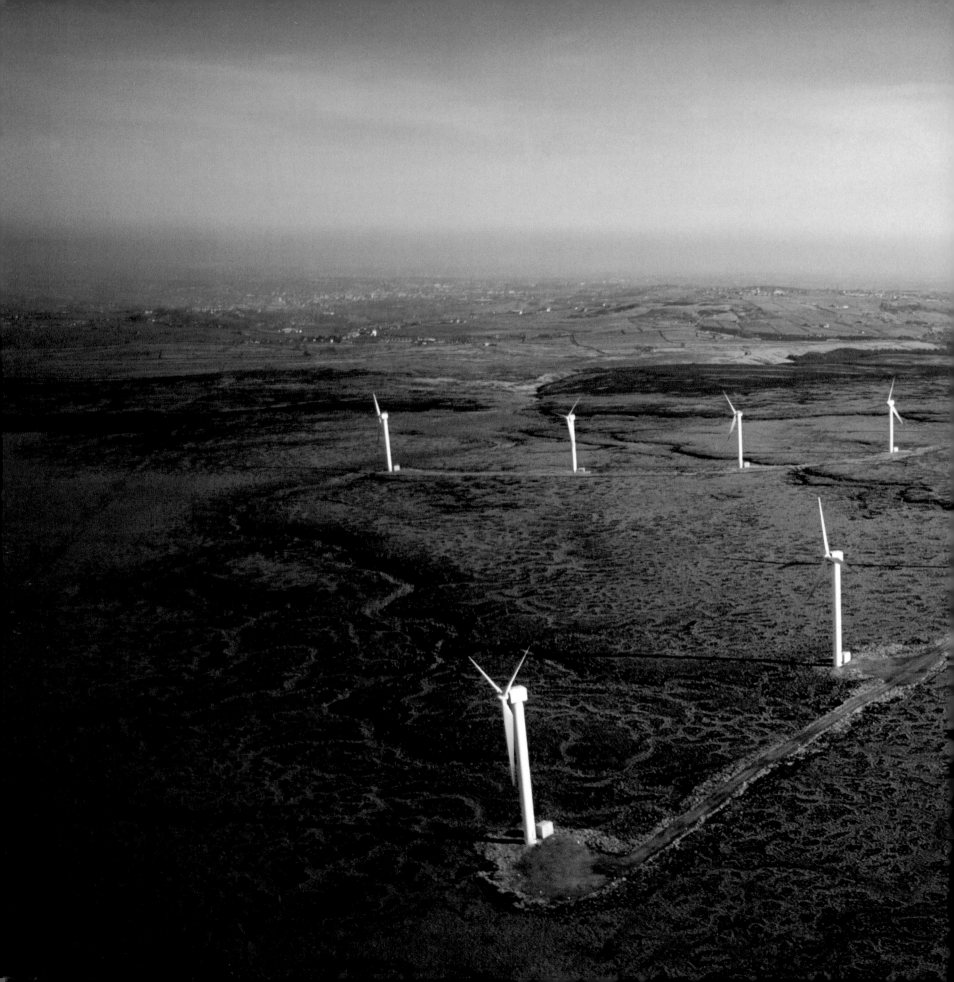

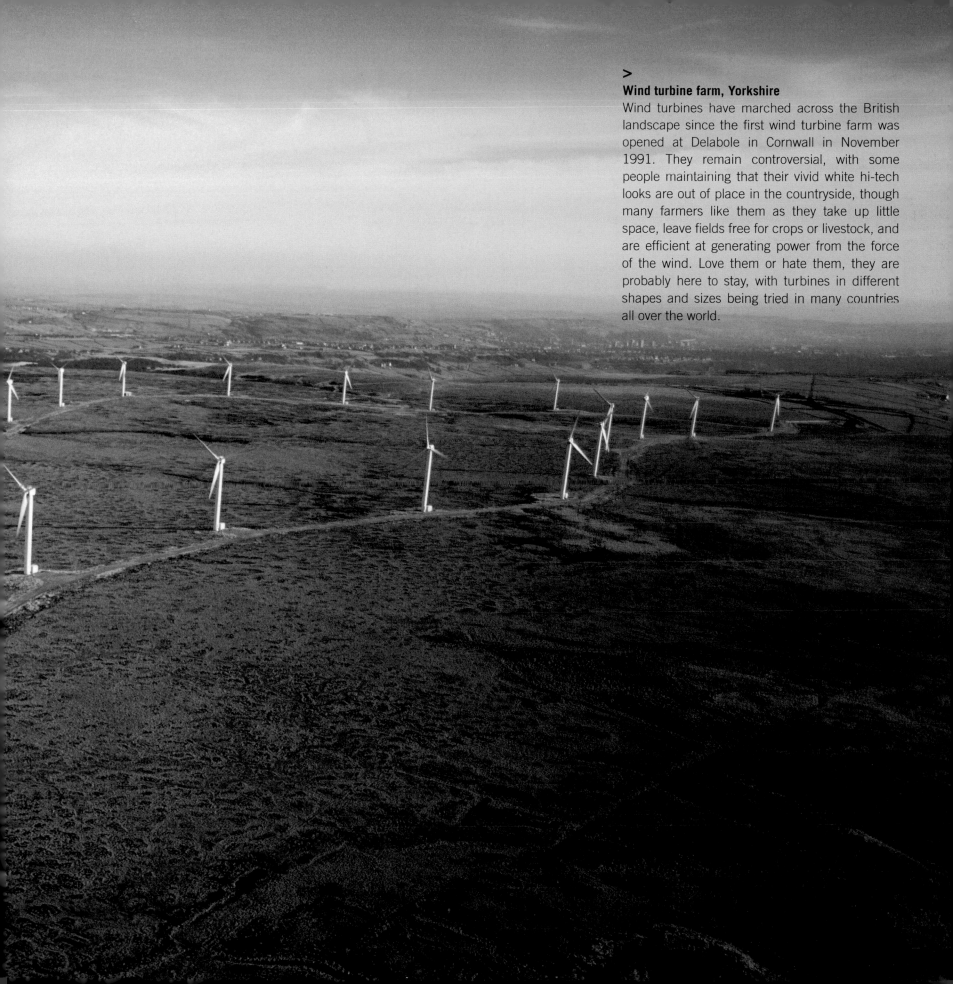

Wind turbine farm, Yorkshire

Wind turbines have marched across the British landscape since the first wind turbine farm was opened at Delabole in Cornwall in November 1991. They remain controversial, with some people maintaining that their vivid white hi-tech looks are out of place in the countryside, though many farmers like them as they take up little space, leave fields free for crops or livestock, and are efficient at generating power from the force of the wind. Love them or hate them, they are probably here to stay, with turbines in different shapes and sizes being tried in many countries all over the world.

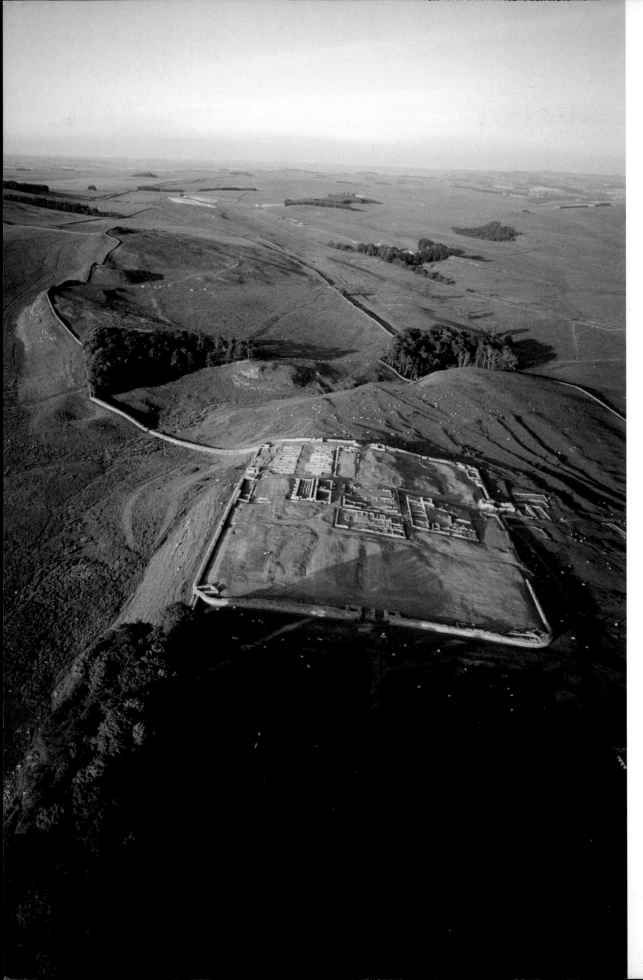

< LEFT
Hadrian's Wall, Northumbria

The significance of the Roman forts which were built into Hadrian's Wall at intervals, like posts in a fence, can be seen from this view of Housesteads. The wall itself snakes off into the distance, and the fort commands the heights and its observation towers would have given fine views of what was happening all around. Housesteads was built in about AD124, only a couple of years after the wall was started, and is one of the most interesting of the Hadrian's Wall sites to explore as a civilian settlement also grew up nearby. It is also one of the best preserved forts, its buildings creating an evocative picture of life at the time.

West Wycombe Estate, Buckinghamshire

The West Wycombe Estate in Buckinghamshire is a fabulous (in the true sense of the word) example of an 18th-century park and country house which embodies the decadence, grandeur and folly of one wealthy aristocrat, Sir Francis Dashwood. The mansion is huge and over-the-top, and the grounds studded with ruins, temples and other follies. One of the few 'real' buildings is the church of St Lawrence, whose golden ball is copied from one on the Customs House in Venice and which can seat 6–8 people. From here there are views for 15 miles in every direction, as far as Windsor Castle in Berkshire.

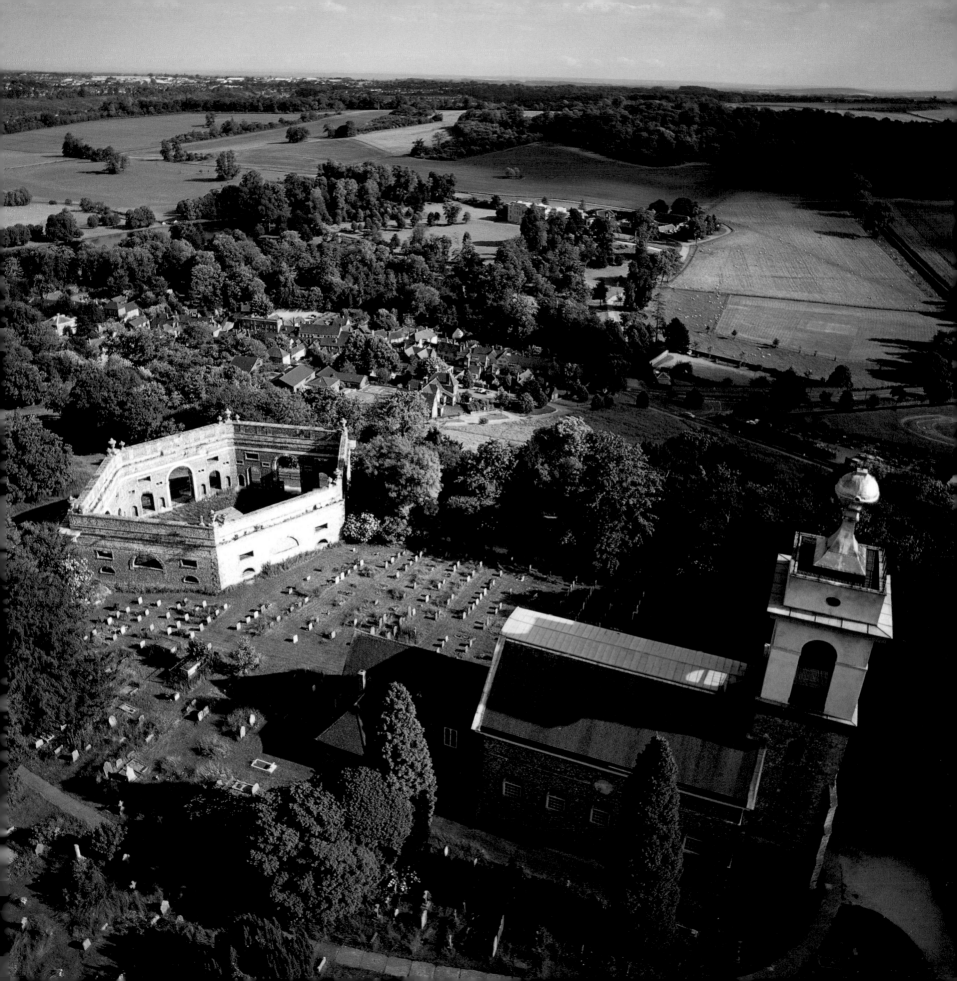

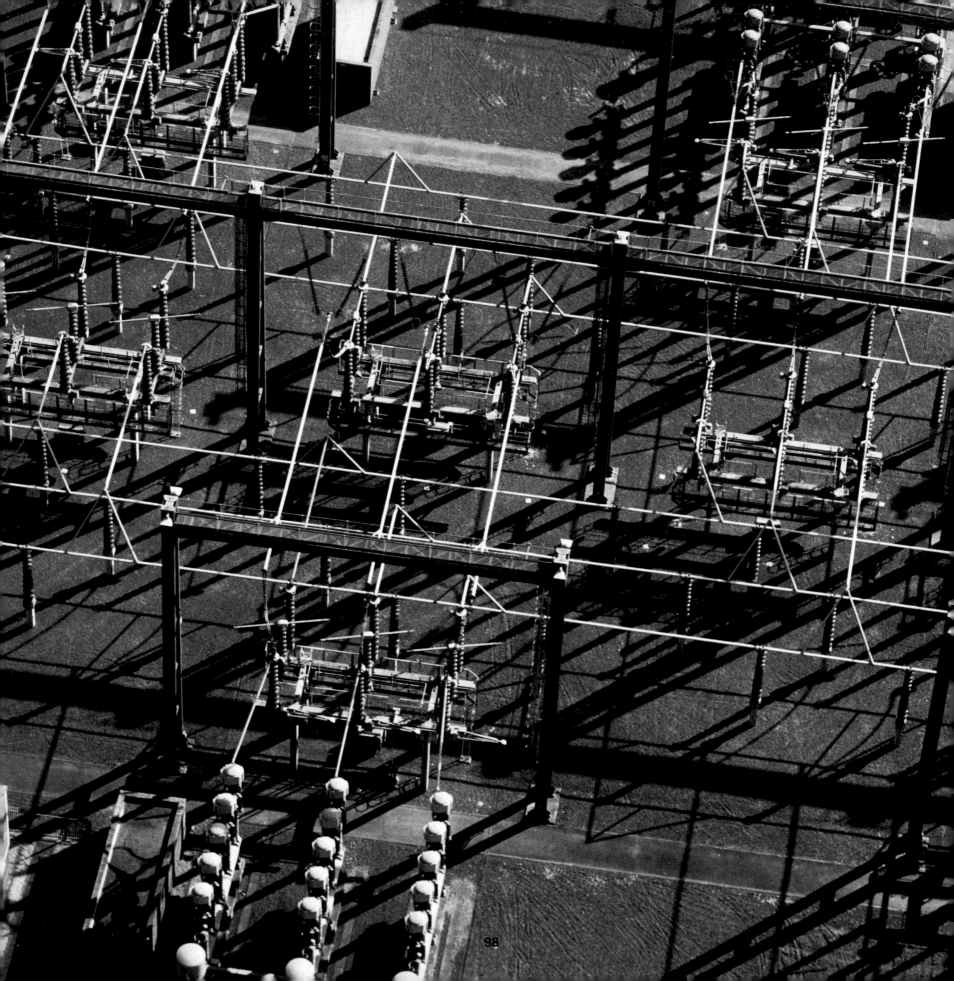

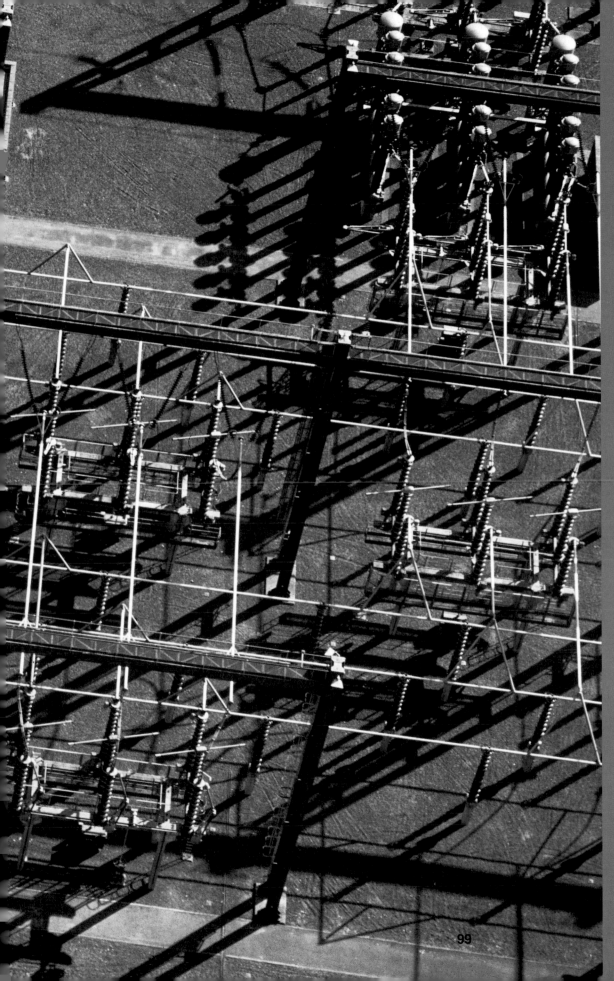

< LEFT
Electricity station, Dorset
Electricity stations like this one in Dorset may not look pretty, although this angle does reveal an interesting similarity with a computer circuit board. Without electricity, though, our lives would grind to a halt. Computers would crash, banks would run out of cash, and many of us would starve. Society has come a long way in two thousand years, as it is roughly this long since the ancient Greeks started to get some idea of what electricity was about.

INDUSTRIAL LANDSCAPES

We tend to think that it was the Industrial Revolution that radically altered the landscape of the British Isles forever, turning the green and pleasant land into a country of dark satanic mills. In fact the whole process had been going on for centuries. Even when the Romans reached these shores in the first century AD, the face of Britain was changing. It continued to change, as towns grew ever bigger, and the seeds were soon sewn, literally, for what became a series of Agricultural Revolutions...

When the Romans arrived in Britain, the native population is thought to have numbered about five million, and was growing fast. At that time about a quarter of mainland Britain was covered in trees, but farmers were already clearing away woodland in order to create pastures for livestock such as cows, to feed this growing population. Wood was also needed to build houses and to heat them, and in some places the lack of available wood was already a problem, and people were starting to build their houses from stone instead.

During the medieval period the building boom continued, and some of the magnificent castles and cathedrals which we see in this book used up wood at a phenomenal rate. The first Canterbury Cathedral was built in the late seventh century, and like many other grand buildings it was destroyed and rebuilt several times over. Initially timber would have been the prime component, which was obviously subject to destruction by fire, but then stone was increasingly used. Vast amounts of timber were still needed, though, some for scaffolding, and an enormous quantity for the building itself. One estimate says that when Salisbury Cathedral was built, it would have needed at least 2,500 of the finest oak trees, wiping out 160 acres (65 hectares) of woodland.

Yet another change to the landscape was brought about by the building of these medieval giants – the need to find sufficient quantities of stone. Quarries, gravel pits and clay pits began to pock the landscapes wherever the material could be found. The industrial landscapes go back a long way before that, though. Tin mining had been an industry in Cornwall since the Bronze Age, but the new scale of progress meant that even in the Middle Ages, Britain was in the early stages of the Industrial Revolution.

There is no one set date when it can be said that the Industrial Revolution began, as it was in fact more of an evolution. Historians disagree on what were the prime factors in triggering the revolution, but it occurred in the period 1750–1850 and it began in Britain, before spreading to the USA and other parts of the developed world.

Before 1750, most people in Britain lived in rural areas, and lived either directly or indirectly from agriculture. By 1850, the majority of the working population was dependent on industry. Vast numbers of people had moved to the towns, turning them slowly into cities, creating the start of the urban sprawl visible in so many of the photographs in this book. Where trees had given way to fields, now fields gave way to people and their houses. This wasn't simply because it was in the towns where new jobs were being created. The introduction of more efficient, large-scale farming methods meant that jobs were harder to find in the countryside too.

Another cause of the Industrial Revolution, and the dramatic changes it caused in the appearance of the British landscape, was the expansion of the British Empire and the fact that Britain, in those days, did rule the waves. Britain had the strongest navy in the world and each of its sailing ships required well over 1,000 trees to be sacrificed in its construction. There was already a brick- and glass-making industry, and a military demand for gunpowder, all of which required charcoal from the country's trees. Again, more of the native forest was being lost.

And then the real Industrial Revolution happened. Manchester was found to have ideal conditions for cotton weaving, so cotton was imported and the textile industry, the real nub of the Industrial Revolution, began. Alongside this were the beginnings of the modern iron and steel industries. The first iron furnaces were deliberately placed close to areas of good woodland, to provide charcoal to keep them burning.

Then came the steam train, a major invention, which also had an impact on the landscape. The trains required fuel and the new tracks required wooden sleepers. By now Britain was heavily dependent on imported wood. The railways themselves had little negative effect on the look of the countryside, as tracks took up tiny slithers of space, and often disappeared completely under the ground through tunnels. Where valleys had to be crossed, elegant viaducts were often built which sometimes even had the effect of enhancing the landscape.

Today only about five or six percent of the British Isles is covered by trees. The industrial towns of the north and midlands, the various capital cities of the different nations, the ports and docklands essential for trade and military use, all have spread into the 'green and pleasant land'. Although it might seem regrettable when car parks replace cow pastures, the process is inevitable, and there are examples of how one-time eyesores can be turned back into attractive parts of the landscape, with great benefits for communities and visitors.

The prime example of this is the conversion of a disused clay pit in Cornwall into one of Britain's biggest tourist attractions: the Eden Project. It was a visionary scheme. The former china clay pit, once a vital part of Cornwall's economy and producing the versatile material called kaolin, was turned not only into a successful tourist project but one that has had a positive impact on locals and visitors alike. The bleak mined-out remains of the clay pit were replaced with the world's largest conservatories. Plants from all over the globe are used to create miniature worlds – tropical forests, deserts and Mediterranean gardens.

The Eden Project is unashamedly educational and 'green'. It has been an astonishing success, since it opened in March 2001 after two and a half years of work, and several years before that, of planning and fundraising. Over eight million people had visited the Eden Project by 2006, well over a million a year. What had been a clay pit which, when it closed down, threw people out of work, now employs several hundred full-time staff, 95 percent of them from the immediate area. It has brought an estimated £700 million into the local economy.

The Eden Project shows what can be done, with imagination and vision, to transform a place. It is a fine example of the modern industrial landscape, in a way turning it back to nature but adapting to the modern world, where one of the biggest industries is tourism. It's notable how many of the places featured in these pages are reliant on tourism – almost every castle in the book, Stonehenge, the piers and the fishing ports, ancient abbeys, country houses, seaside towns. All rely on the visitor, taking the time to appreciate them.

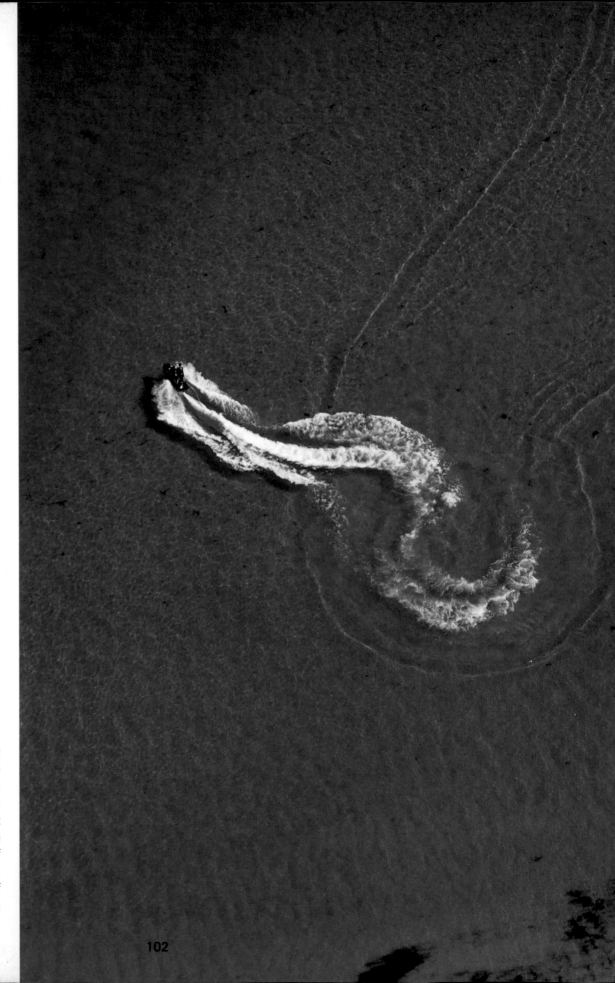

> RIGHT
Jet skiing, Devon

Jet skis have been around since 1973, when the Japanese company Kawasaki produced the first machines, and their brand name for them became a general term, just as Hoover came to mean a vacuum cleaner. The skier here is enjoying the crystal-clear waters off the Devon coast, though as with any water sport, he will need to take care. Every year British coastguards rescue dozens of jet skiers who stray out of the sight of land, and become disorientated.

> OPPOSITE
Eastbourne bandstand, East Sussex

A far more sedate picture of the British seaside is created by this image of the Eastbourne bandstand. Bandstands began in the Victorian era, when brass bands boomed in popularity and people started to travel more for leisure. Most seaside towns had their own bandstand, where people could relax for an afternoon or evening of music. The semi-circular Eastbourne bandstand, with its blue-tiled roof strangely reminiscent of more exotic places like Samarkand, is unique in the British Isles.

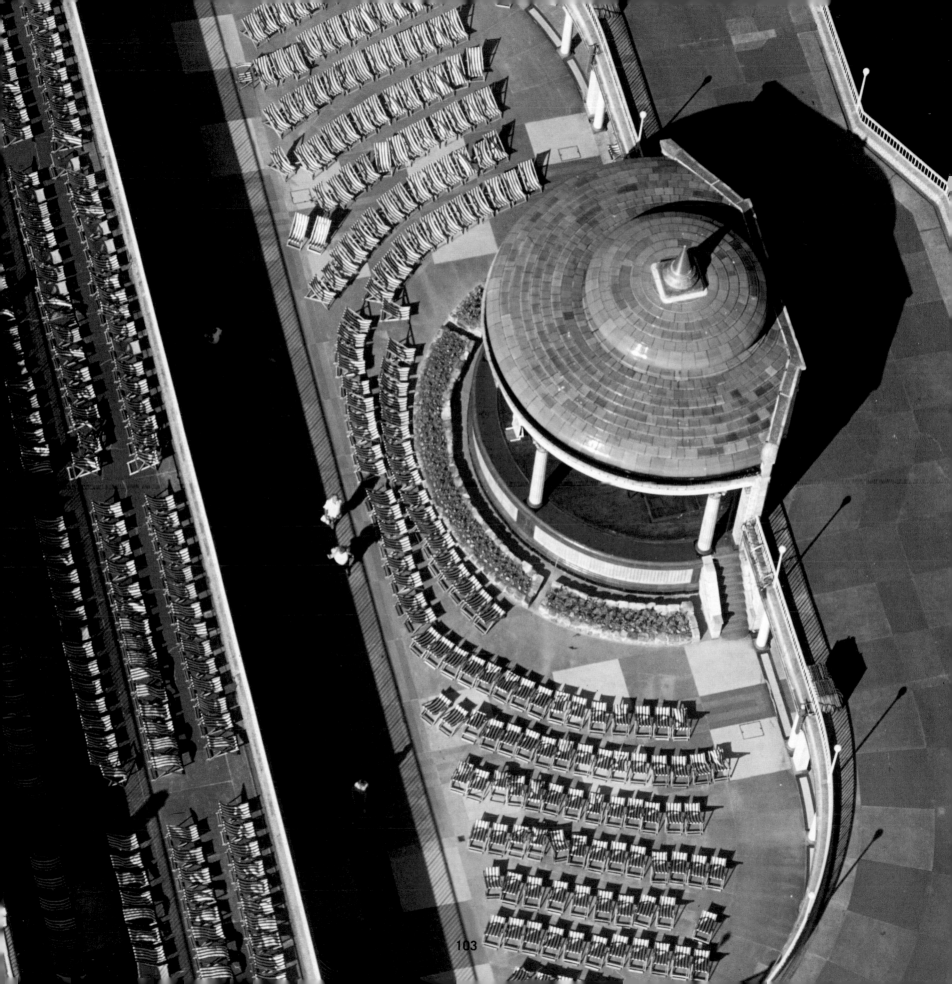

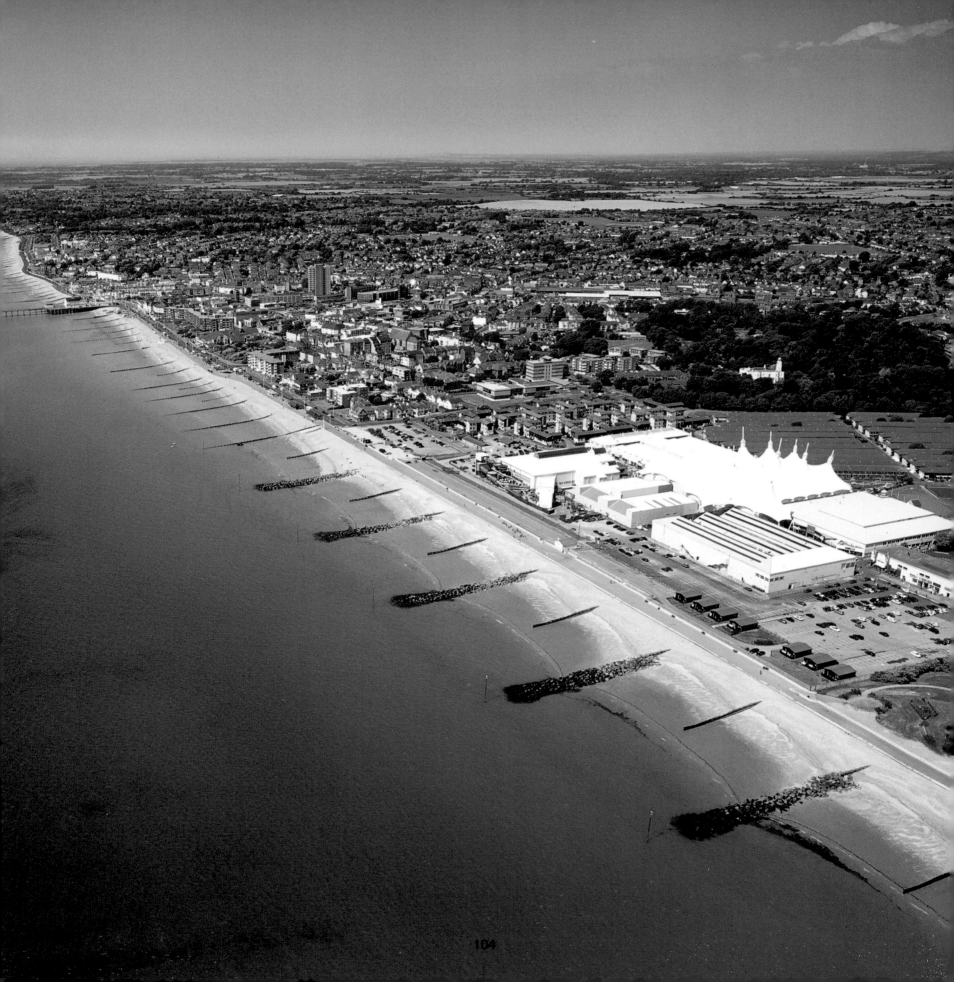

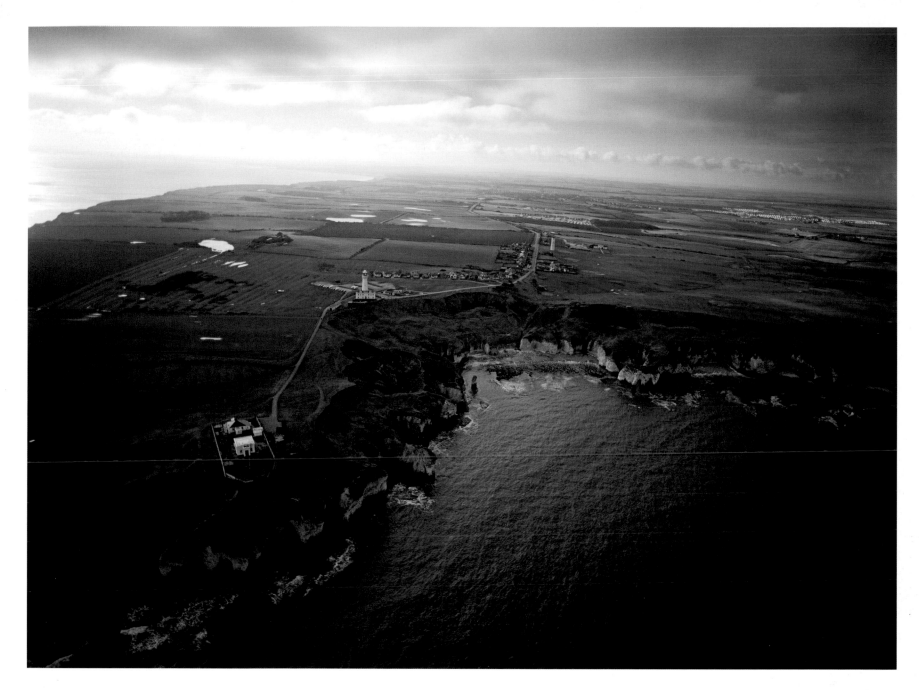

< OPPOSITE
Bognor Regis, West Sussex

Bognor was, for a long time, just another fishing village on the south coast of England, until the late 18th century when visitors began coming to enjoy the sands and the waters. It is less than 70 miles from London, making it an easy day trip when the railways developed. It gained the suffix of 'Regis' after King George V visited in 1927, and eventually retired there as the clean air was deemed to be good for his health, after a lifetime of heavy smoking.

^ ABOVE
Flamborough Head, Yorkshire

Protruding into the North Sea on Yorkshire's east coast, and close to some of the highest sea cliffs on the whole of Britain's east coast, Flamborough Head is a seven-mile long chalk promontory. The hard pounding of the sea has resulted in the carving out of numerous caves along the coast, despite the usual resistance of chalk to erosion. Its cliffs and caves, and its projection out into the sea, make it a magnet for migrating birds – and for the British 'twitchers' who follow them.

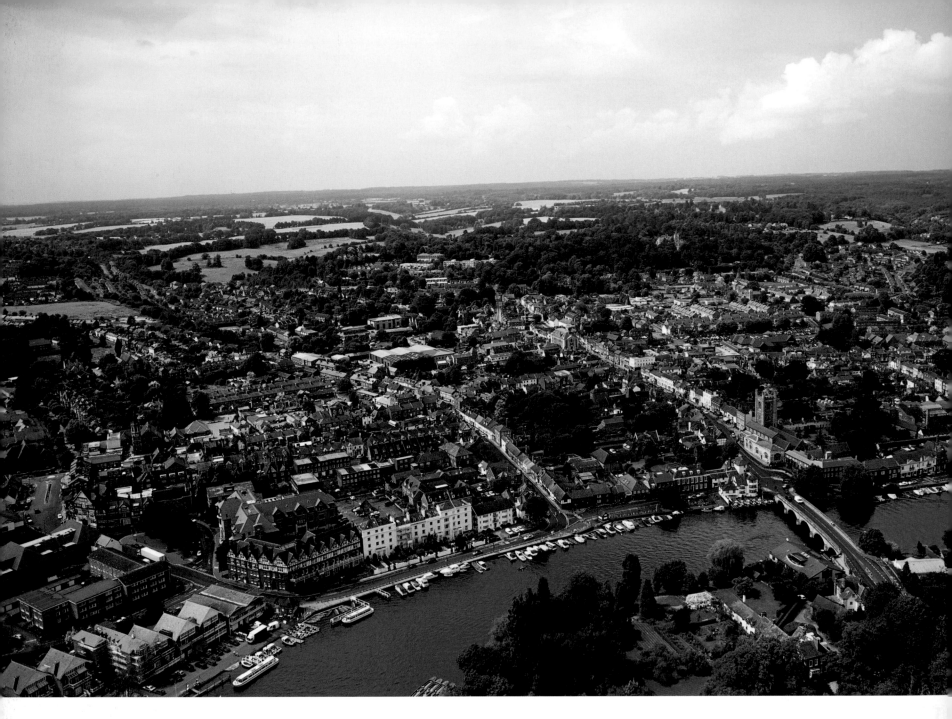

^ ABOVE

Henley-on-Thames, Oxfordshire

Visitors to Britain who only go to London don't get a full picture of what the River Thames means to people. Here upstream at Henley, the Thames is a narrower and gentler river, very much at the heart of town activity. Henley Bridge has five stone arches and has linked the two riverbanks – one in Berkshire, one in Oxfordshire – since 1786, although there was a wooden bridge here for many years before its construction.

> OPPOSITE

Chesil Beach, Dorset

Part of the Jurassic Coast World Heritage Site, Chesil Beach is a unique stretch of Dorset coastline that runs for 18 miles (29km) from the Isle of Portland to West Bay, near Bridport. For much of its length, the sand and shingle beach is separated from the mainland by the Fleet Lagoon. It is an offence to remove stones from the beach, although people from Portland are sometimes called 'slingers', from the days when they would use Chesil stones in their slingshots.

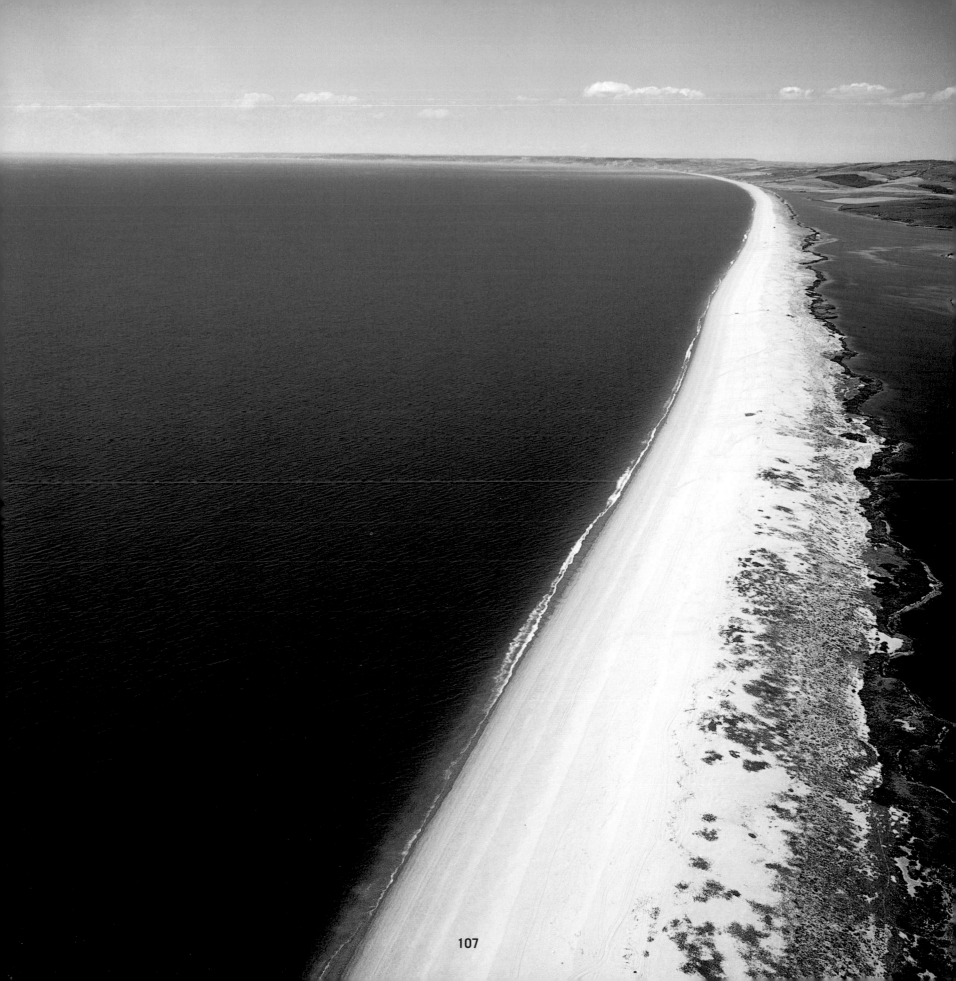

>
Longleat Maze, Wiltshire

This hedge maze at the Longleat country house and estate is a modern version of an ancient tradition. Mazes and labyrinths go back thousands of years to the Ancient Egyptians, and turf and stone mazes have been popular in Northern Europe since at least the Bronze Age. Hedge mazes developed from these and have been found in Britain since the 16th century. Here at Longleat the Marquess of Bath is following in a noble tradition: Louis XIV had a hedge maze in his palace gardens at Versailles.

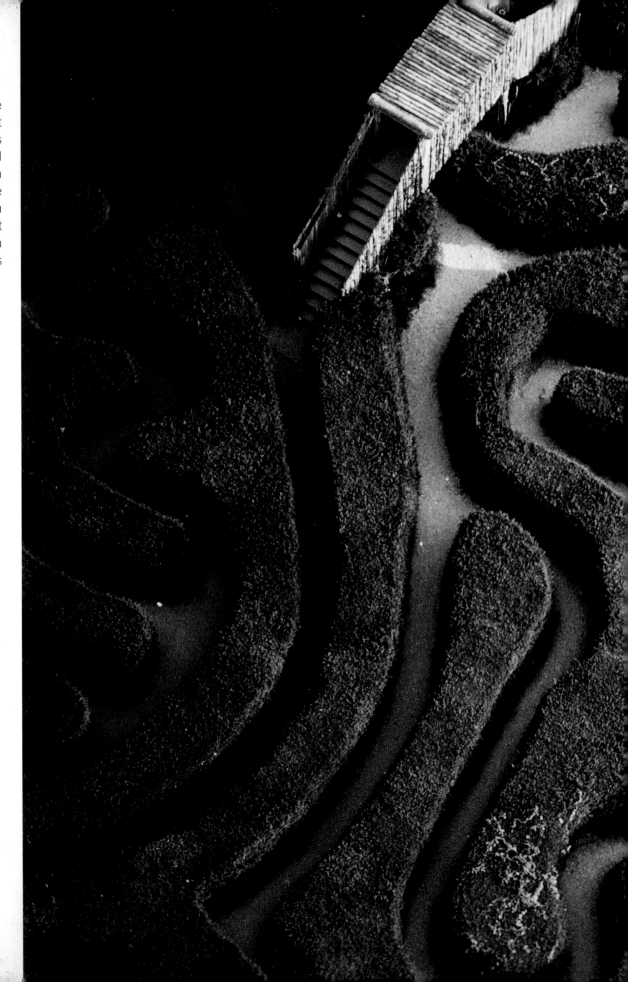

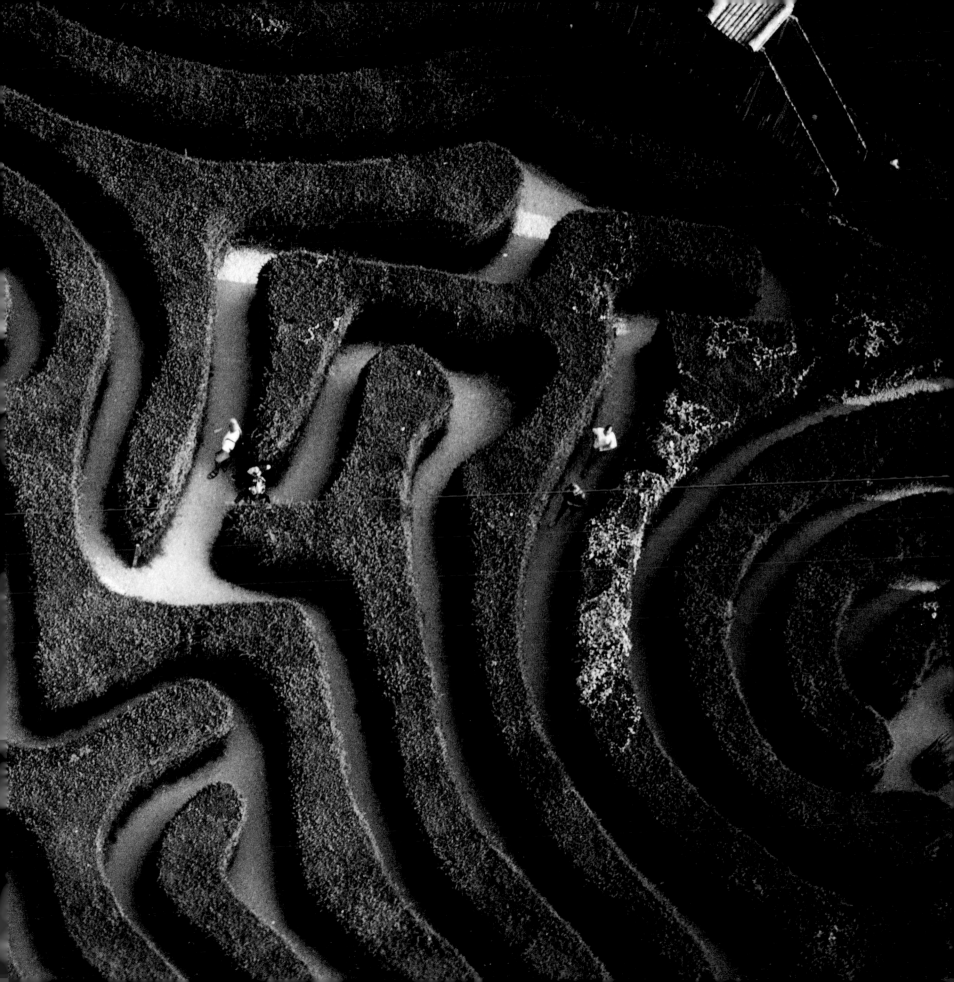

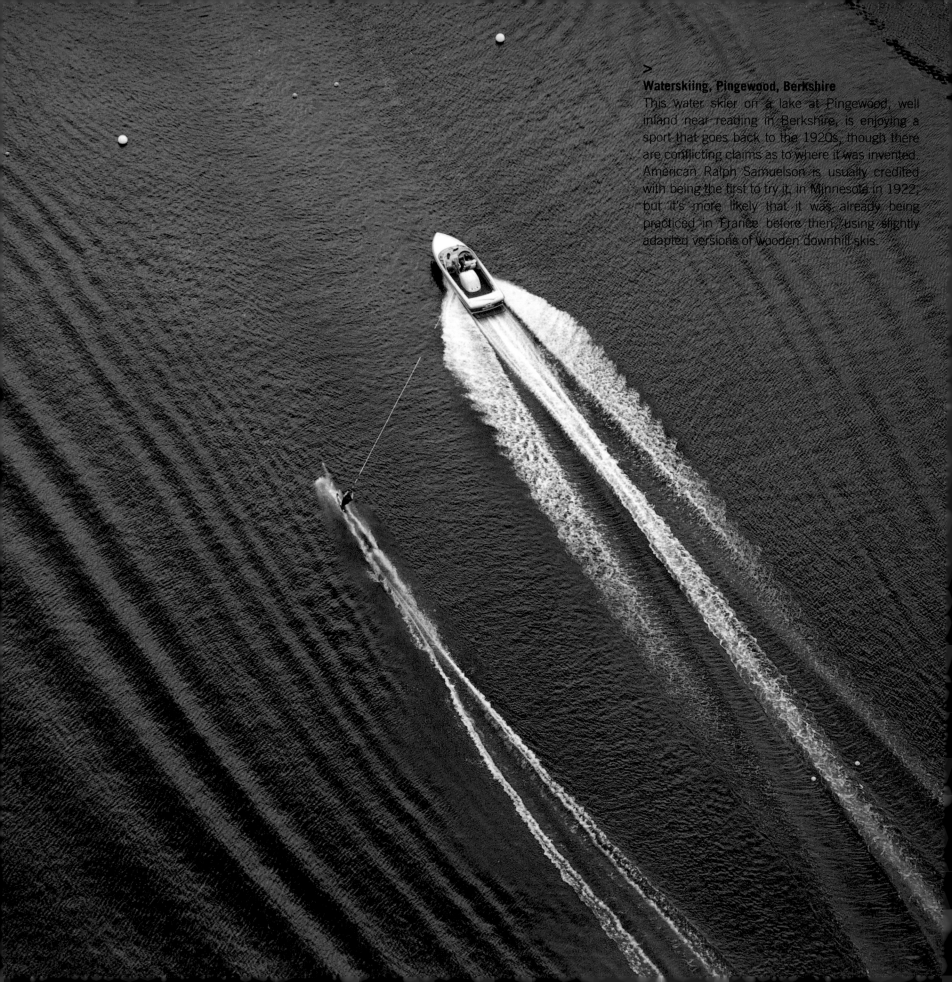

> **Waterskiing, Pingewood, Berkshire**
This water skier on a lake at Pingewood, well inland near reading in Berkshire, is enjoying a sport that goes back to the 1920s, though there are conflicting claims as to where it was invented. American Ralph Samuelson is usually credited with being the first to try it in Minnesota in 1922, but it's more likely that it was already being practiced in France before then, using slightly adapted versions of wooden downhill skis.

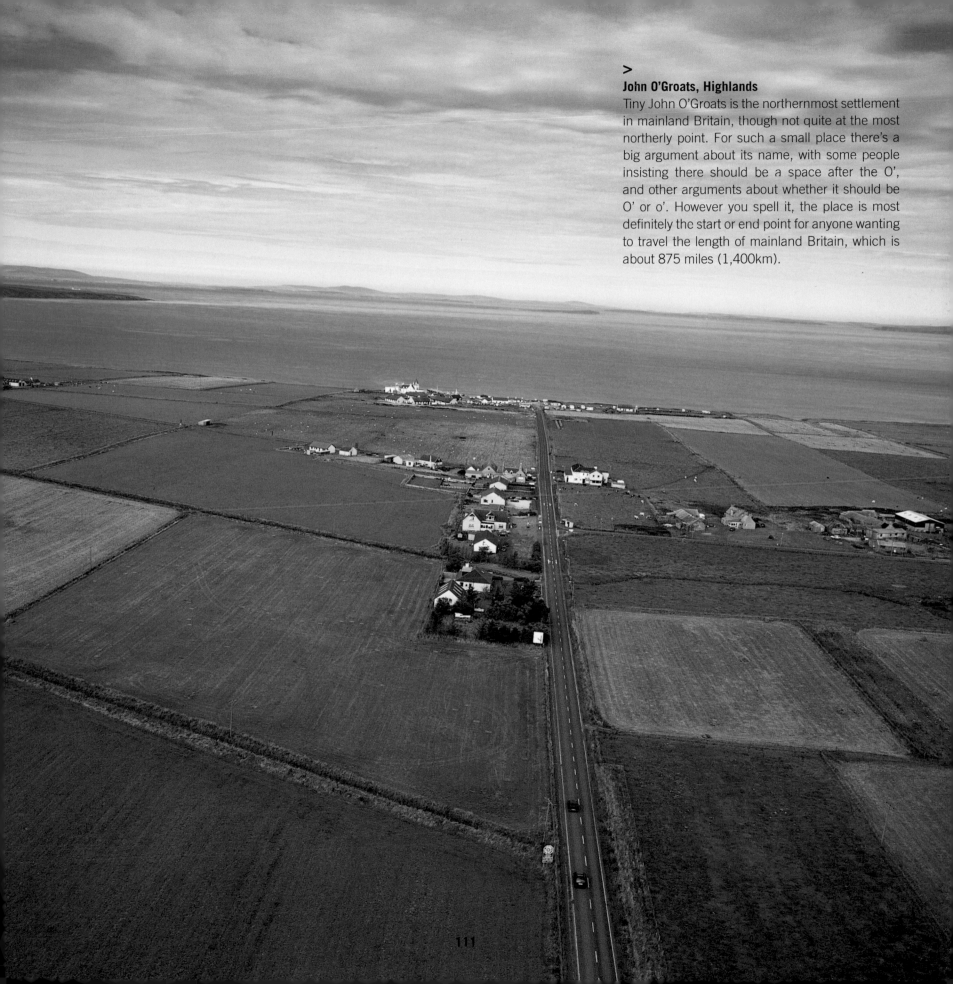

>
John O'Groats, Highlands

Tiny John O'Groats is the northernmost settlement in mainland Britain, though not quite at the most northerly point. For such a small place there's a big argument about its name, with some people insisting there should be a space after the O', and other arguments about whether it should be O' or o'. However you spell it, the place is most definitely the start or end point for anyone wanting to travel the length of mainland Britain, which is about 875 miles (1,400km).

111

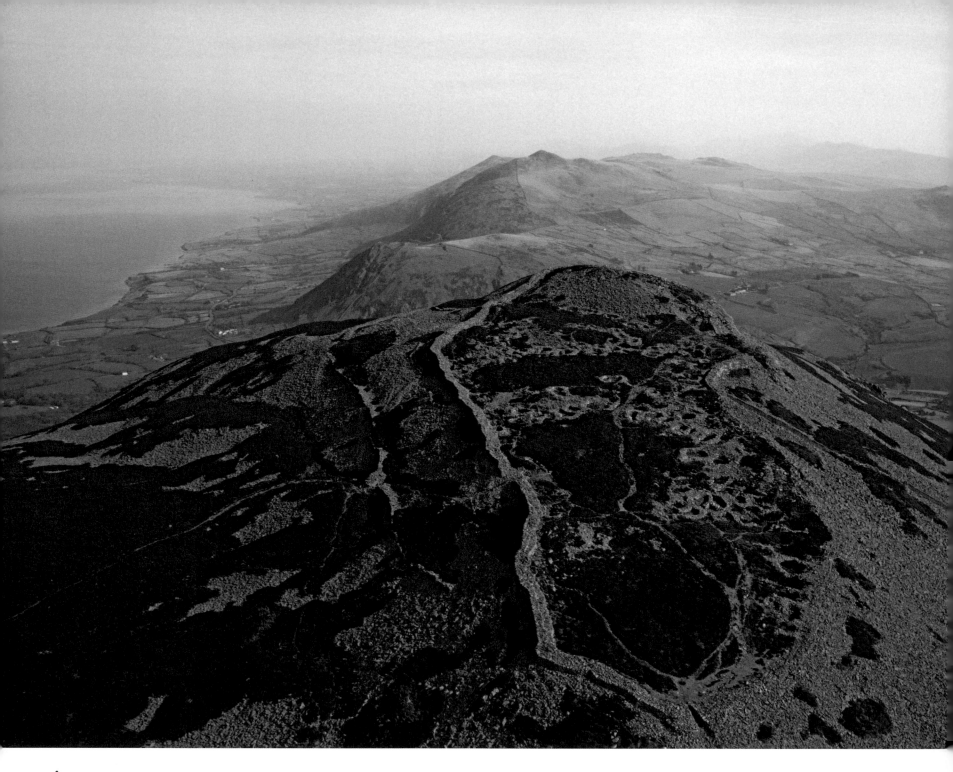

^ ABOVE
Tre'r Ceiri hill fort, Caernarfonshire
The spectacular location of this hill fort in northwest Wales can really be appreciated in this view from the air. The remains of some 150 or so houses can be found within its perimeters, and although most of these date from the Roman period, AD150–400, it's thought that the hill fort was here in at least 100BC.

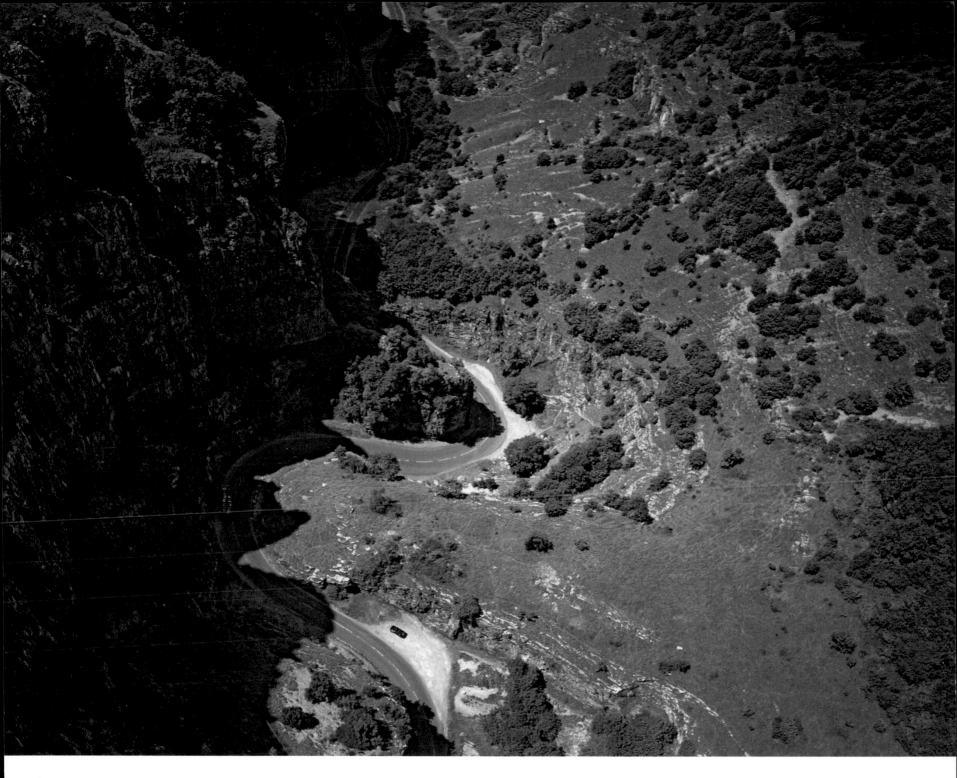

^ **ABOVE**
Cheddar Gorge, Somerset
Somerset's Cheddar Gorge is the biggest gorge in the British Isles. It is known that people lived here up to 40,000 years ago. The oldest complete human skeleton, the youthful 9,000-year-old Cheddar Man, was found here too, in one of the many caves that exist in what was originally an Ice Age river bed.

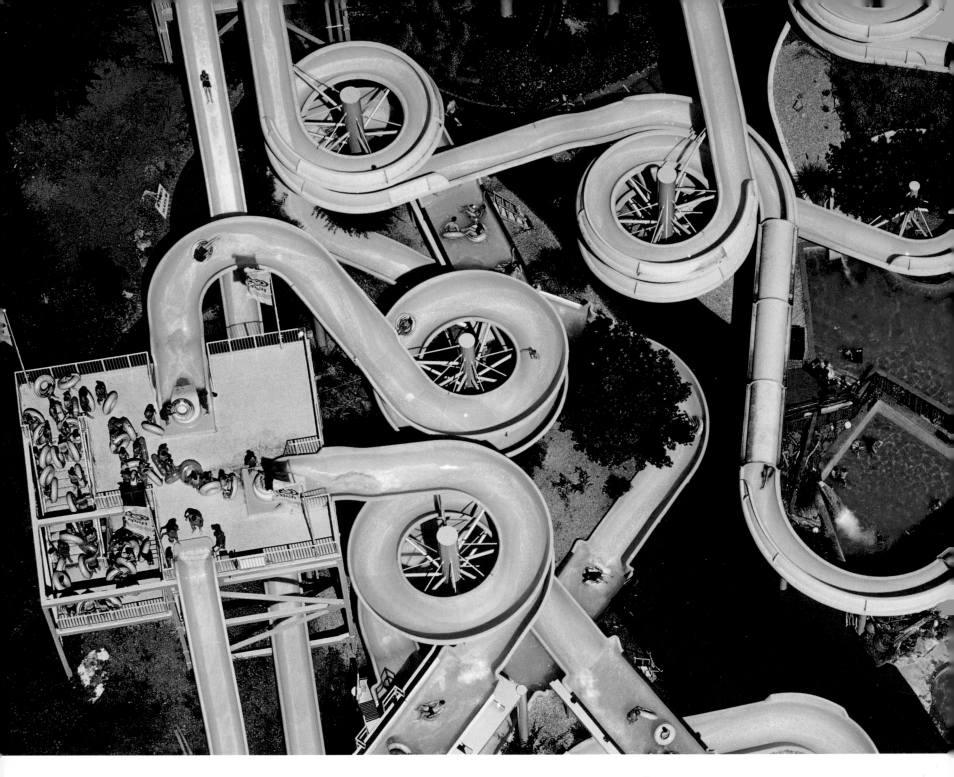

Waterpark near Paignton, Devon

The Quaywest waterpark near Paignton in Devon, with rides like the Devil's Drop and Wild Kamikaze, is a typical example of the kind of fun waterpark that has spread round the world since they were first developed in, where else, 1950s America.

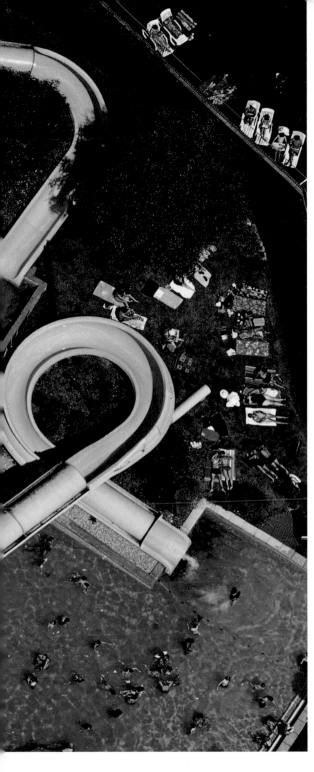

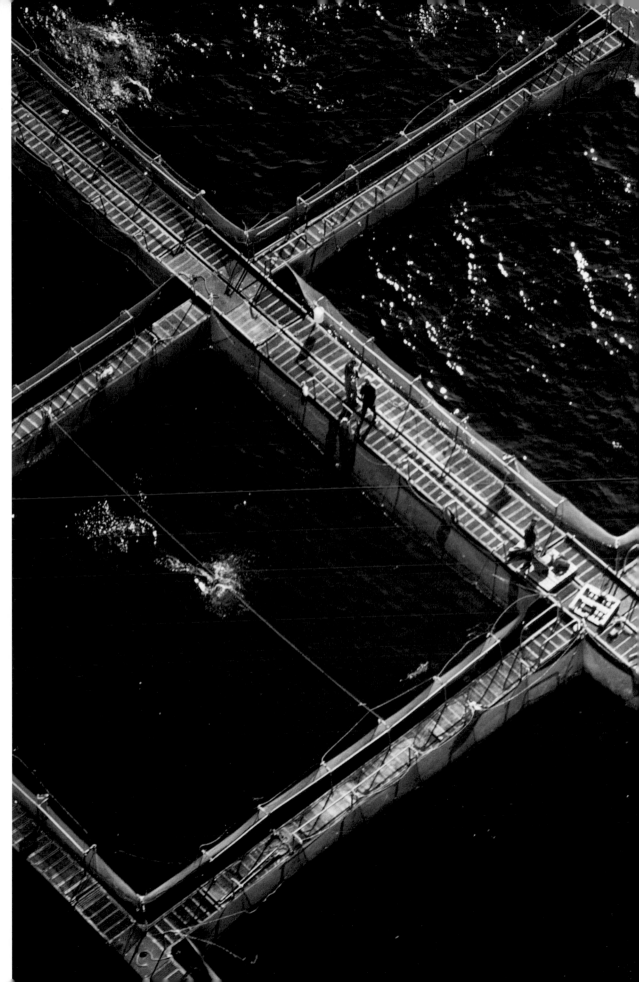

> **RIGHT**
Salmon farming, Loch Duich
People's increasing awareness of the need to eat healthily, especially oil-rich fish like salmon, has resulted in a growing salmon farming business. It is now a large part of the Scottish economy, as salmon need good, clean water in order to flourish, so they do well in Scotland's rivers and lochs.

> RIGHT
Edinburgh

In the distance, the Firth of Forth, to the right the heights of Arthur's Seat and below that the Royal Palace of Holyroodhouse and the new Scottish Parliament Building. From there the Royal Mile leads up to Edinburgh Castle. The city of Inspector Rebus and Miss Jean Brodie spreads out in a panorama before us, revealing just some of its many layers.

∨ BELOW
Forth Bridge, Edinburgh

The final one of the eight million rivets that hold together the Forth Bridge was driven home by the then Prince of Wales, later King Edward VII, when he declared the bridge open in 1890. Almost a hundred workers are thought to have lost their lives in the seven years it took to build the bridge.

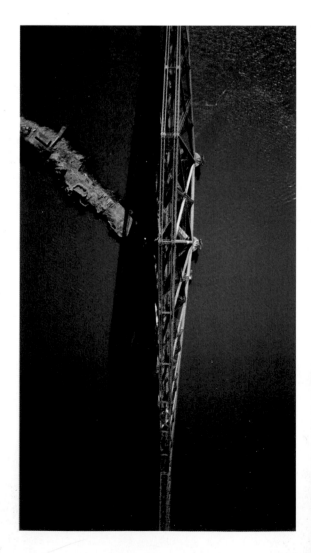

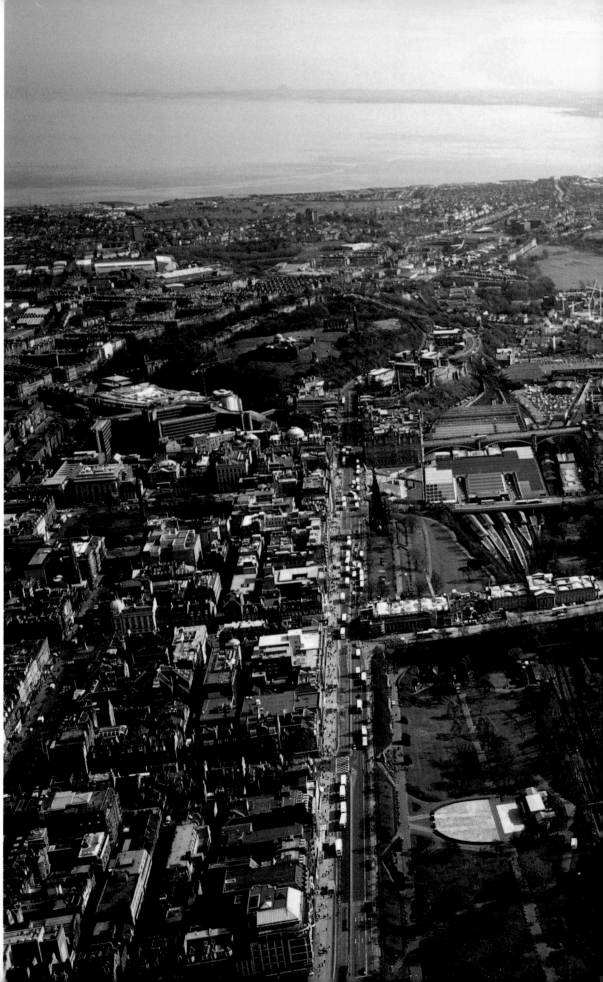

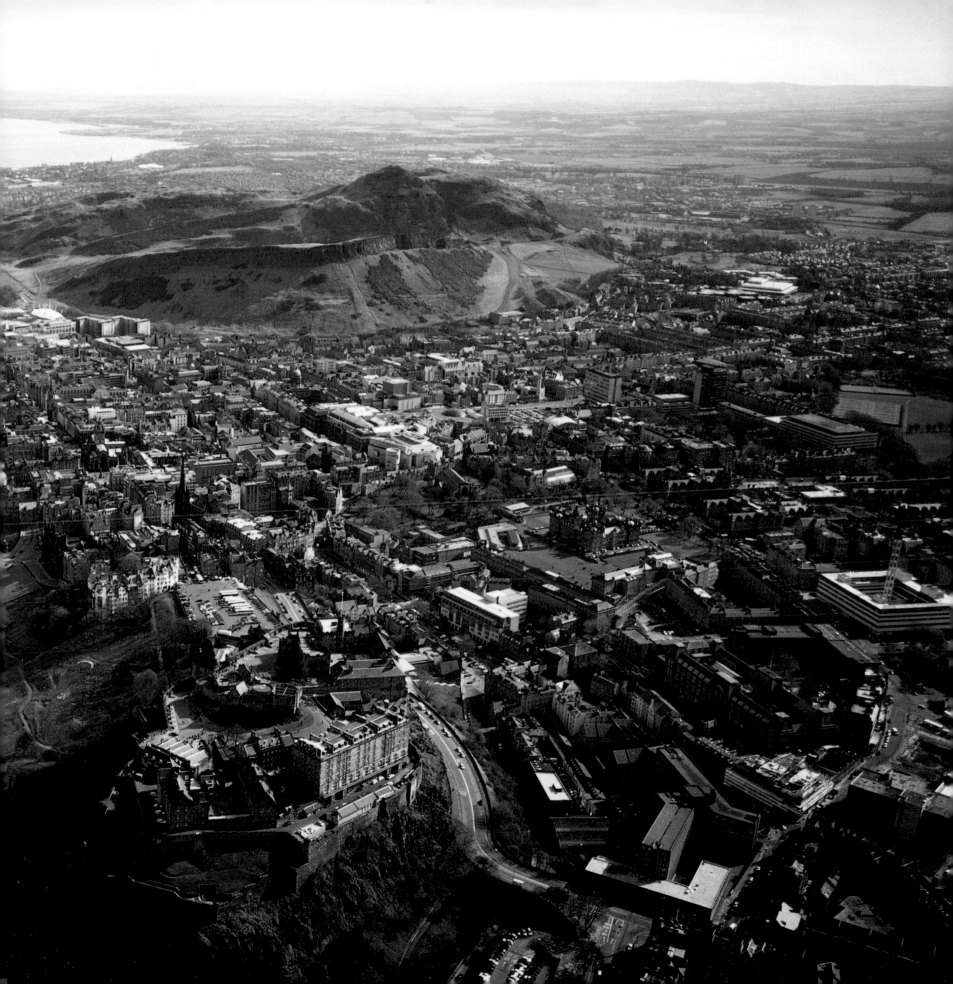

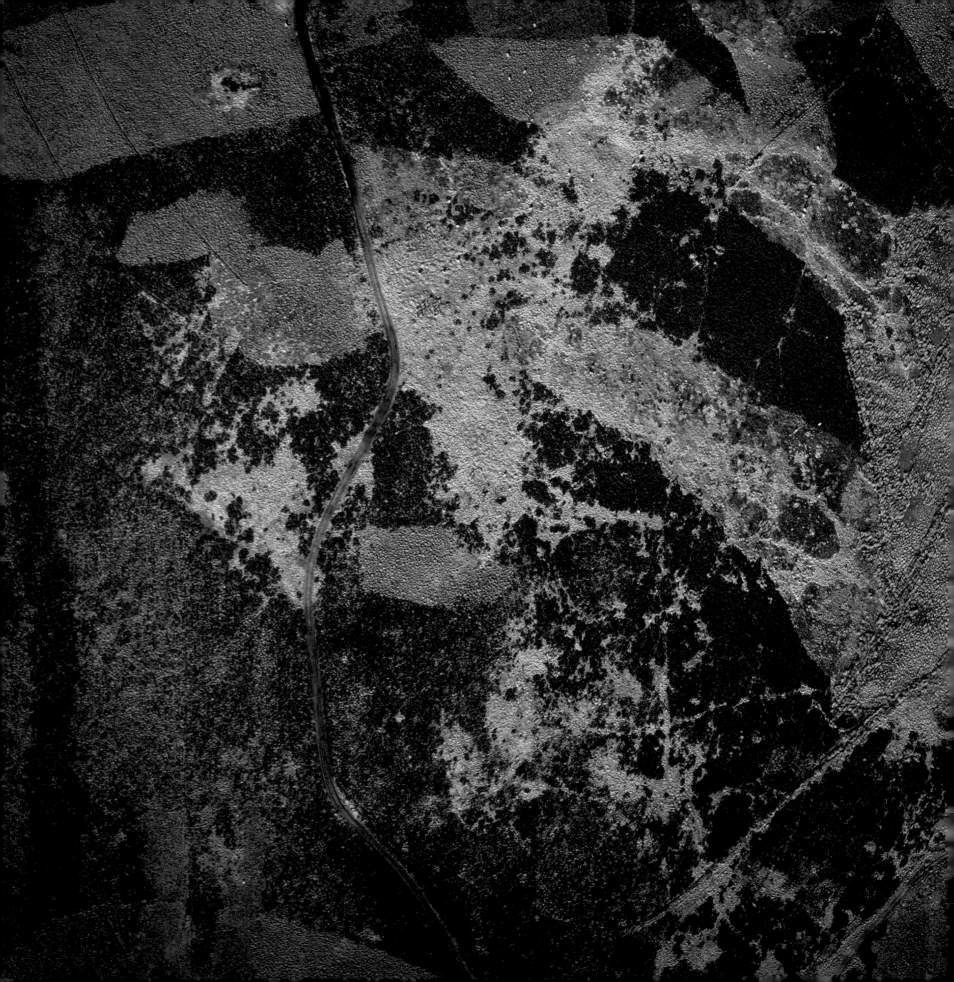

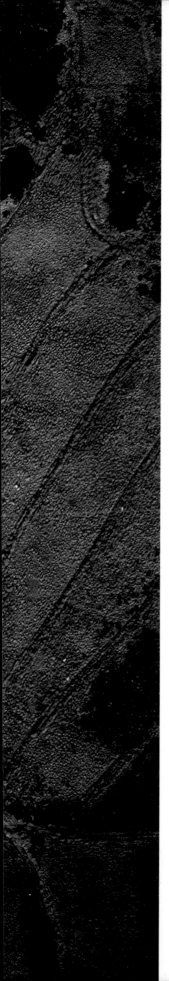

< LEFT
Moorland, Angus

Moorlands like this form a large part of the British landscape, and feature in British life socially as well as geographically and historically. Mention Ilkley Moor and the average British person will think of a song about Yorkshire, while Elmey Moor means a TV transmission mast. Say Saddleworth Moor and awful child murders are remembered, while Dartmoor creates an image of a prison and a rather bleak landscape.

> RIGHT
Rhuddlan Castle, Denbighshire

These striking twin towers guarding the gatehouse of Rhuddlan Castle in northeast Wales have stood for almost 750 years, as it was the late 13th century when the castle was built. Even then, there had been some kind of settlement here for about 500 years, as this was the best point for fording the River Clwyd, which runs near Rhuddlan Castle. A canal was built from the river to the castle, to enable construction materials to be brought in more easily, as in those days there was no convenient coastal road – just marshland leading down to the sea.

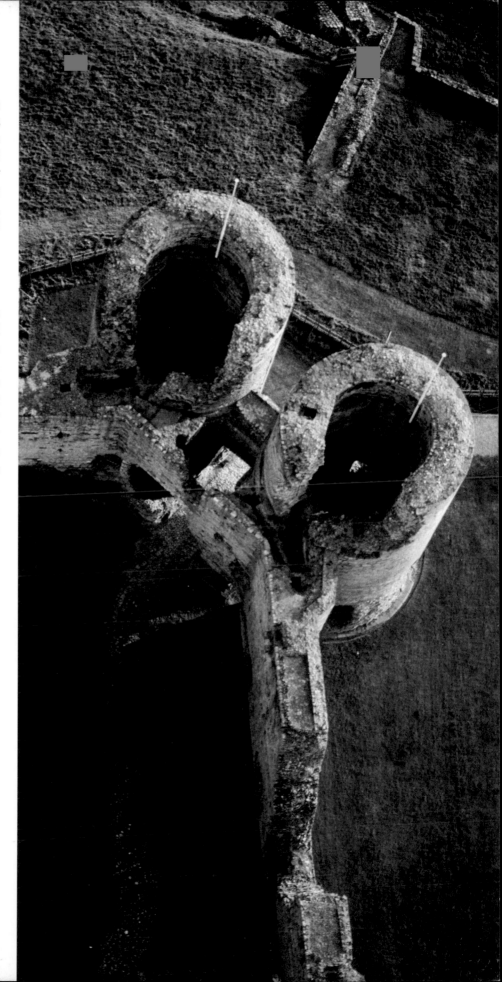

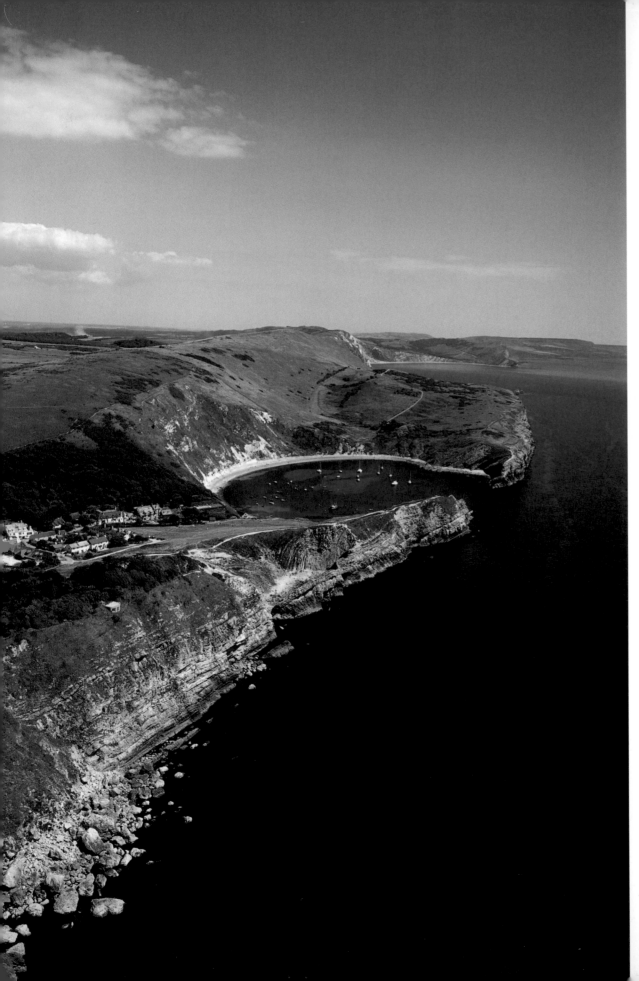

< LEFT
Lulworth Cove, Dorset

Lulworth Cove looks almost too good to be true, and it is indeed regarded as a fine example of a cove – a naturally-made protected inlet with a small entrance. It took millions of years for the cove to achieve this perfect shape, and a million visitors a year come to enjoy it, though there can be no more impressive view than this one from high in the air.

> OPPOSITE
Boat and water lilies, County Sligo

County Sligo in the northwest of Ireland is an area noted for its links with the poet WB Yeats, as well as for its natural features, especially its mountains and lakes. This beautiful view seems almost an intrusion onto the private peace of a fishing boat and the hundreds of water lilies look like an Impressionist painting.

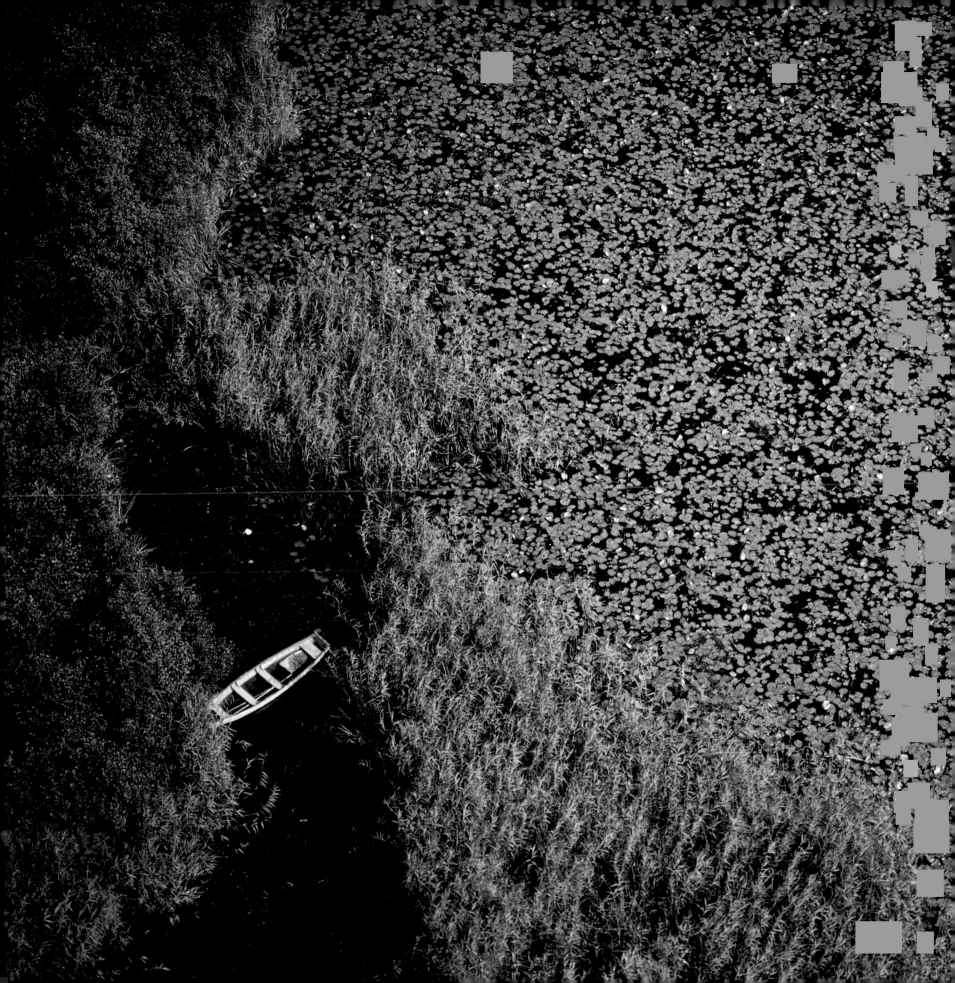

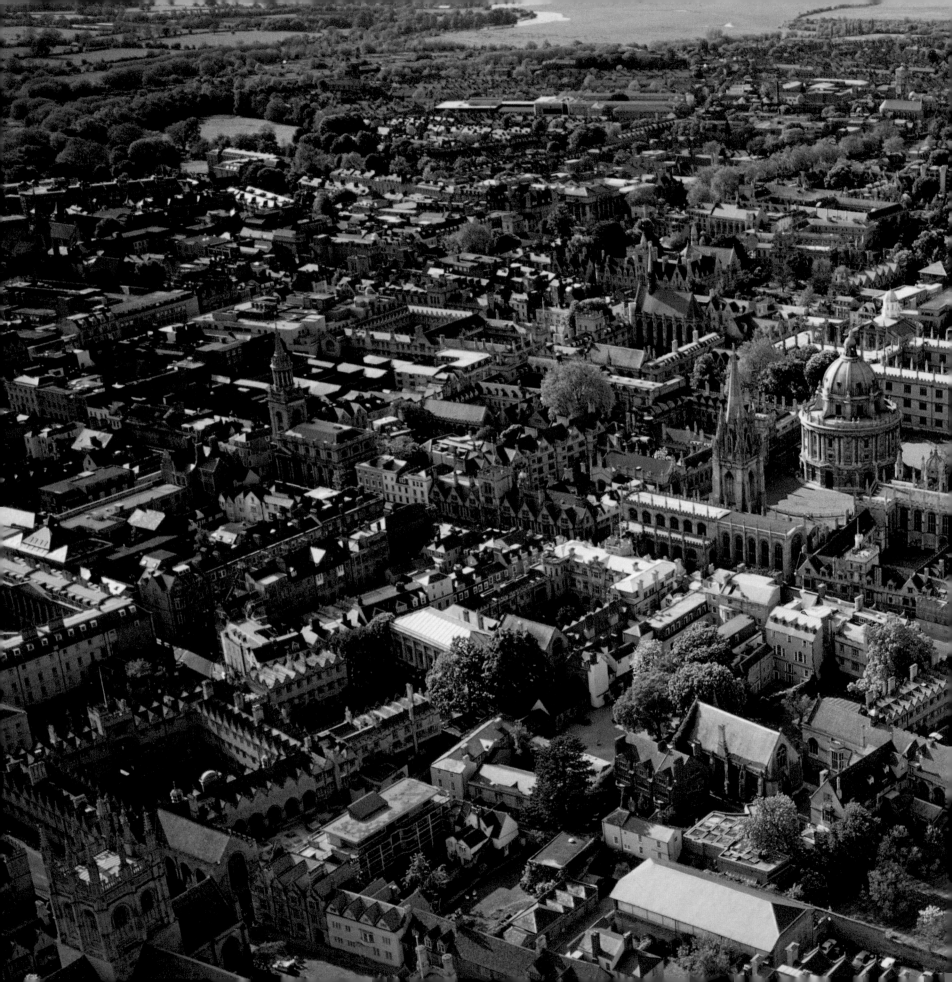

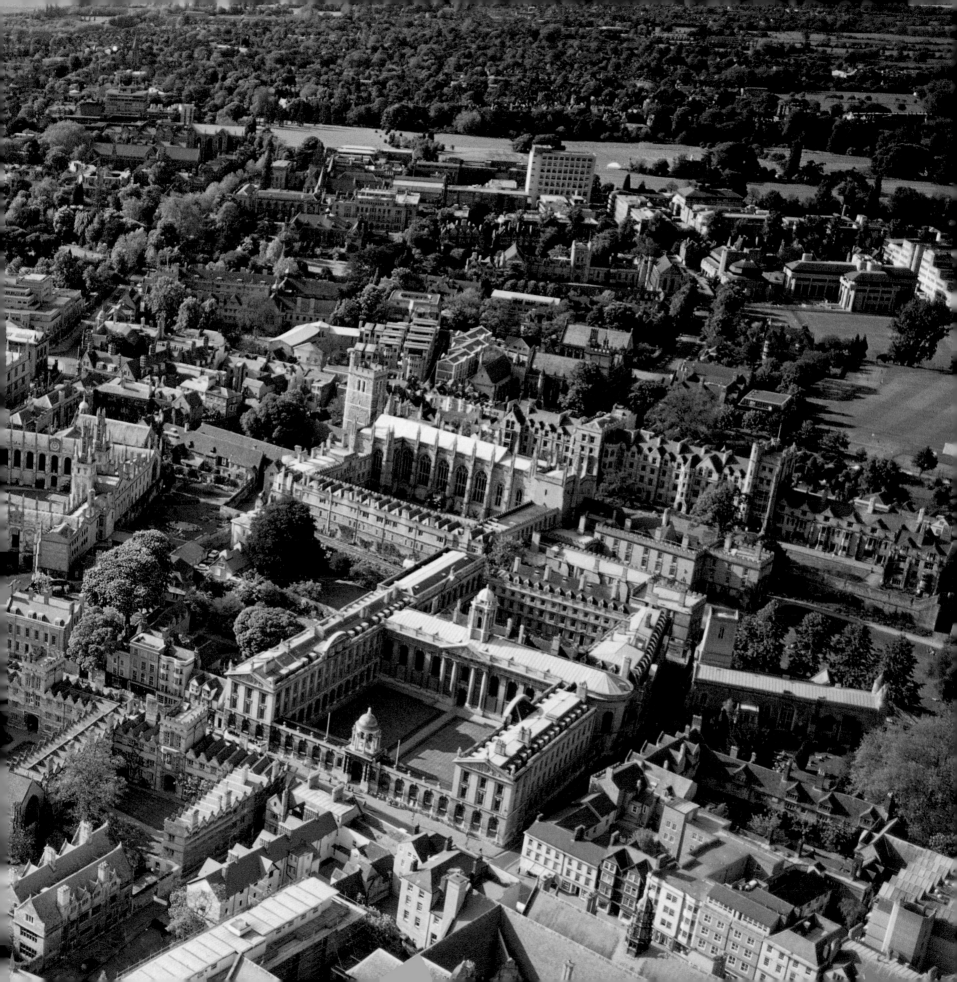

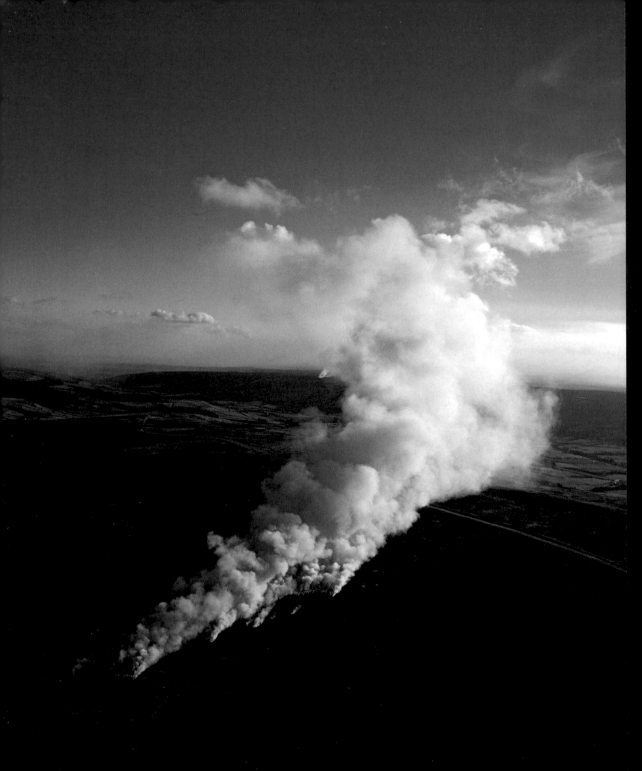

« PREVIOUS
Oxford, Oxfordshire

The symmetrical beauty of Oxford and its colleges is perhaps best seen like this, from above, a view which also shows how green the city really is, and how close to the countryside. Oxford has existed as a town for almost 1,200 years, and in that time has developed enormously as one of the world's great centres of learning, yet England's fields and woods are but a short walk away.

< LEFT
Heather burning, Yorkshire

Though it looks destructive, the burning of heather, as seen here in Yorkshire, is actually good for agriculture and also for the wildlife that enjoys this kind of habitat. Strict regulations exist on the burning of heather, which can only be done at certain times of year, and cannot be started between the hours of sunset and sunrise.

> RIGHT
Hay bales, Berkshire

There are many reasons why farmers make hay while the sun shines, the main one being that the best hay has to be dry to avoid becoming rotten later. An intense period of sunshine dries the hay perfectly, and it then has to be gathered in and stored quickly before the notoriously fickle British weather changes.

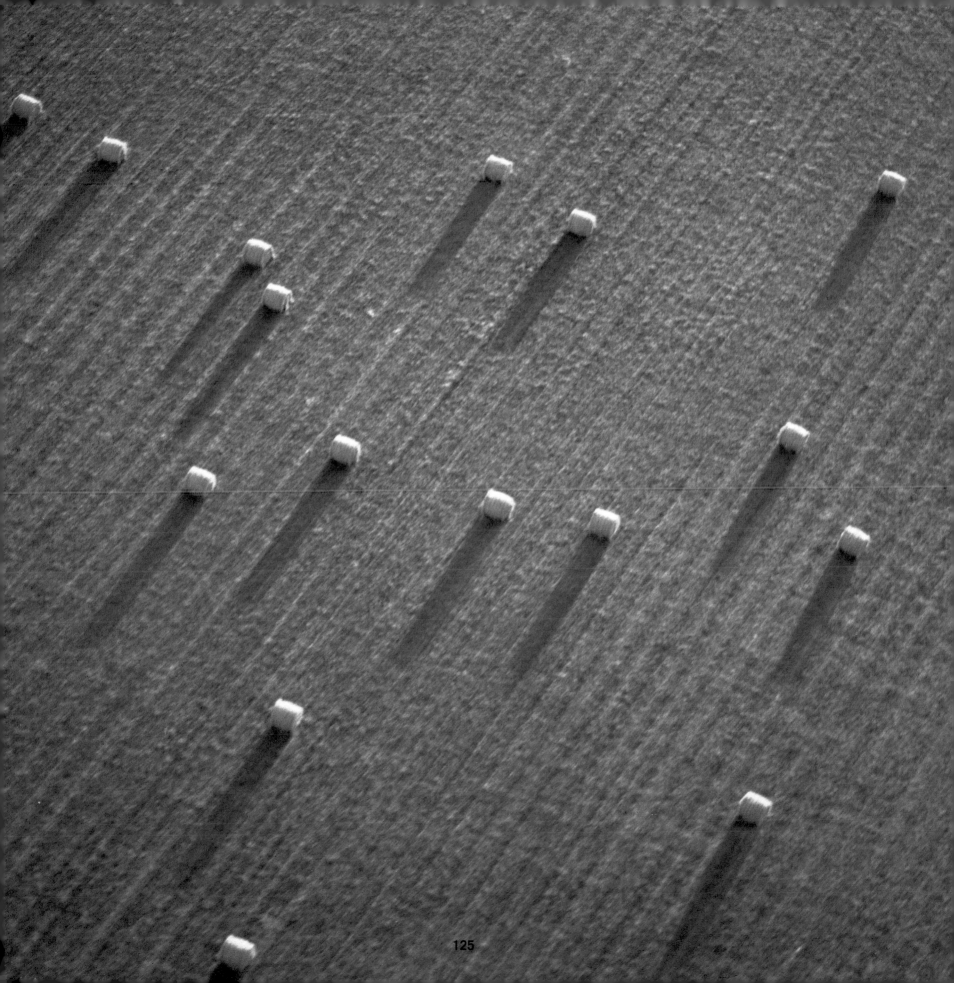

> **RIGHT**

Fort Augustus & Loch Ness, Highlands

Loch Ness is known for one thing, its monster, and so enduring is this belief that the eyes are immediately drawn to the water's surface in any photo of the loch. This detracts sometimes from the awe-inspiring scenery, here in the Great Glen, the glen that runs the whole width of Scotland. The villagers of Fort Augustus must have one of the best views in the British Isles.

> **OPPOSITE**

Glasgow, Strathclyde

In the distance is the busy and historic city centre while in the foreground are the symbols of regeneration. The Glasgow Tower stands alongside the ultra-modern look of the Glasgow Science Centre, while across the river and right in the centre of the photograph is the equally modern-looking Scottish Exhibition and Conference Centre, known as the SECC for short, and as the Armadillo by Glasgow's residents.

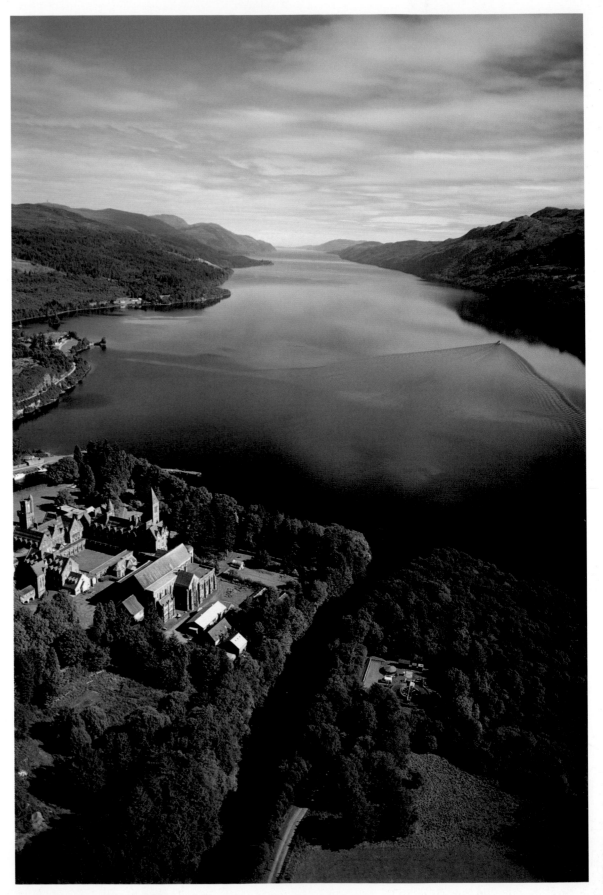

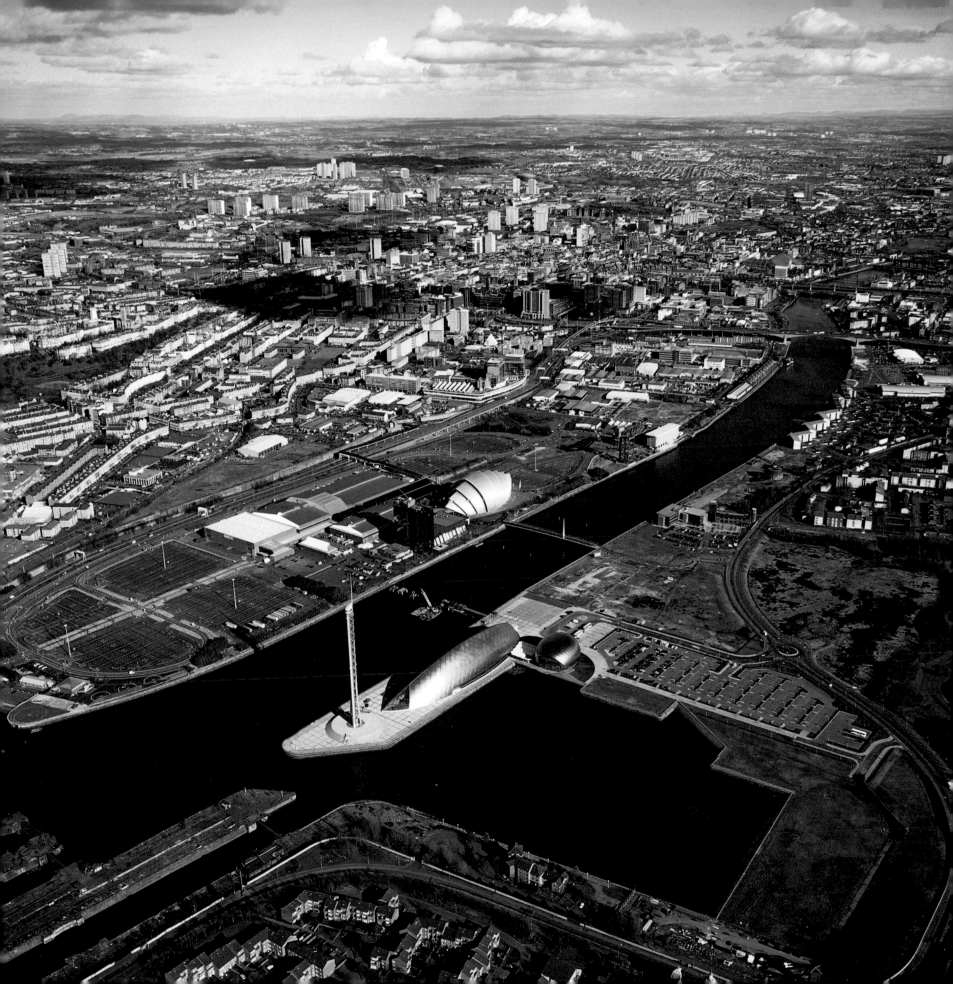

LAND OF WRITERS

The British Isles has produced more winners of the Nobel Prize for Literature than any other part of the world. Only France can claim the same number of winners, thirteen, but as one of those declined the prize, Jean-Paul Sartre in 1964, it leaves Britain and Ireland at the top of the literary league table. The first British winner was Rudyard Kipling in 1907, and the tradition continues through to the present day, with Harold Pinter being given the award in 2005.

The Nobel Prize isn't the only benchmark for literary achievement, as many fine writers have never won it. They include one writer who countless literary critics regard as the finest writer of them all – James Joyce. For the comparatively small island of Ireland to produce Joyce and four Nobel Prizewinners (Samuel Beckett, Seamus Heaney, George Bernard Shaw and WB Yeats) is a remarkable achievement. It suggests two things. One is that the Irish have a natural way with words, and the other is that Ireland is an inspiring country.

Inspiration doesn't need to come from the landscape itself, although Ireland has more than its fair share of inspirational places. Villages, small towns and cities provide equal stimulation for the observant writer. Nor does inspiration have to come from actually living in the country, as some of the best works frequently come from writers in exile, such as James Joyce himself, who spent many years in Italy.

Joyce was born in the fashionably affluent suburb of Rathgar, in the south of Dublin, in 1882, though when he was five the family moved to the nearby seaside town of Bray. He spent much of his student life in Dublin, but by the time he was 22 he had eloped to the continent with his future wife, Nora Barnacle, living variously in Trieste, Zurich and Paris. It was another ten years until his first collection of short stories, *Dubliners*, was

published, and although he was living abroad when writing the stories, they present a vivid portrayal of Dublin society at that time, with many of the characters based on people Joyce met, and involving incidents that actually happened to him. It's a critical view of Dublin society, but despite that, the city absorbed Joyce for the rest of his life.

What many people regard as his greatest novel, and some as the greatest novel of the 20th century, was *Ulysses*. This difficult book paints a picture of Dublin on one day, 16 June 1904, which was the day of his first date with Nora Barnacle. There are many aspects to this complicated book, but one of them in particular is interesting in relation to this set of photos of the British Isles from the air. If you trace the day's wanderings on a map of Dublin, of the main character, Leopold Bloom, they make the shape of a question mark.

Another Irish writer writing at the same time as Joyce was WB Yeats. Much of his inspiration came from the other side of the country, in more ways than one. He wrote extensively on the natural – and supernatural – world of Ireland, and especially about the west of the country, whereas Joyce wrote about the urban world of Dublin in the east.

One of Yeats's best-loved poems was an early poem, *The Lake Isle of Innisfree*. The poet has described how, when he was growing up in Sligo, he read the work of Henry David Thoreau and wanted to live in his own hut, on an island on the nearby Lough Gill. The island was called Innisfree, which means Heather Island. A sense of the wildness and solitude of some of the loughs in the west of Ireland can be gleaned from these pages, and we can also see another of Yeats's sources of inspiration, the mountain of Ben Bulben. So powerful was Ben Bulben to the poet that he wanted to be buried beneath it – and he was. He died in Menton in the south of

France in 1939, and was first buried nearby at Roquebrune-Cap-Martin, but later was moved to Drumcliffe in County Sligo and buried 'Beneath Ben Bulben,' in accordance with his wishes. He himself once said that 'the place that has really influenced my life most is Sligo.'

If ever a place was influenced by a poet, then it is the Lake District in Cumbria, in the northwest of England. The poet is William Wordsworth, who lived with his sister Dorothy in Dove Cottage close to Grasmere from December 1799 until May 1808. He was such a celebrity at that time that admirers would make their way to Dove Cottage and sometimes surprise him while he was trying to write. It didn't please the poet greatly, and nor did the coming of the railways which brought even more visitors to the Lake District. He protested greatly about that, although he was partly to blame because he himself had written a guide to the Lake District.

Of the millions who still visit the Lake District, many come in spring to try to see the daffodils that Wordsworth wrote about in his best-known poem, which begins: 'I wandered lonely as a cloud.' It is a poem that can probably be found somewhere in every school, library and bookshop in the land. In the pages of this book of photographs we can see the magnificence of some of the Lake District's lakes, while Wordsworth's poet's eye was drawn to the vivid colour and the delight of just one of the flowers to be found on the ground there, the ordinary daffodil. It's a harbinger of spring, and a welcome and cheerful sight for those who have suffered through the cold of a British winter.

Anyone wanting to experience that cold and see if they can still be inspired can now rent Thomas Hardy's cottage in Dorset. The cottage was built by Hardy's grandfather, and the poet and novelist was born there in 1840. He lived there until he was 34, and during that time wrote two of his Wessex novels: *Under the Greenwood Tree* and *Far from the Madding Crowd*. The cottage was left to the National Trust in 1948, and although it has always been open to visitors during the summer, it can now also be rented out during the winter months.

Hardy was inspired by the Dorset scenery, and the rural life of that time, which he wrote about in his series of Wessex novels such as *Jude the Obscure*, which features fictionalised versions of places such as Oxford and Salisbury, both seen in these pages. Hardy borrowed the name of the old Anglo-Saxon kingdom of Wessex, which gave his stories of rural life a timeless quality.

Greatly influenced by Hardy's work was the writer John Fowles, who made his home in Lyme Regis, and made the coastal town the setting of one of his most famous books, *The French Lieutenant's Woman*. The subsequent film, which featured Meryl Streep as the book's main character, Sarah Woodruff, made Lyme Regis famous throughout the world. Sarah Woodruff, whose nickname is 'Tragedy', spends much of her time brooding on one of Lyme's most famous features, the Cobb. The Oscar-nominated script for the film was written by Britain's most recent winner of the Nobel Prize, Harold Pinter.

The southwest of England seems to have inspired more writers than any other area of Britain, perhaps because of the strange and haunting beauty of the area, and the fact that Hardy's Wessex still seems to live on there. One of the most recent examples of its literary inspiration is *On Chesil Beach*, by Ian McEwan. One look at Chesil Beach and you know it is a unique place that has atmosphere, history and mystery. So many corners of these British Isles provide that, and will no doubt continue to inspire writers in years to come.

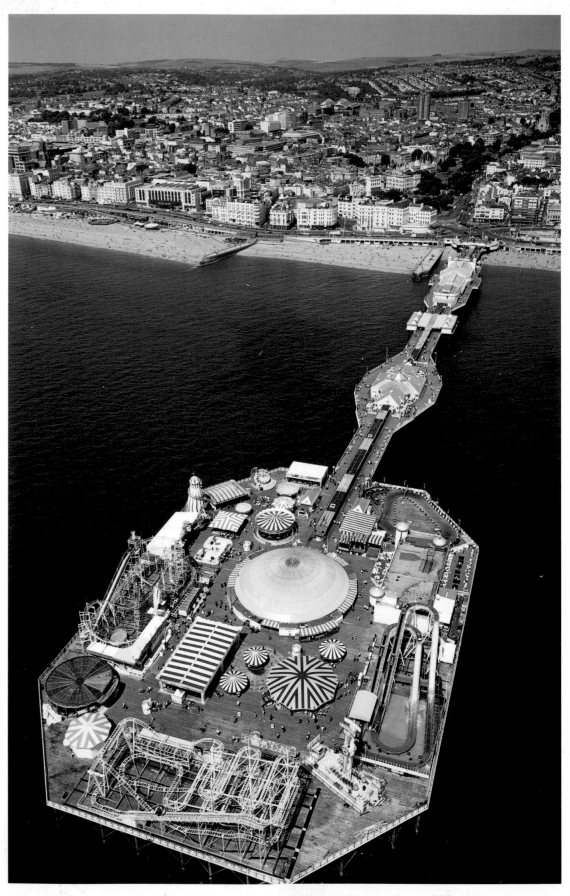

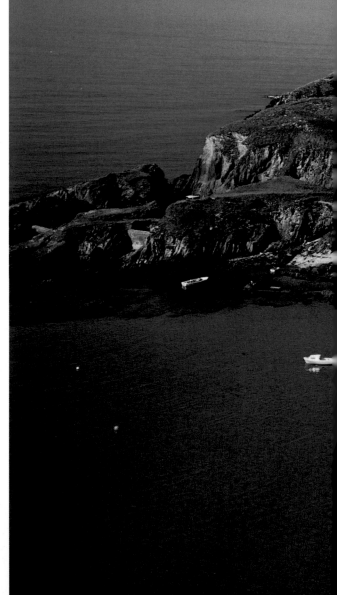

Brighton Pier, Sussex

Brighton Pier from the air looks appropriately enough like a child's toy, made up of different shapes and different sizes, in a rainbow of colours. Despite its modern look from above, it was opened back in 1899 after eight years of work, and it was then the third pier in Brighton giving some indication of the popularity of piers in their heyday.

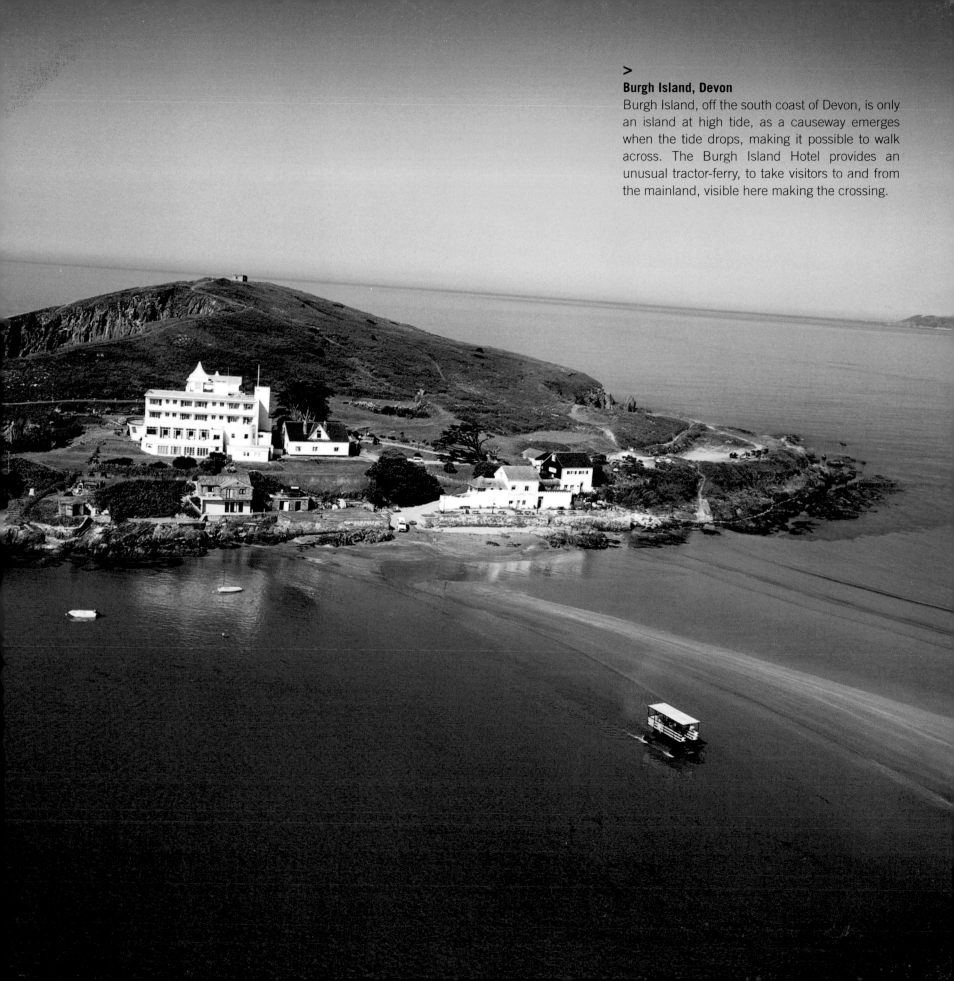

Burgh Island, Devon
Burgh Island, off the south coast of Devon, is only an island at high tide, as a causeway emerges when the tide drops, making it possible to walk across. The Burgh Island Hotel provides an unusual tractor-ferry, to take visitors to and from the mainland, visible here making the crossing.

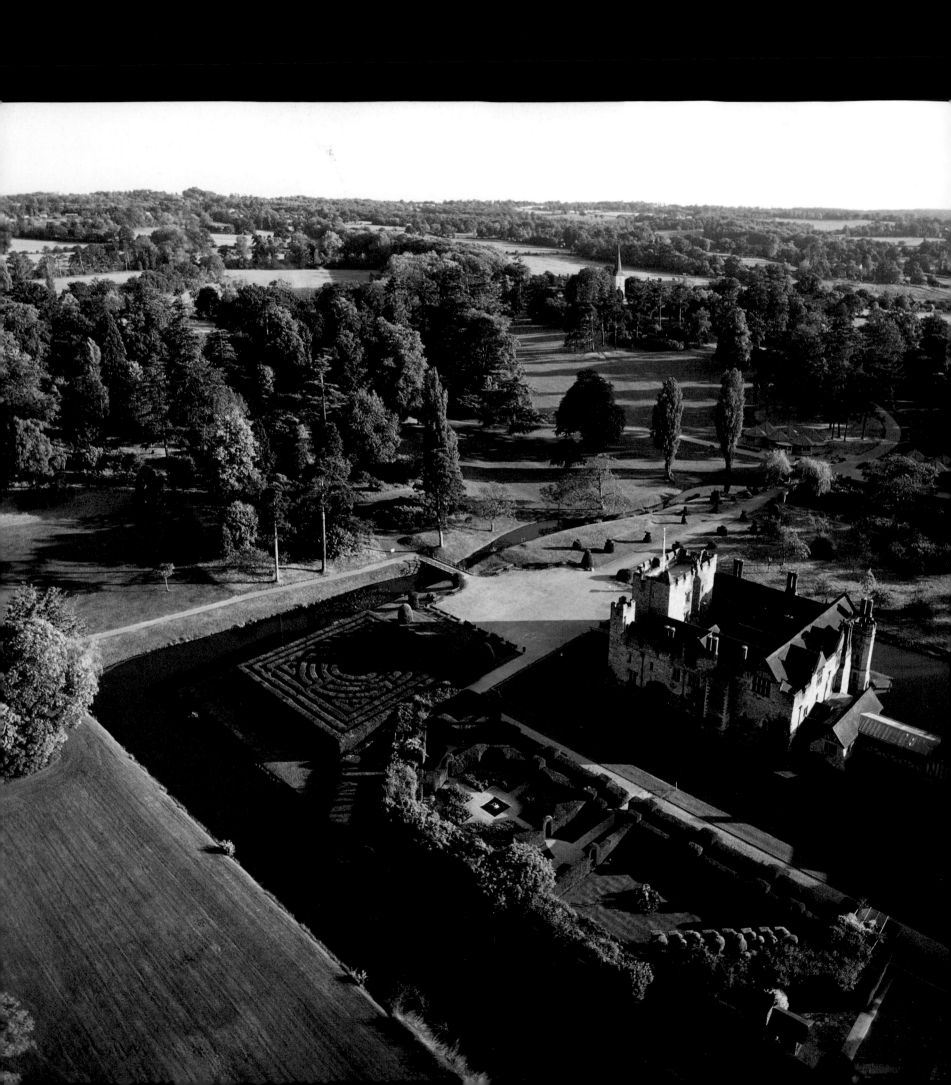

< OPPOSITE
Hever Casle, Kent

Going back as it does to the 13th century, when it was first built, Hever Castle in Kent overflows with history. It was once owned by Geoffrey Boleyn, when he was Lord Mayor of London, and his daughter Anne – later to wed and then be beheaded by King Henry VIII, spent part of her childhood in the castle.

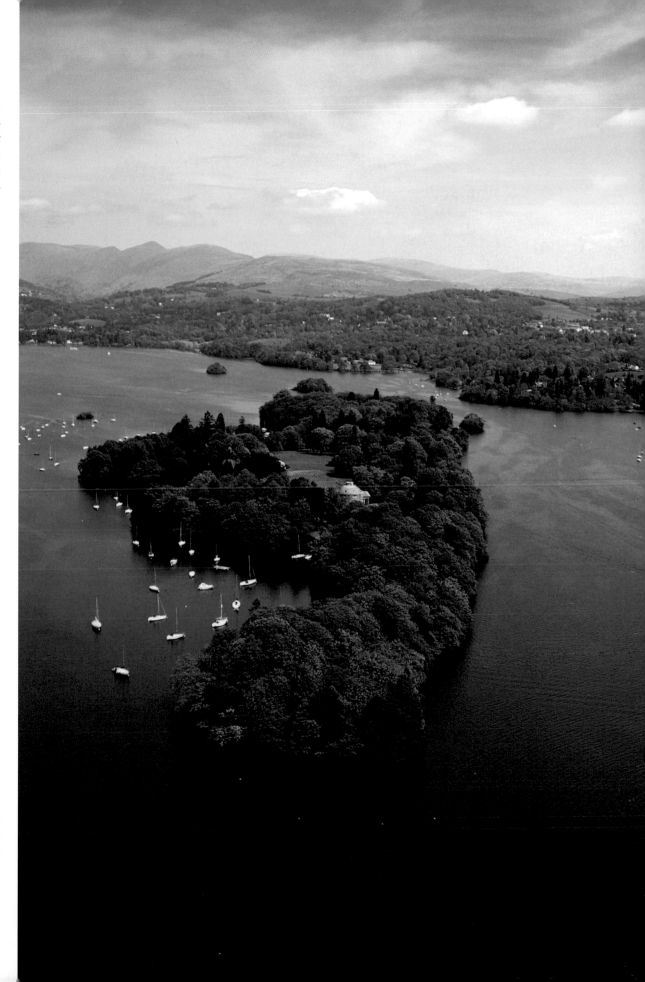

 > RIGHT
Windermere, Cumbria

At 5.7 square miles (14.7 sq kms), Windermere is the largest natural lake in England. It is a long and thin body of water, stretching for 10.5 miles (17km), and in places is as much as a mile wide. The lake is big enough to contain 14 islands, many of them simply called Holme, a local word for 'island' which derives from the Norse language.

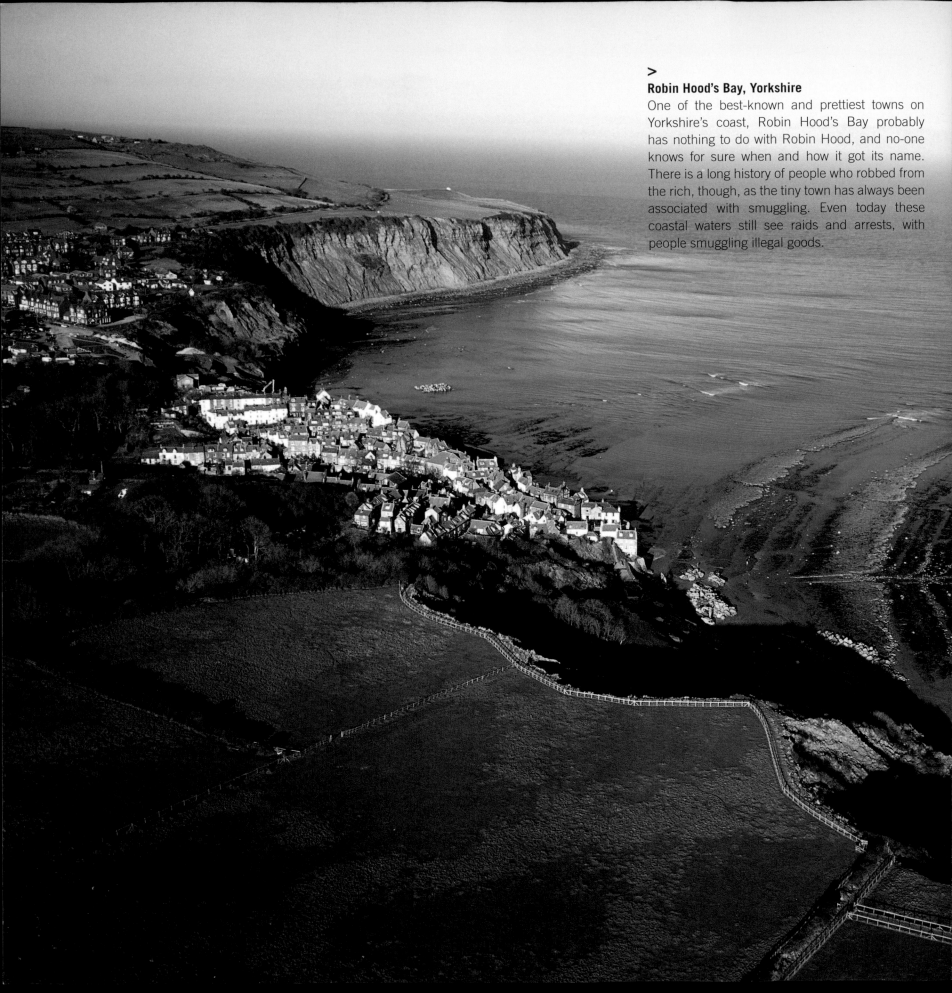

> **Robin Hood's Bay, Yorkshire**
One of the best-known and prettiest towns on Yorkshire's coast, Robin Hood's Bay probably has nothing to do with Robin Hood, and no-one knows for sure when and how it got its name. There is a long history of people who robbed from the rich, though, as the tiny town has always been associated with smuggling. Even today these coastal waters still see raids and arrests, with people smuggling illegal goods.

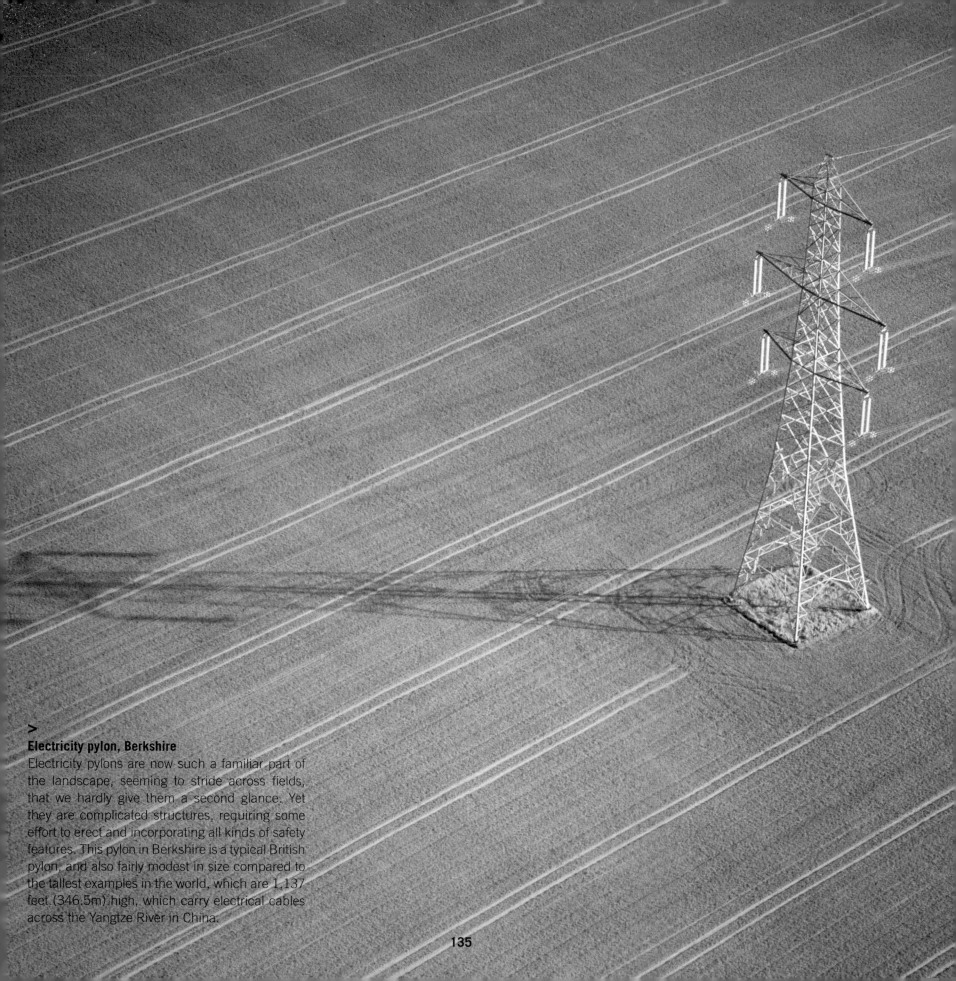

> **Electricity pylon, Berkshire**
Electricity pylons are now such a familiar part of the landscape, seeming to stride across fields, that we hardly give them a second glance. Yet they are complicated structures, requiring some effort to erect and incorporating all kinds of safety features. This pylon in Berkshire is a typical British pylon, and also fairly modest in size compared to the tallest examples in the world, which are 1,137 feet (346.5m) high, which carry electrical cables across the Yangtze River in China.

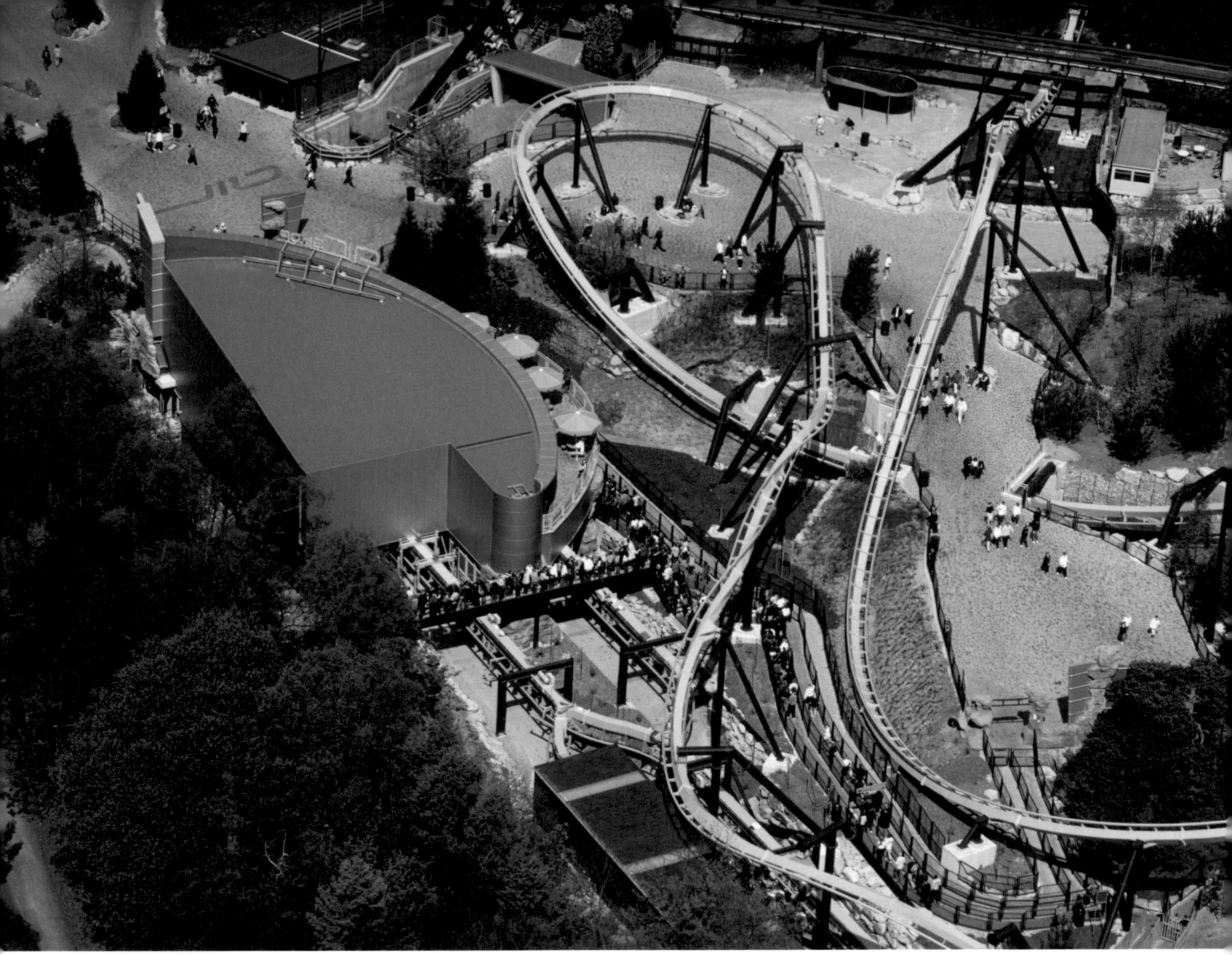

^ **ABOVE AND OPPOSITE >**

Alton Towers, Staffordshire

Alton Towers theme park in Staffordshire is one of the biggest and most famous in the British Isles. Its name comes from the old country house which stood on this spot and which was in ruins prior to the arrival of the theme park. It was once the seat of the Earls of Shrewsbury, and Alton Towers does work with Staffordshire University in order to preserve and ultimately present the heritage of the park to the public. The park was a visitor attraction back in the 19th century, although not attracting the 2.5 million annual visitors that arrive at its gates today. The park is constantly changing to maintain its appeal, so these modern photographs may soon become historical records.

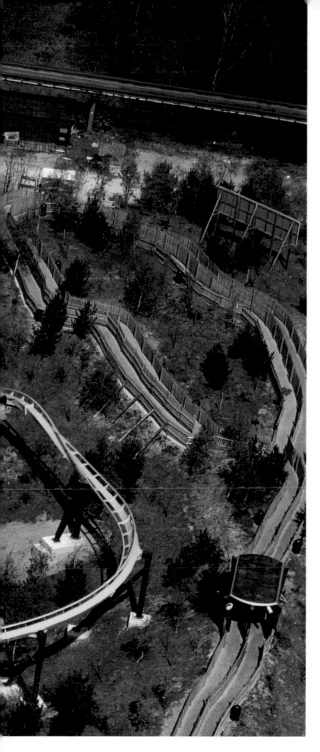
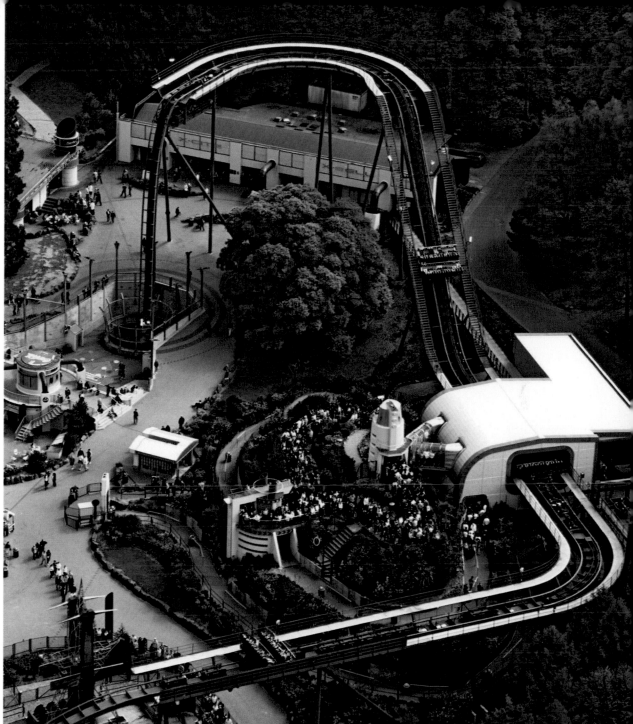

Oil rig, North Sea

The extraction of oil from the earth, and especially from under the sea as shown here, is a hugely expensive business. Platforms like this are not only costly to construct in the first place, it can take weeks and the labour of hundreds of men to dismantle them to the point where they can be moved to another site.

Longships Lighthouse, off Land's End, Cornwall

Not everyone welcomed lighthouses. Here on the Longships rocks, off Land's End, the locals boosted their income when ships were destroyed in the fierce storms, and their cargoes could be plundered. Then a light was established here in 1795 though the locals still had their booty from time to time as during bad storms the seas were frequently higher than the lighthouse. A new one was built in 1873, which today is unmanned.

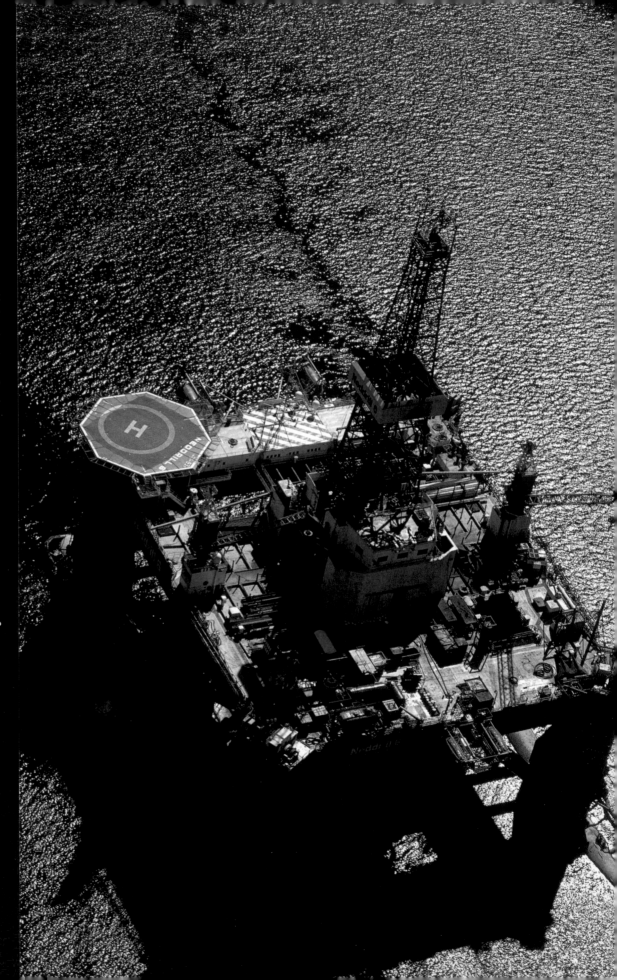

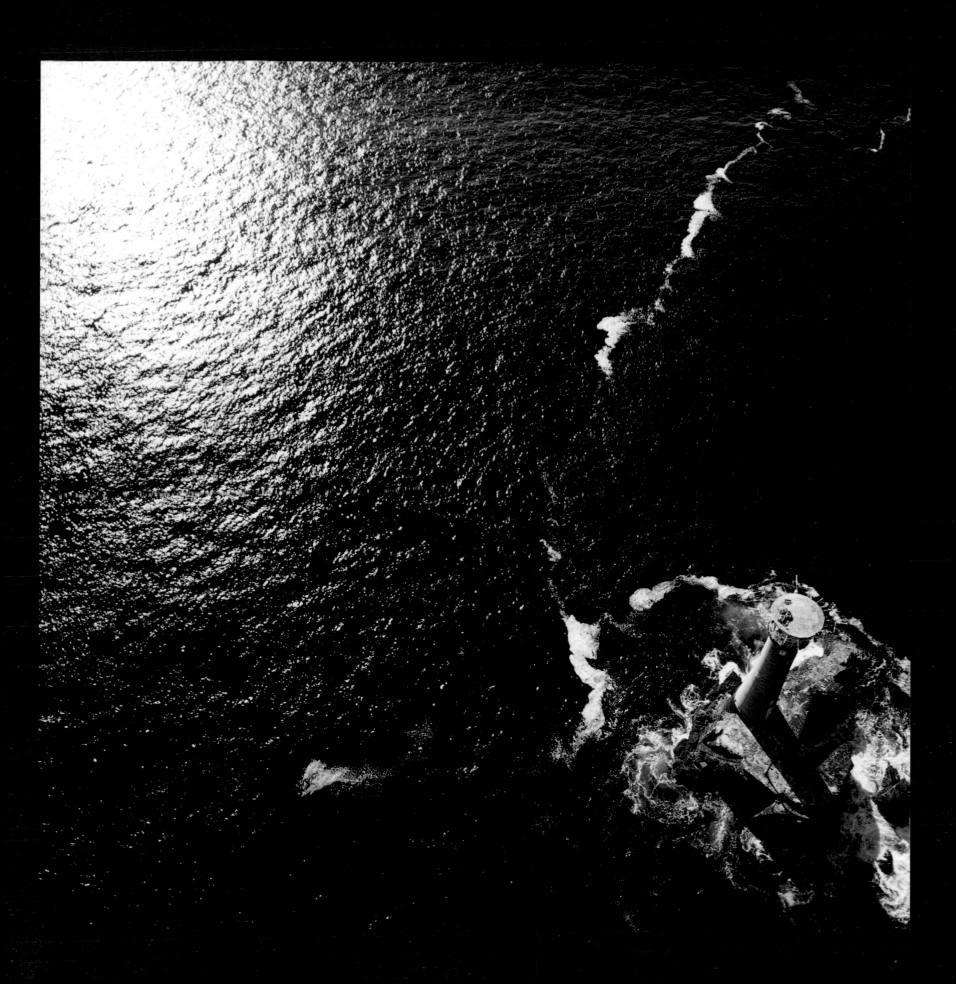

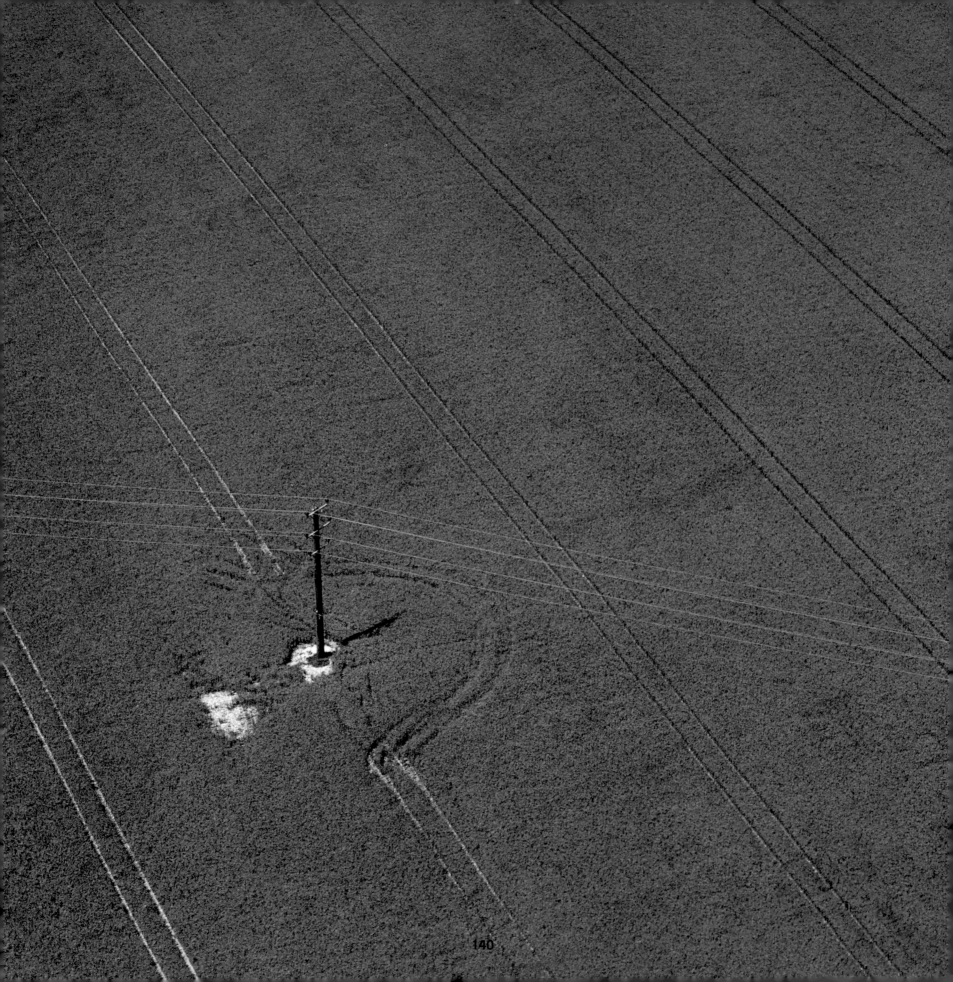

140

< LEFT
Fields of linseed, Buckinghamshire
As well as providing stunning fields of colour, like this in Buckinghamshire, the flax plant, or linseed, produces oil which has numerous uses. Linseed oil can be used as a lubricant, as a food supplement for humans and animals, in putty and paint, to treat leather, make linoleum and, that most English of uses, to act as a preservative on the willow wood used to make cricket bats.

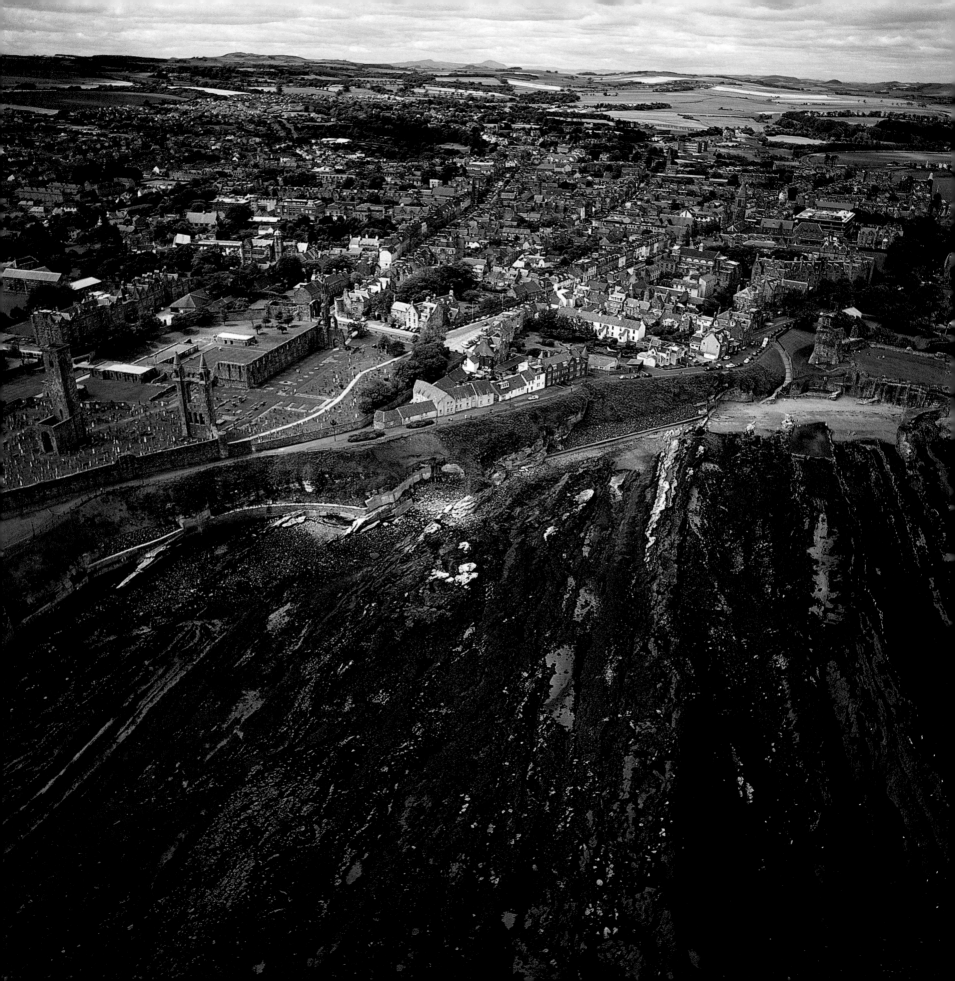

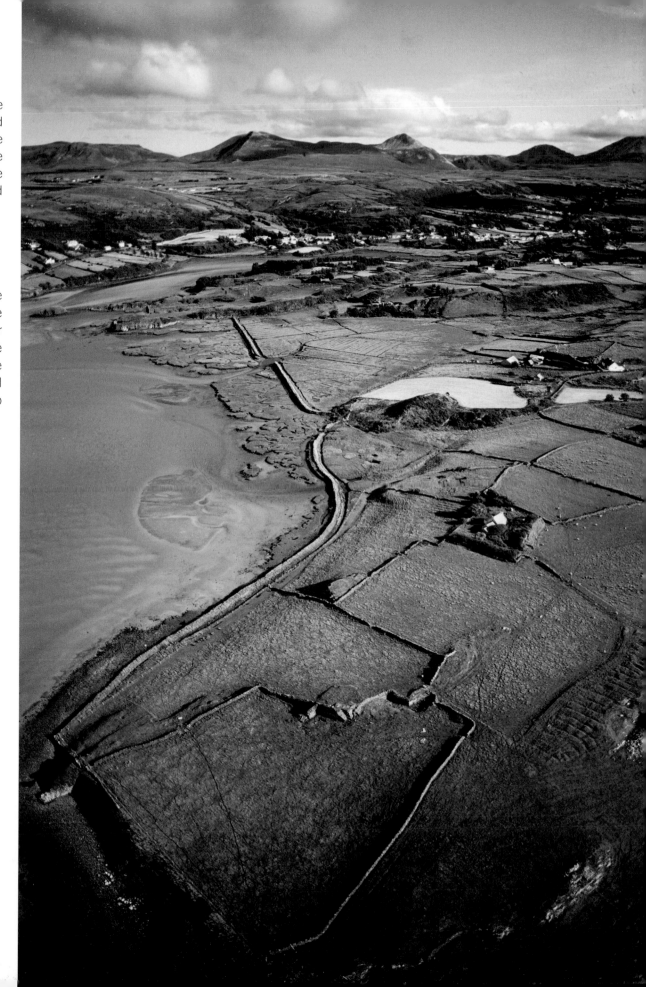

< OPPOSITE

St Andrews, Fife

St Andrews on the Fife coast is known as the home of golf, as here you'll find the Royal and Ancient Golf Club, founded in 1754. It isn't the oldest club in Scotland, but it quickly became the dominant body and the rules for golf around the world, except for the USA and Mexico, are laid down in this small Scottish seaside town.

> RIGHT

**Coastline and Derryveagh Mountains,
County Donegal**

The distant Derryveagh Mountains provide some of the most dramatic scenery in Donegal, in the northwest of Ireland, and none more so than their highest point: Errigal Mountain. Errigal is visible here as the pyramid-like peak in the centre of the photograph, 2,466 feet (751m) high, beautiful but deadly, having claimed the lives of some who would try to conquer her.

∨ BELOW
Portsmouth Harbour, Hampshire
Once a Saxon fishing village, Portsmouth became a military town and later the home of the British Royal Navy. Along with London, it was one of the hubs from which the British Empire spread. It still has the oldest working dry dock in the world, and you can still see famous ships such as Lord Nelson's HMS *Victory* here.

> OPPOSITE
Bluewater, Kent
The triangular shape of Bluewater, the huge shopping centre in Kent, is no accident. It was deliberately chosen after surveying shoppers about their shopping experiences, and the optimum design was thought to be a triangle, with three distinct shopping malls and a huge, recognisable store at each point of the triangle. It must work, as the average visitor spends three hours there.

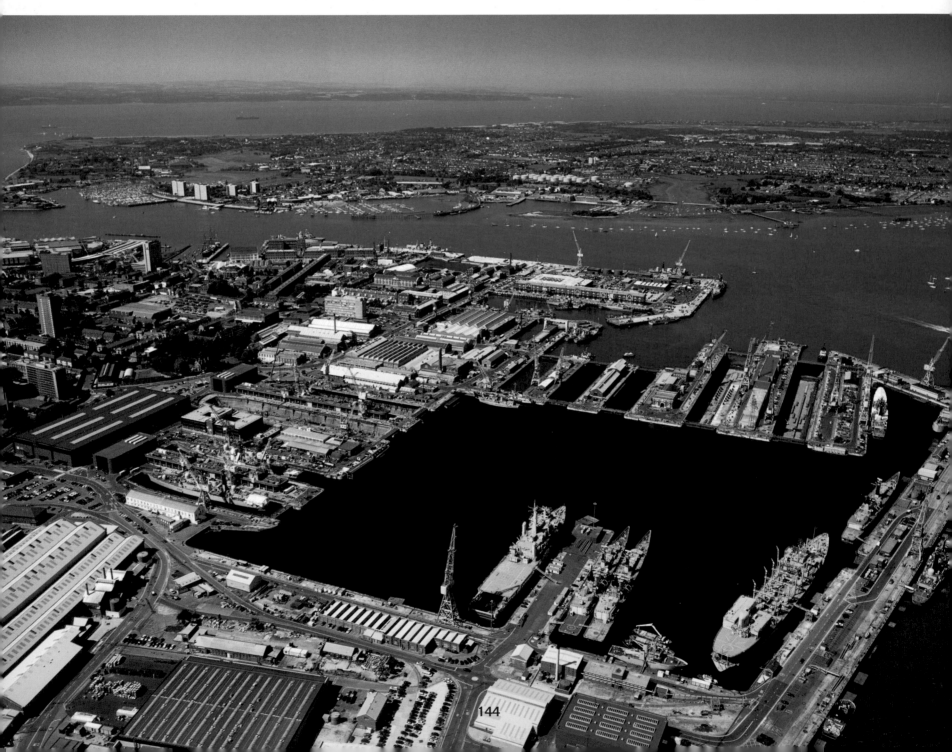

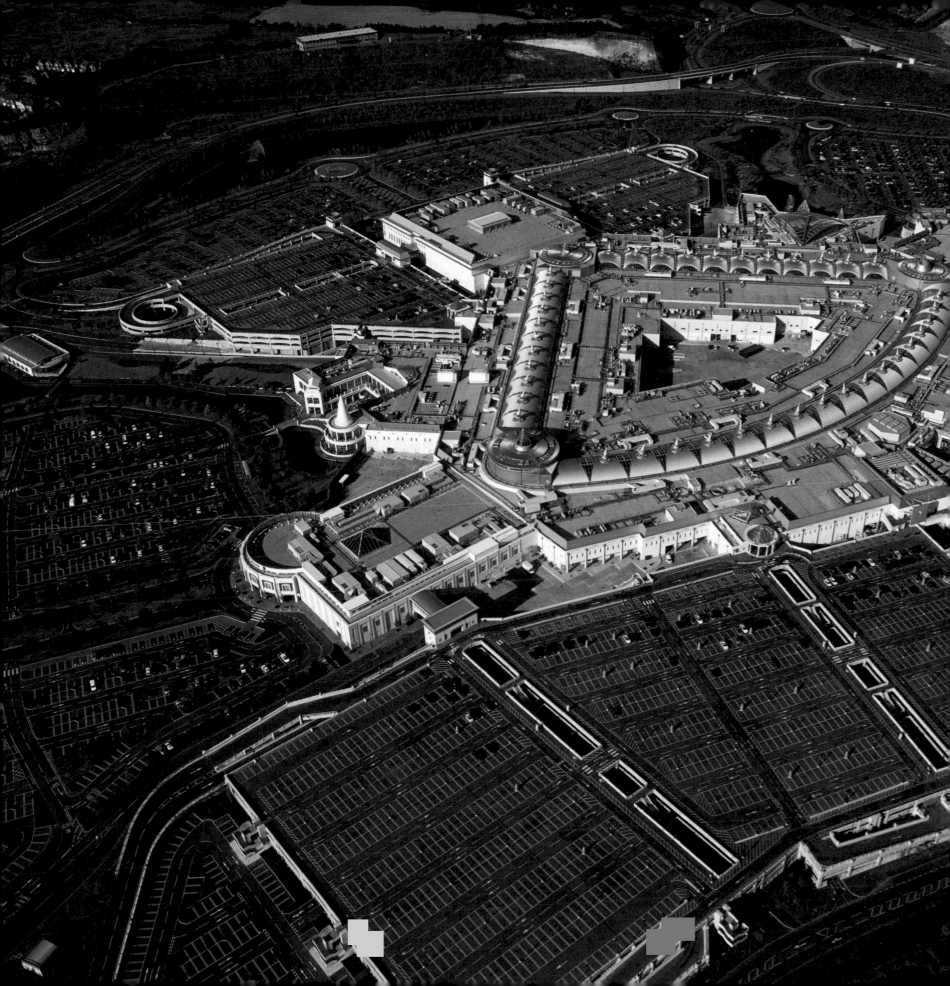

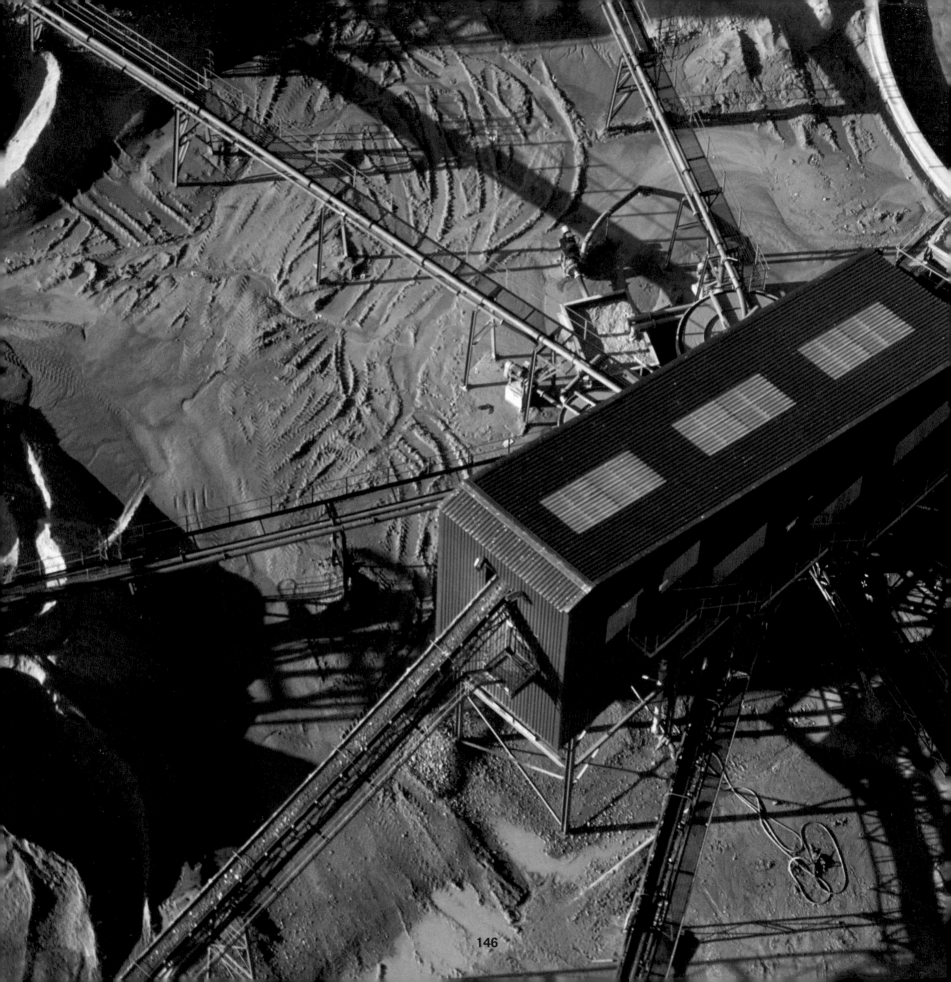

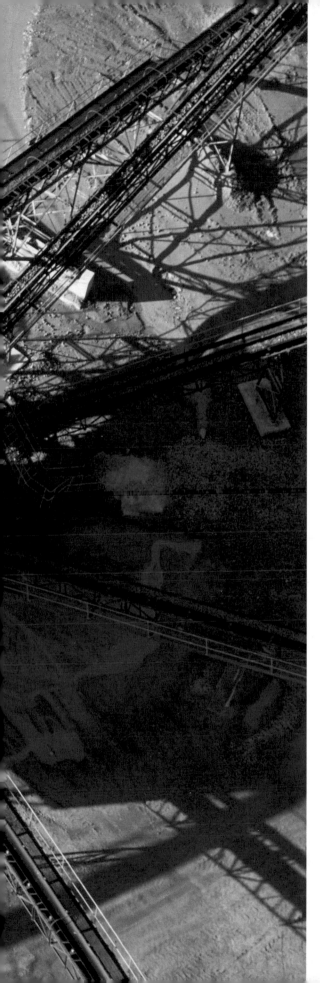

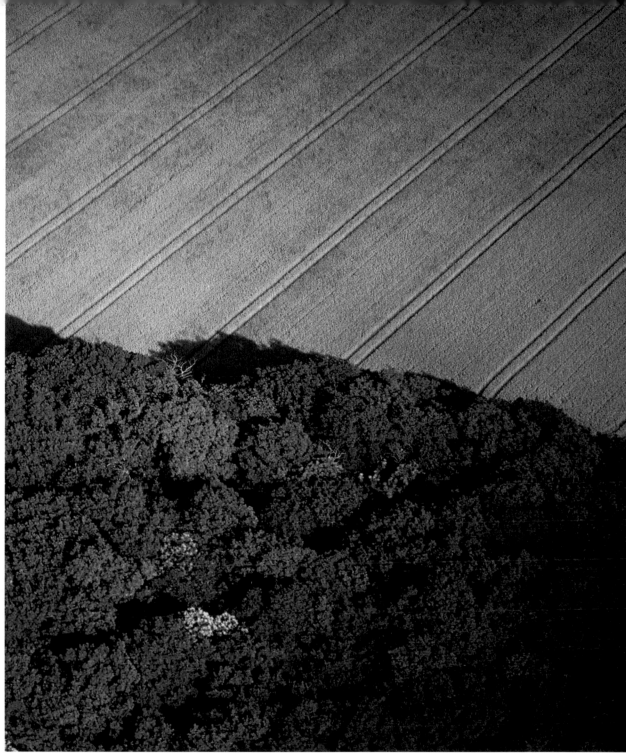

Gravel pit, Buckinghamshire
Looking at the moment like a film set for a sci-fi movie, perhaps the colonisation of a far-distant barren planet, this gravel pit will probably one day become a lush part of the English landscape. Many pits, when they have served their purpose of providing gravel for building and other projects, have been turned into wildlife reserves.

Woodlands and field, Gloucestershire
This simple English countryside scene reminds us that close to where it was taken, in Gloucestershire, the poet Laurie Lee grew up. He described his rural childhood, during and shortly after the First World War, in his best-selling book *Cider with Rosie*. This view of woods and crops shows that not all of that world has yet been lost.

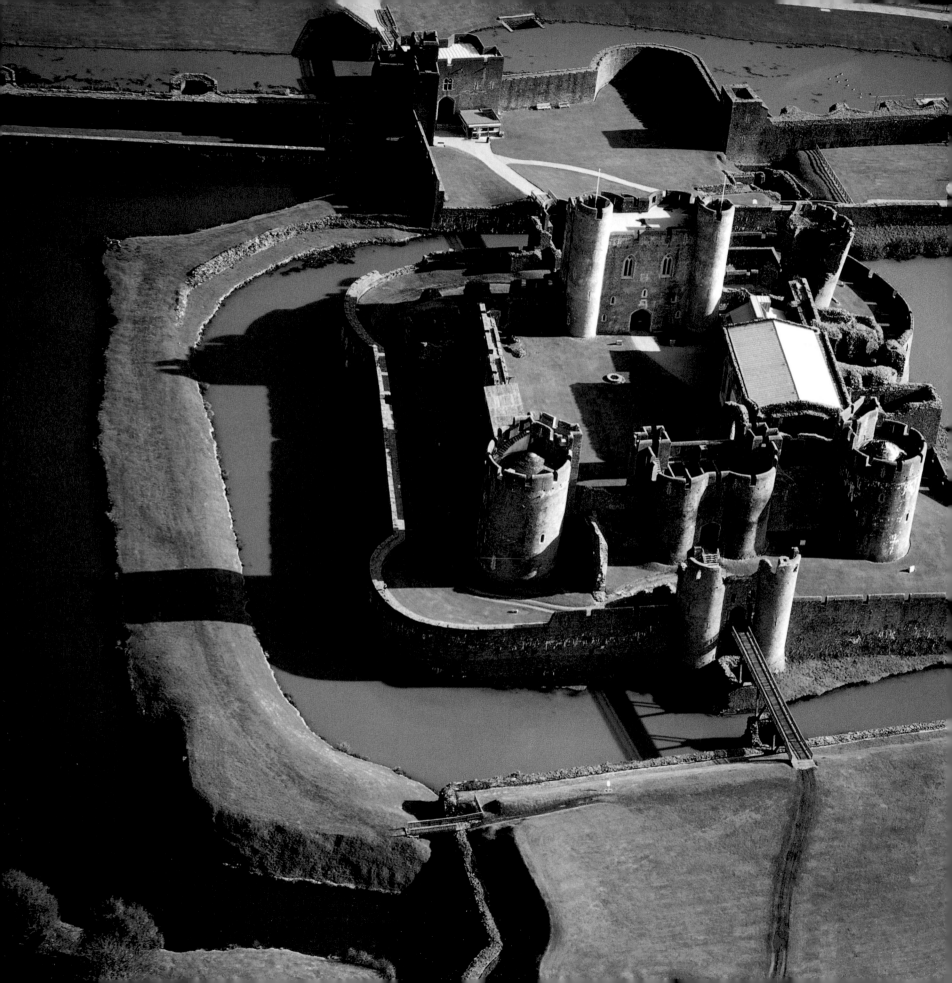

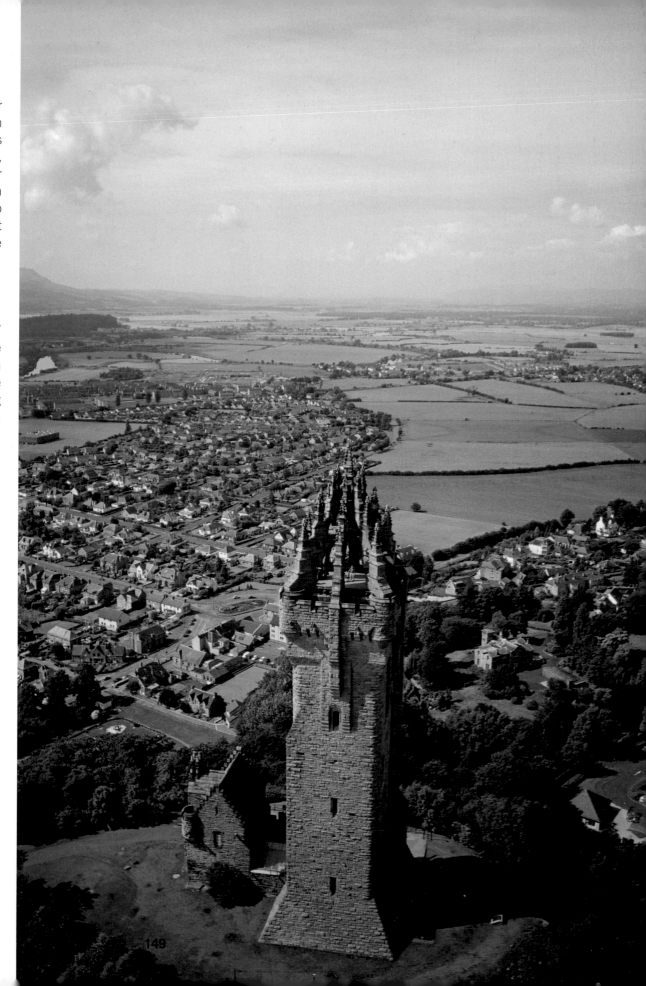

< OPPOSITE
Caerphilly Castle, Glamorgan
In Britain, only the royal castle at Windsor is larger than Caerphilly, which has stood in Glamorgan in South Wales since the late 13th century. It's an unusual example of a series of fortresses, surrounded by a mix of moat and lakes, to hinder the enemy's approach. After standing firm for a few hundred years the castle eventually fell into disrepair, and renovations began with the First Marquess of Bute, who made his fortune from the nearby coalfields.

> RIGHT
Wallace Monument, Stirling
The power and significance of William 'Braveheart' Wallace is shown by this shot of the Wallace Monument, towering over Stirling. It stands on Abbey Craig, from where Wallace is said to have watched the massing of the armies under King Edward I, before the Battle of Stirling Bridge – a significant victory for Wallace over the English.

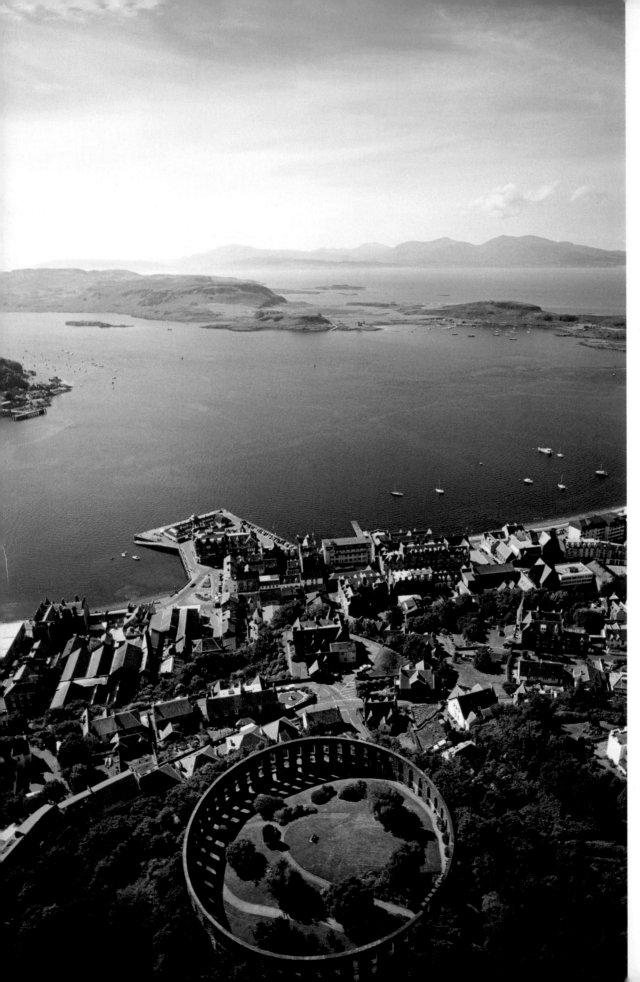

< LEFT
Oban, Argyll

Little Oban in Argyll, on the west coast of Scotland, is dominated by McCaig's Folly, as this photo shows. It was built by a wealthy local banker, John Stewart McCaig, though he died in 1902 before his plans could be fully realised. He was an admirer of Ancient Greece and Rome, and he intended the building to be modelled on the Colosseum and to contain a museum. He left money to continue his work but his family successfully challenged his will and the building remained unfinished.

> OPPOSITE
Marlow and the Thames, Buckinghamshire

On one side of the River Thames stands Marlow in Buckinghamshire, on the other side Bisham in Berkshire. The two have been linked by a bridge since the 14th century, although the present impressive suspension bridge was opened in 1832. The engineer behind the project, William Tierney Clark, was one of the first to work with suspension bridges, and this one in Marlow was a prototype for his later work on the Széchenyi Chain Bridge, the first bridge to be built across the River Danube, in Budapest.

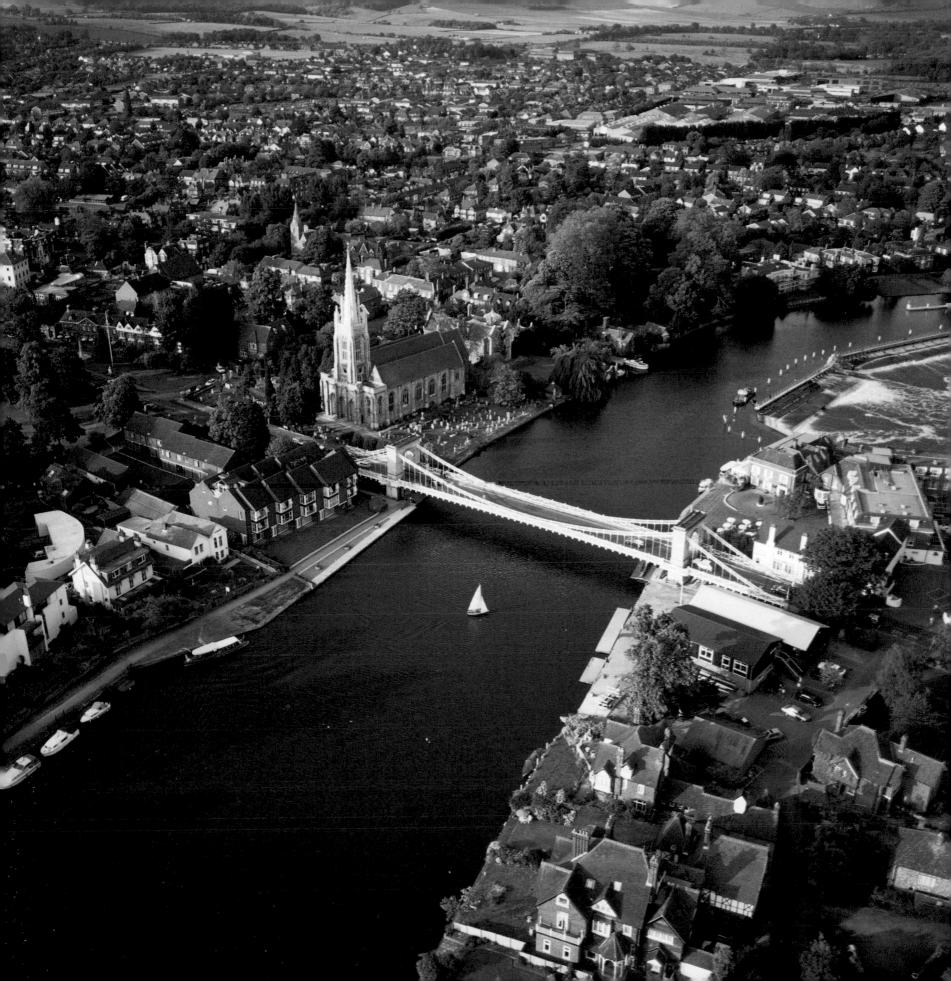

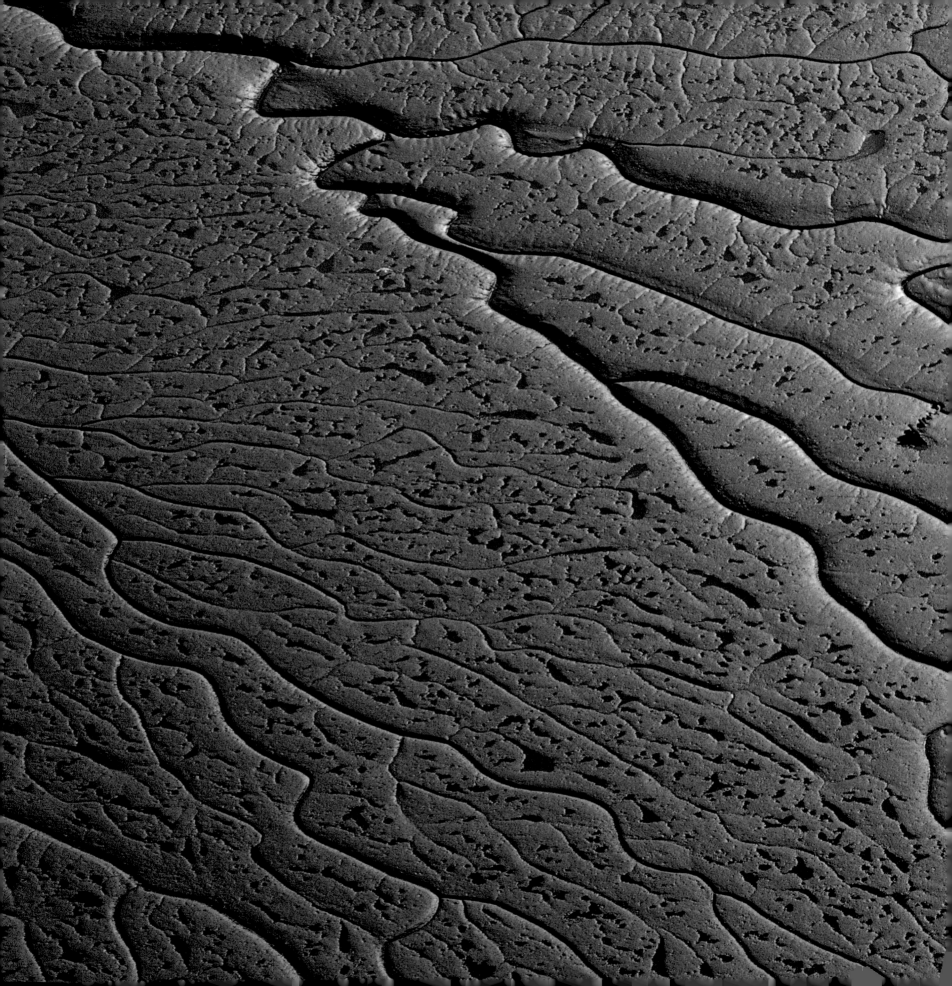

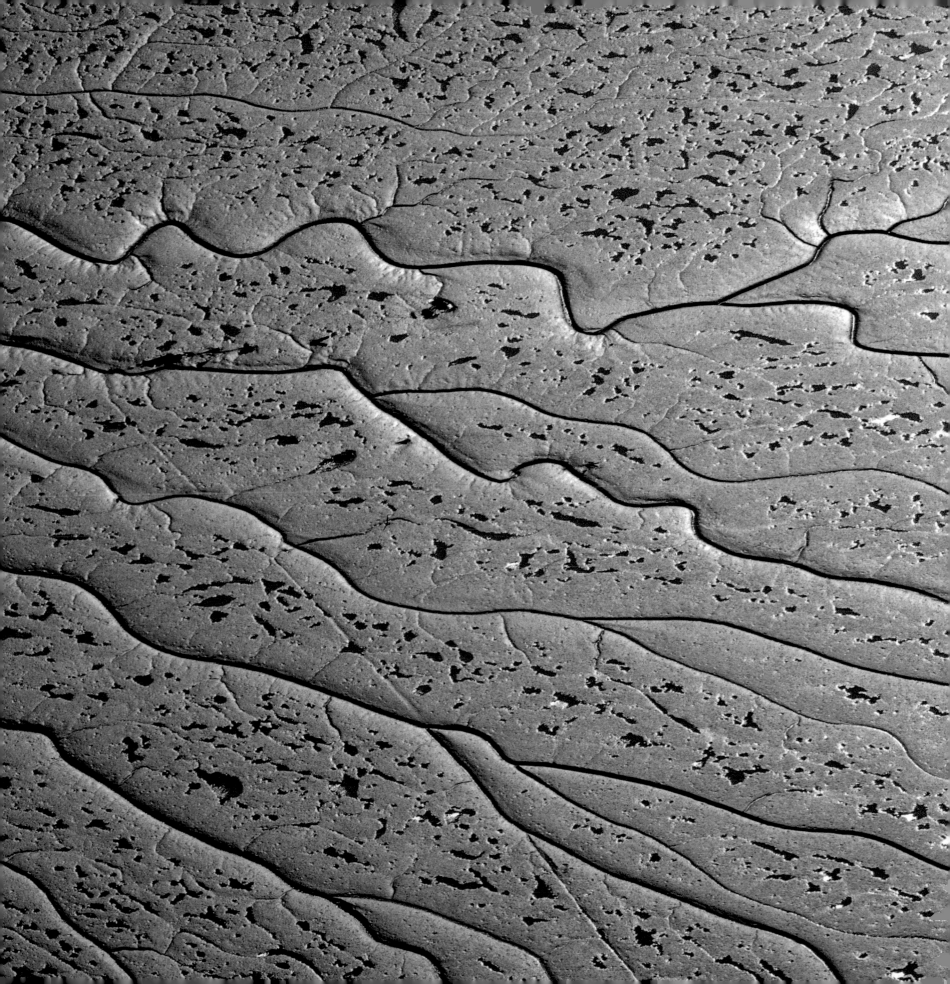

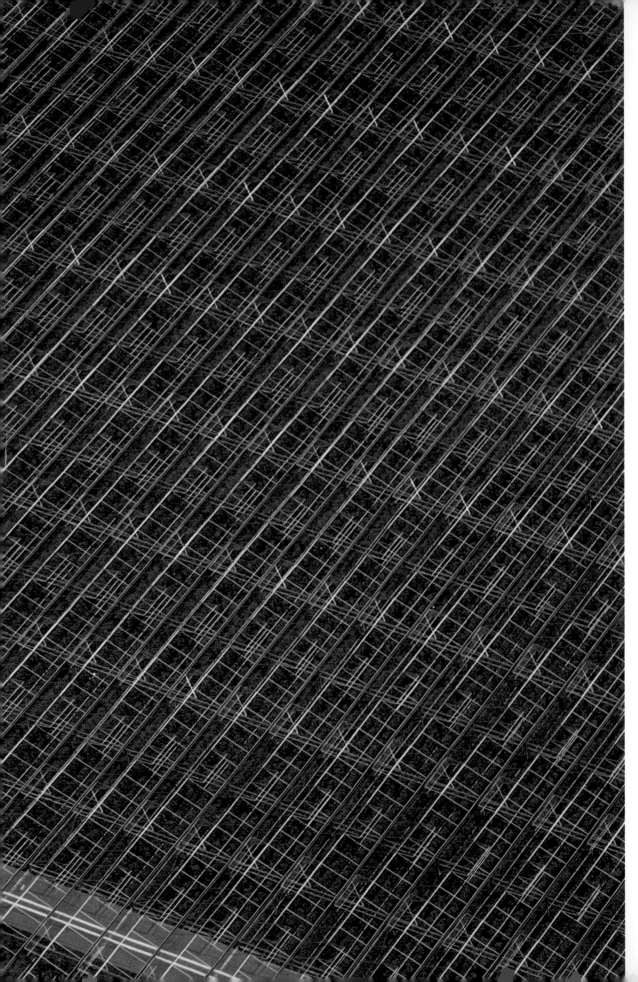

« PREVIOUS
Mudflats near Cardiff Bay, Glamorgan
Looking from the air like a patch of elephant hide, these mudflats near Cardiff Bay are, like mudflats everywhere in Britain, a much more important part of the landscape than they may at first look. They are vital in providing food for wildlife, particularly for migrating birds. They also help to prevent coastal erosion, although as sea levels rise due to global warming, we will start to lose our mudflats and the benefits they provide.

< LEFT
Greenhouses, Kent
The advantage of growing plants under glass or some other clear covering has been known since at least Roman times, and by the 16th century the Italians had developed the first examples of what we would regard as modern greenhouses. They were initially used to try to create a climate in which to keep the tropical plants that were brought back from overseas explorations, and they spread to countries like England and the Netherlands, two great plant-importing nations who were in even greater need of greenhouse warmth. Today's population growth means that greenhouses must be used intensively, like these in Kent.

> OPPOSITE
Ackergill Tower, Caithness
Ackergill Tower stands near Wick in Caithness, just a few miles south of John O'Groats in the extreme northeast of the Scottish mainland. It dates back to the early 15th century when it was built as a tower house for the clan Keith, a prominent local clan, but today it has some unusual distinctions, one being that it is the most northerly opera house in the United Kingdom.

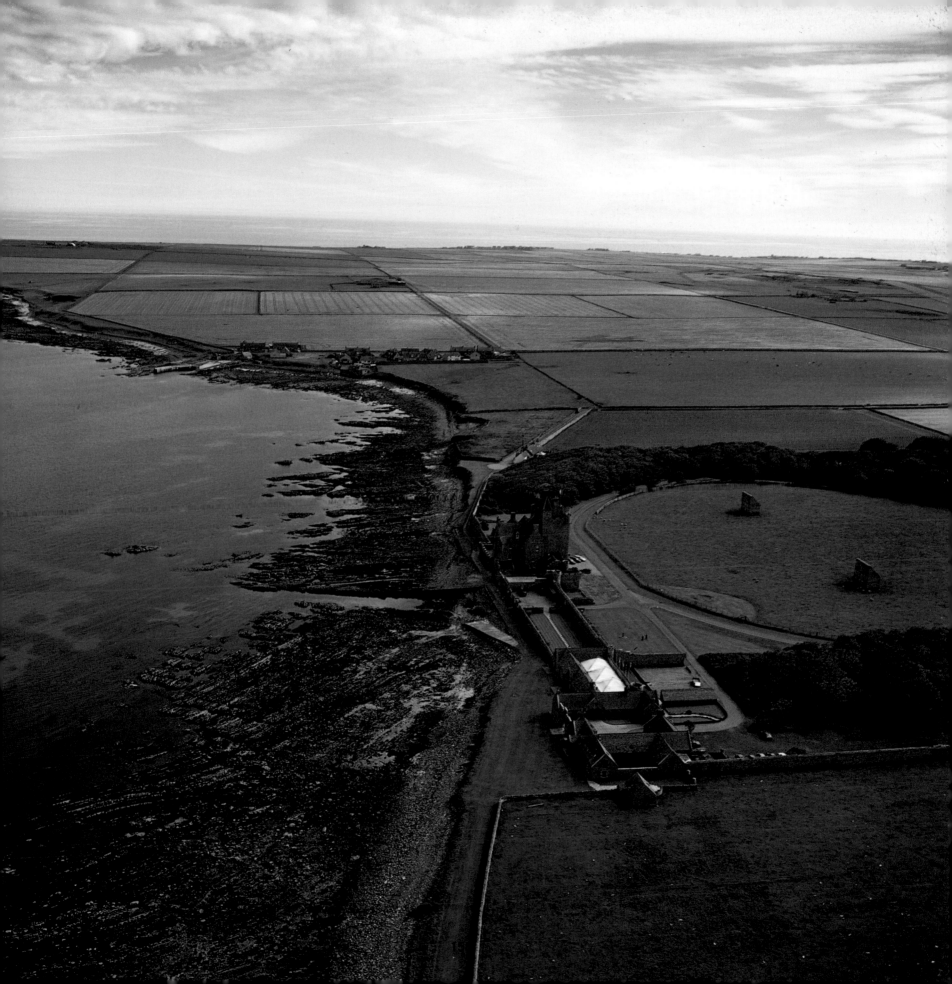

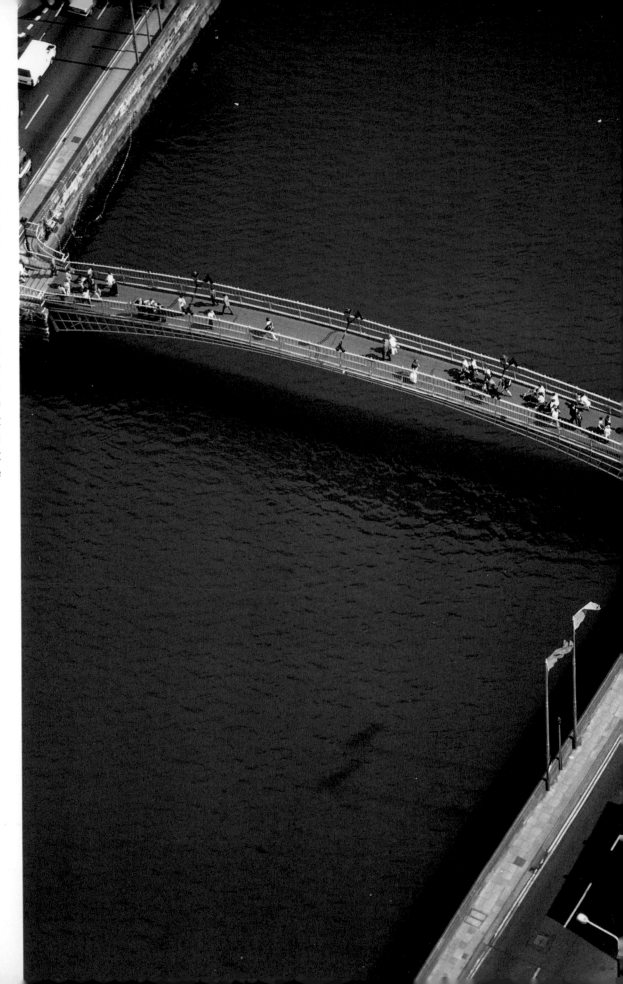

> RIGHT
Ha'penny Bridge, Dublin

Dubliners love giving their own names to the city's features, regardless of the official names. The Wellington Bridge that was opened in 1816 immediately became the Ha'penny Bridge because people had to pay a toll of half a penny to use it. The toll went to the ferry operator, who was instructed by the authorities to either build a bridge or stop operating his ferries, which were in a dangerous condition. The toll lasted just over 100 years, but the name has lasted longer.

> OPPOSITE
Lough Carra, County Mayo

In Mayo in western Ireland, Lough Carra is a very shallow lake, as can be seen from the clear waters in this view. It attracts trout fishermen, especially looking for brown trout as the lake is filled with them. There is a lot of lake to fill, too, as the lake is six miles long and covers 4,000 acres (about 1,620 hectares). The fish are also larger than in any of the other lakes in the area, and a trout weighing 18lb (almost 8,200 grams) was once caught here.

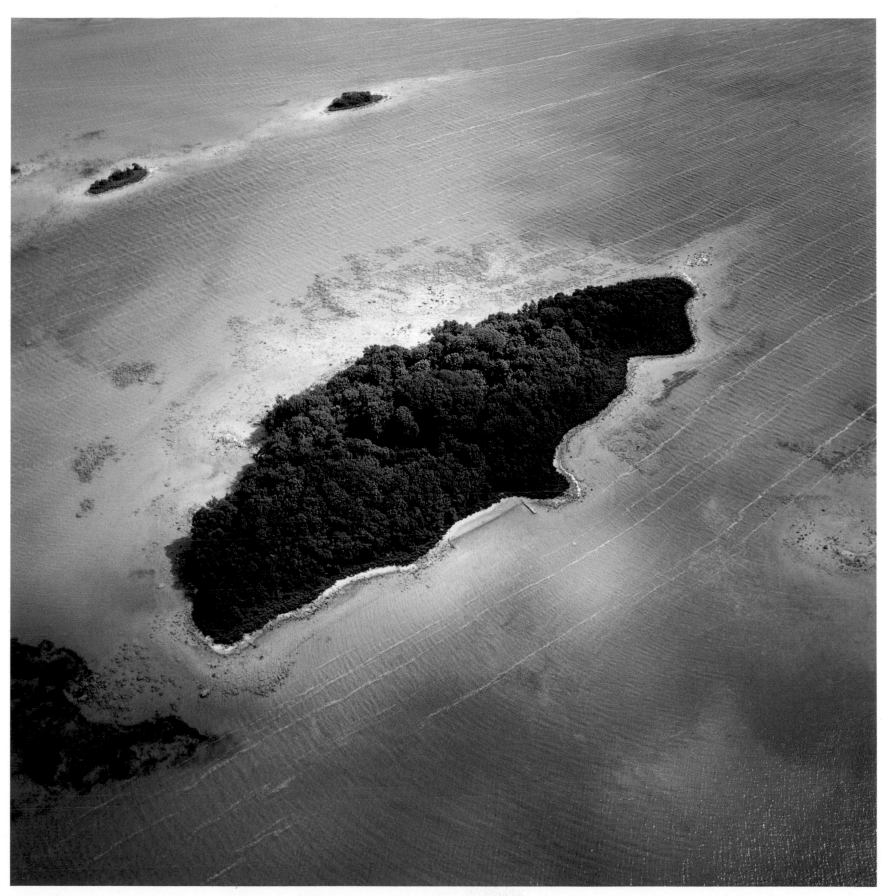

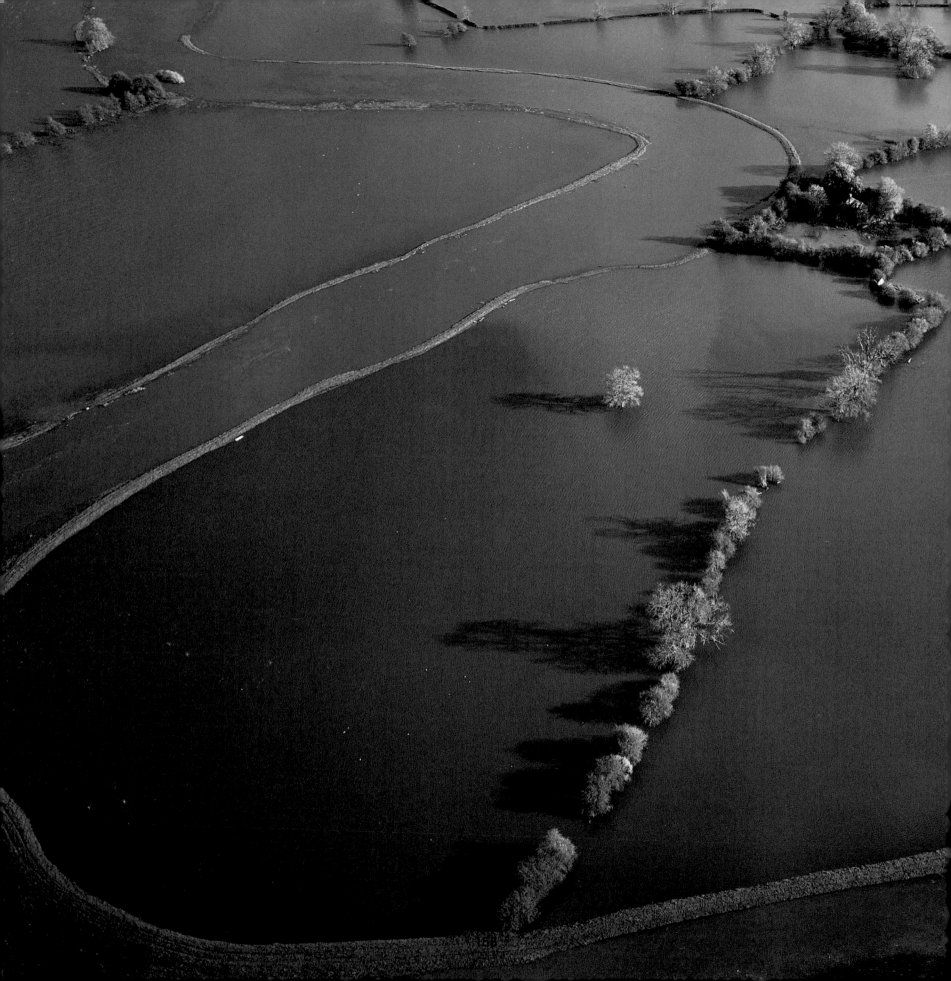

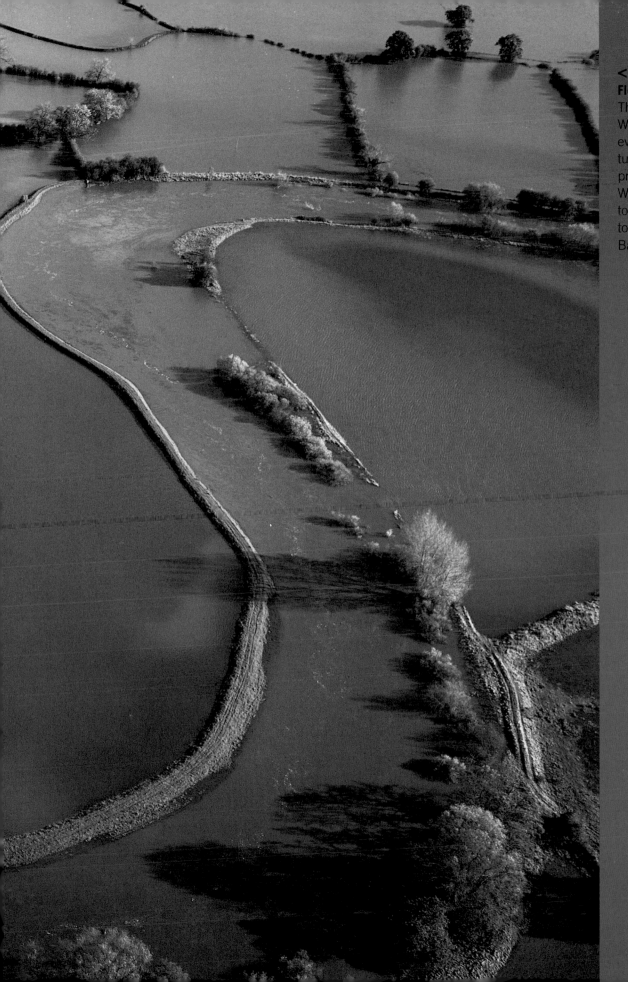

< LEFT

Flooded fields, east of Wrexham, North Wales

The River Dee flows east of Wrexham in North Wales, and north to the Dee Estuary, its waters eventually becoming part of the Irish Sea. It often turns the land into a kind of sea because it is very prone to flooding. The land is low-lying and the Welsh mountains attract plenty of rain, sometimes too much for the riverbeds to contain. The nearby town of Bangor-on-Dee might better be called Bangor-under-Dee, so often does it flood.

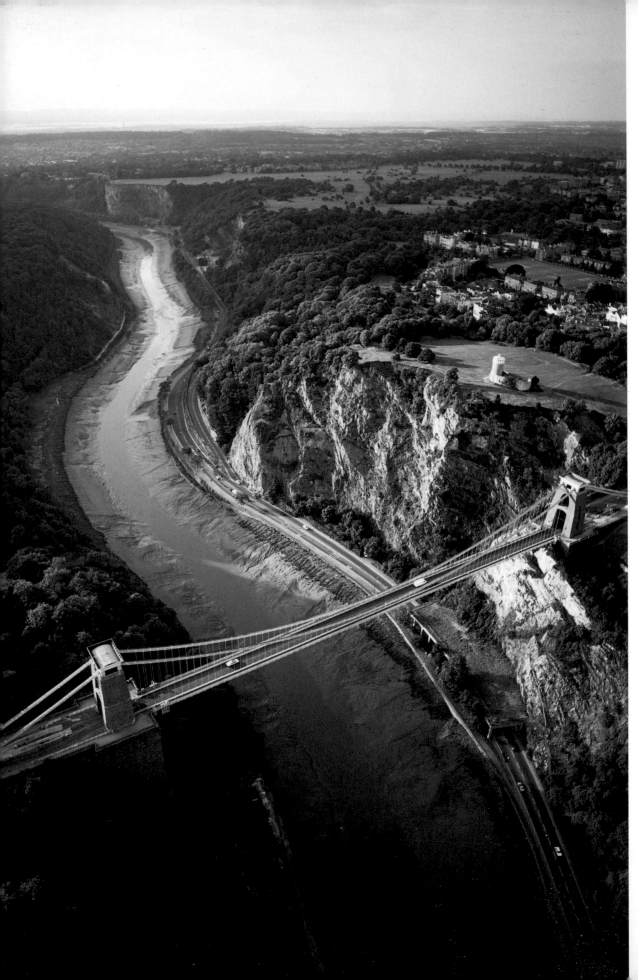

< LEFT
Clifton Suspension Bridge, Bristol

The impressive Clifton Suspension Bridge spans the Avon Gorge, linking the city of Bristol with North Somerset. The bridge was designed by the great Victorian engineer, Isambard Kingdom Brunel, though he did not live to see it completed. There were major delays in the building of the bridge, due to practical, financial and political reasons. While work on the bridge began in the 1830s, it wasn't opened until 1864, five years after Brunel's death.

> OPPOSITE
Dryburgh Abbey, Scottish Borders

Dryburgh Abbey was built on the banks of the River Tweed, which meanders its way through the Scottish Borders. The spot had been known as a holy place for over 500 years before the Abbey itself was built, in 1152. Despite being destroyed by fire three times, and suffering even more at the hands of passing armies, many of the walls and other structures remain intact and give visitors a real feeling of medieval monastic life.

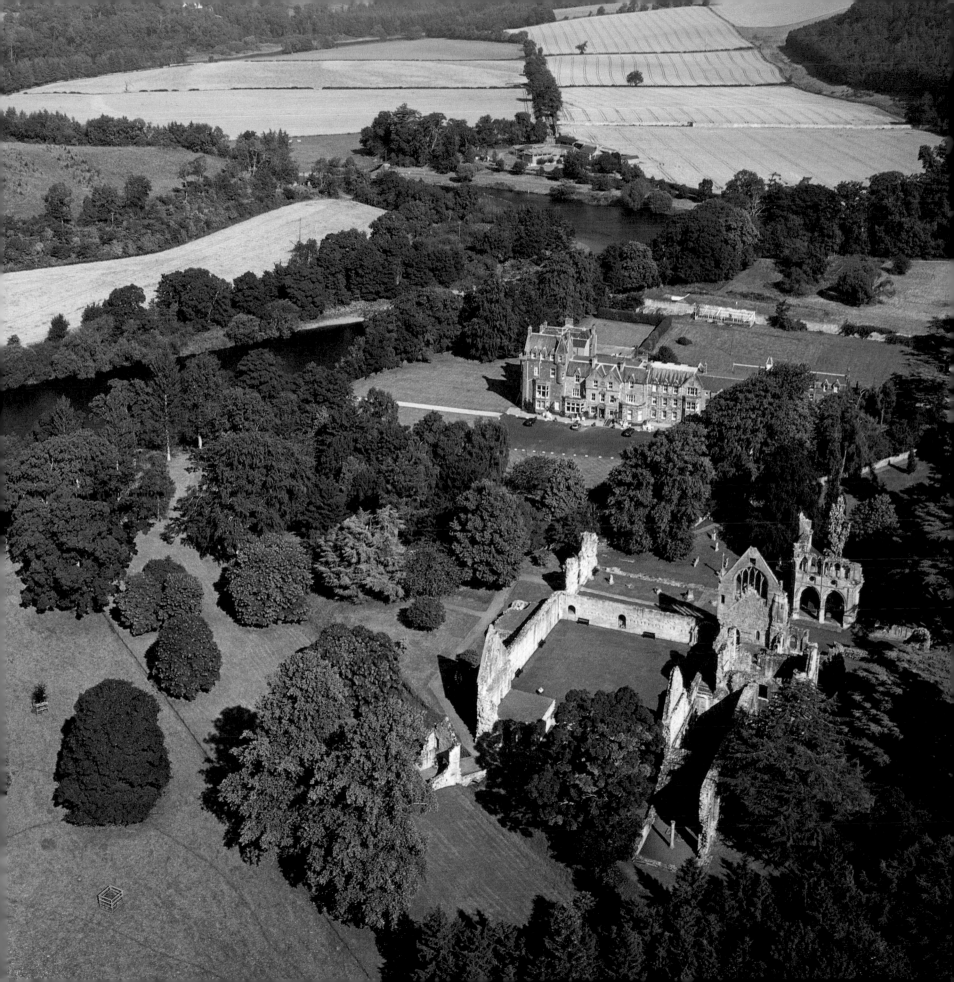

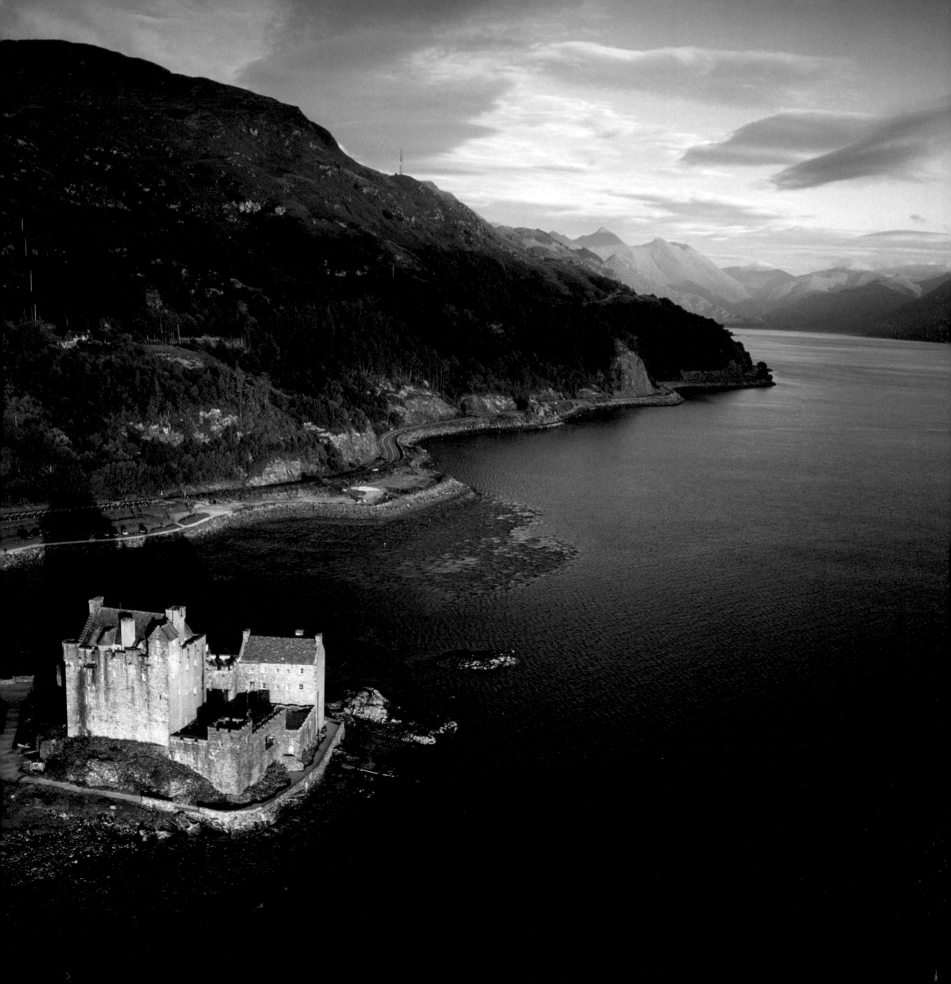

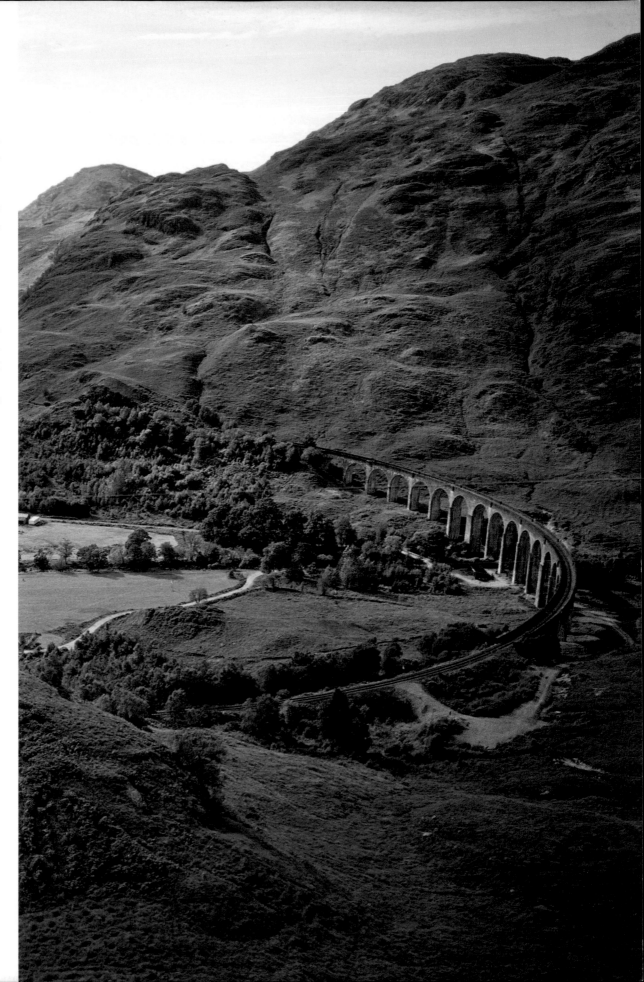

< OPPOSITE

Eilean Donan Castle, Western Highlands

Eilean Donan Castle on Loch Duich in the Western Highlands may appear idyllic, but it has seen some turbulence in its times. Marauding Vikings were the reason for a castle first being built on this spot, back in 1220, and since then it has been besieged and taken by clans and Spaniards alike. Today it is besieged by visitors, and also movie companies looking for locations. James Bond is one of the more recent fictional visitors.

> RIGHT

Glenfinnan Viaduct, Northern Highlands

The Glenfinnan Viaduct was designed by the engineer Sir Robert McAlpine, also known as 'Concrete Bob', and was completed in 1901. It was to gain more fame a hundred years later when it was seen carrying the Hogwarts Express in the film *Harry Potter and the Chamber of Secrets*. In the real world the viaduct is on the West Highland Railway, and the tallest of its 21 arches reaches a height of 100 feet (30m).

> RIGHT

Fishing trawler, Camel Estuary, Cornwall
The River Camel runs for 30 miles (48km) through north Cornwall, and passes Padstow as it emerges into Padstow Bay and on out into the Celtic Sea. The fishing industry, epitomised by these tiny but brave trawlers, has been a livelihood here since long before the celebrity chef Rick Stein made the town famous as a gastronomic destination. The river's unusual name has no exotic connections, but comes from the Cornish for 'the crooked one', describing the route it takes to the sea.

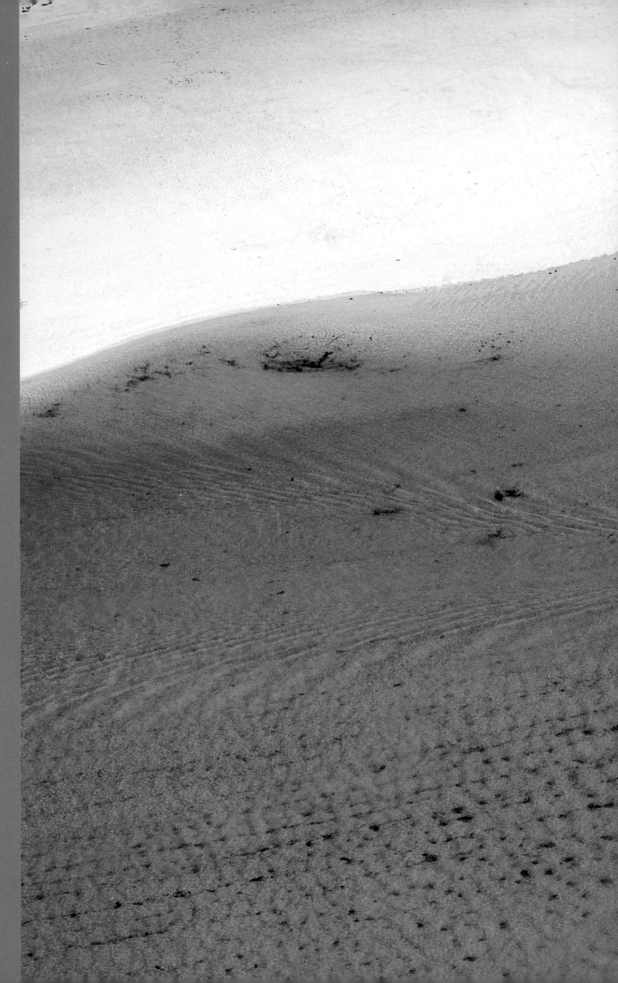

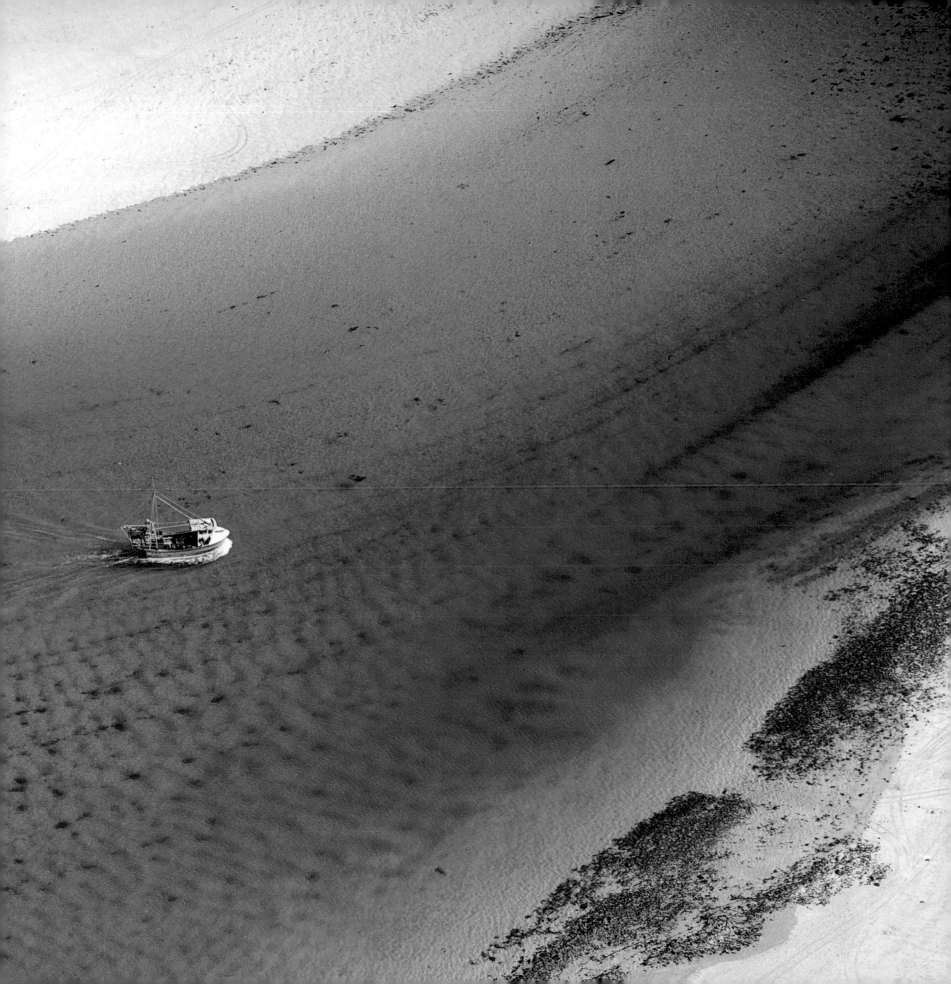

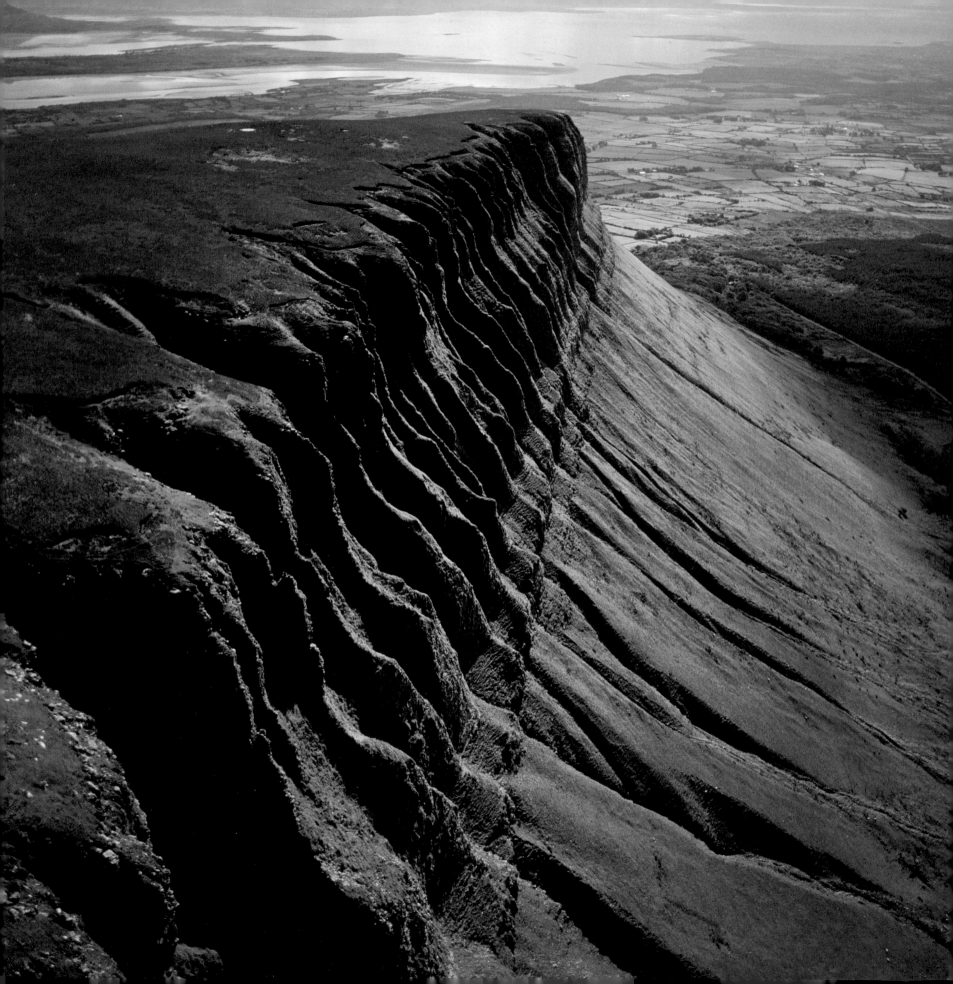

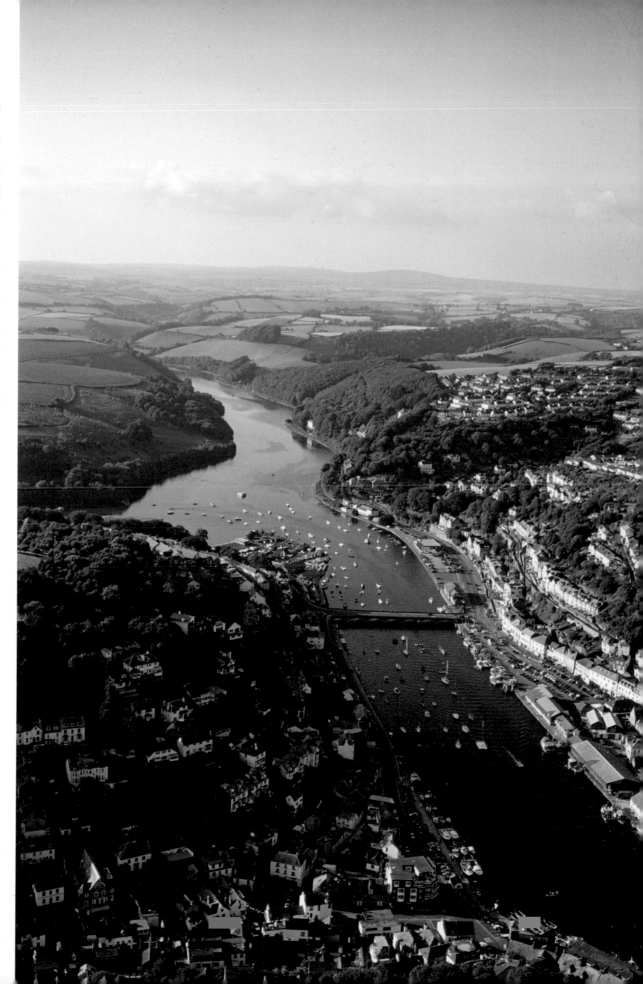

< OPPOSITE
Ben Bulben, County Sligo

Under Ben Bulben, the awe-inspiring mountain in County Sligo, the poet WB Yeats lies buried. *Under Ben Bulben* is also one of the finest, and the last, poems that the Nobel Prizewinner wrote, and the final three lines from the poem are carved on his gravestone in the cemetery at Drumcliffe from where the striking outline of Ben Bulben can clearly be seen.

> RIGHT
Looe, Cornwall

For at least 3,000 years mankind has lived here on the banks of the River Looe, in Cornwall. There are two towns either side of the river, East Looe and West Looe, and just offshore (and out of the picture) where the river emerges into the English Channel, is Looe Island. The two towns were joined by a bridge across the river, the first in Cornwall, as early as 1411.

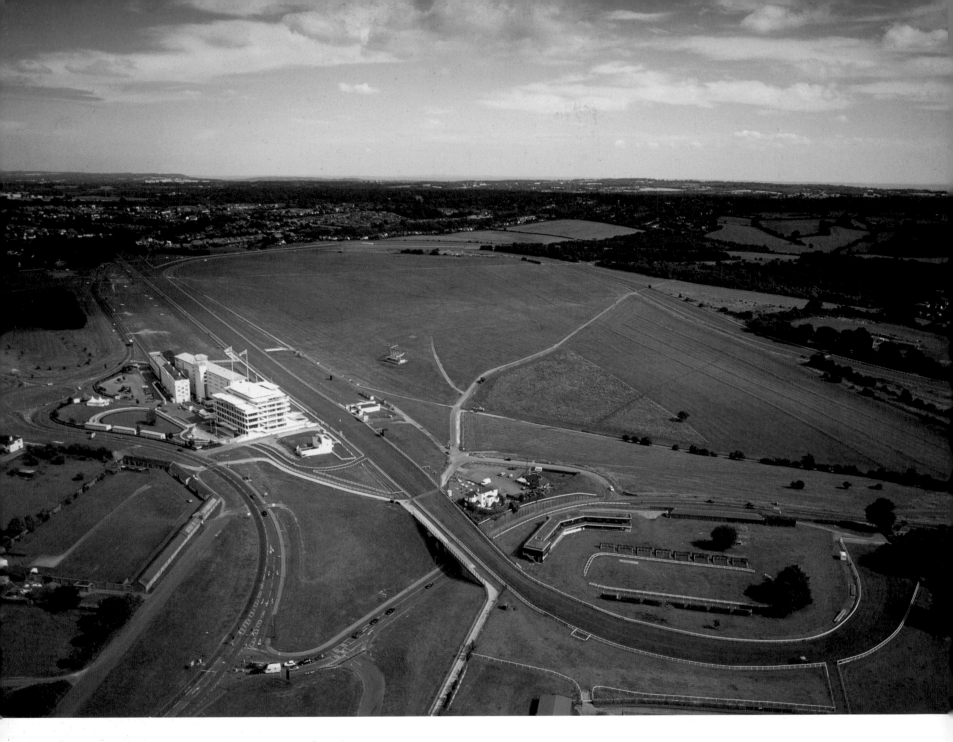

^ **ABOVE**

Epsom racecourse, Surrey

The Epsom Derby rivals the Grand National at Aintree for being the most famous horserace in the British Isles, and it has an unusual history. In 1618 a local farmer took his cattle to a watering hole he had found on Epsom Downs, and thought the water had great healing properties. Soon Londoners were coming here for their health, and racing began to entertain these visitors in 1661.

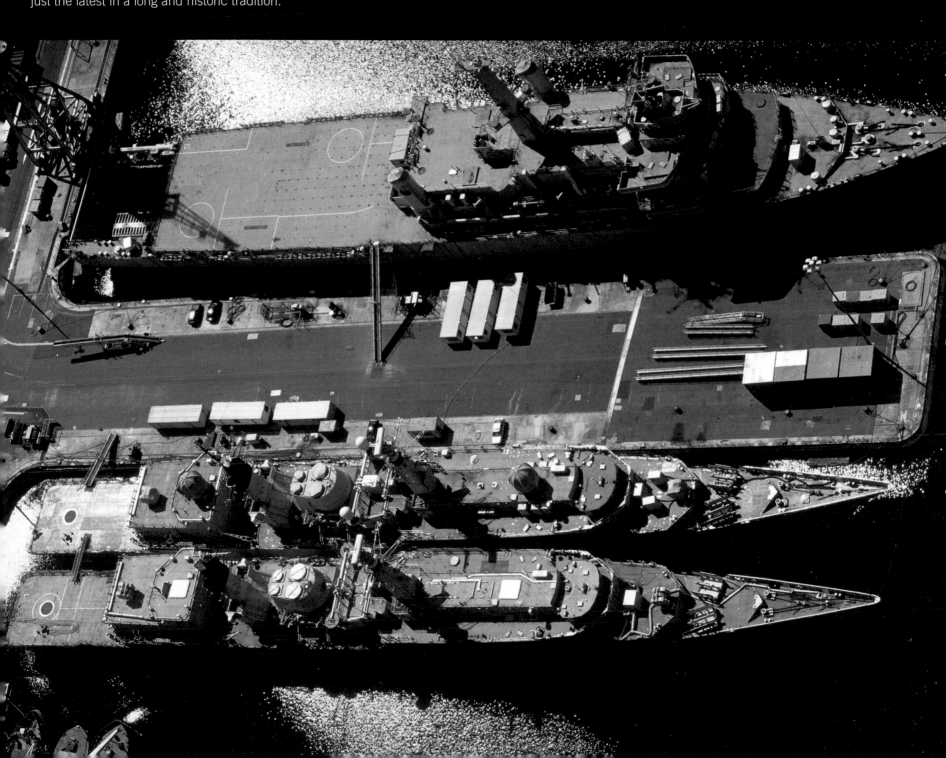

∨ BELOW
Portsmouth, Hampshire
As an island, Britain has always been reliant on a navy to help defend its territory, and the earliest recorded naval battle in British waters was in 719. King Alfred (c.849-899) is often credited as being the founder of the navy, as he used longships in sea battles against the Vikings. These modern navy vessels in Portsmouth Harbour are therefore just the latest in a long and historic tradition.

MARITIME BRITAIN

The people of the British Isles, like those of all island nations, have always looked outwards to the sea, and the lands beyond. Britain became one of the world's great maritime nations, perhaps only rivalled by the Netherlands as a small country which eventually conquered, controlled and traded with a large part of the known world. From early explorers like St Brendan to recent adventurers such as Dame Ellen MacArthur, and including such well-known men of the sea as Sir Francis Drake, Lord Nelson and Sir Francis Chichester, Britain has always respected and honoured its sailors.

And with good cause. If St Brendan did indeed make his journey to the Americas in the early sixth century, it would have been a remarkable achievement (and would mean that his visit preceded Christopher Columbus's trip by almost a thousand years). St Brendan was born in about 484 near Tralee, County Kerry, in the southwest of Ireland. He would have grown up looking out to sea in the direction of the Americas, wondering what lay beyond the horizon. Legend has it that in about 530 he set out into the Atlantic Ocean with a number of fellow pilgrims, to find out just what was out there, looking for the Isle of the Blessed.

Whether, in heading westward, St Brendan eventually reached the Americas, is not known for sure, and there are different versions of the story, most dating from several centuries after the event, and it may well have been a religious allegory blended with a real exploratory journey. No proof exists that St Brendan did discover the Americas, although he has plenty of believers. Another great British explorer and adventurer, Tim Severin, made a journey in 1976 to see whether it was even possible for St Brendan to have made such a long trip in the boats that were used at the time. He built a leather currach, like the ones in use in western Ireland in those days, and sailed it across the Atlantic to Newfoundland.

St Brendan aside, it was not until the fifteenth century that Britain and other European nations set sail to explore – and colonise – the rest of the world. It was Britain's power at sea, not to mention a combination of diplomacy and ruthlessness, that helped create the British Empire, the largest the world has ever seen. By 1921 the British Empire covered about a quarter of the world, and controlled about a quarter of its population.

The beginnings of the British Empire were at the end of the 15th century. One of the first major explorations, from the port of Bristol in 1497, was led by an Italian. John Cabot had been recruited into Britain's service because neither of the other great exploring nations, Spain and Portugal, were interested in him. As a result, Britain financed this 1497 expedition which led to him reaching his new-found-land.

One of the earliest English explorers and heroes – if you overlook some unheroic features such as slave trading and piracy – was Sir Francis Drake. He was born in about 1540 in Tavistock in Devon, a few miles inland from the great port city of Plymouth. His family were Protestants and his father was a preacher, and during the Roman Catholic Prayer Book Rebellion in southwest England in 1549, the family fled to Kent. It was from here that Drake first went to sea at the age of 13, working on a cargo vessel. Within ten years he was sailing from Plymouth to the New World.

In 1577 Queen Elizabeth I commanded Drake to go and deal with the Spanish, on the Pacific coast of the Americas. He set sail from Plymouth on his famous ship which was later renamed the *Golden Hinde*, and became the first man to venture into Antarctica, albeit inadvertently. He was rounding Cape Horn to get to the Pacific when a storm blew his ship further south than any other vessel had ever been, making him and his crew the first to enter Antarctic waters. From there he headed north, plundering Spanish and Portuguese ships and settlements as he went. He went further north than the most northerly Spanish settlement, in San Diego, and is known to have landed there, staying for some time repairing and restocking his ships, and may even have left some of his men behind to start a small colony – though no one knows where it was.

From here Drake headed west and made his way to Indonesia, picking up spices in the Spice Islands (then literally worth their weight in gold), and travelled around the Cape of Good Hope to return to Plymouth a hero, the first Englishman to circumnavigate the globe, and probably only the second after Magellan. He also returned a wealthy man too, and a hero to the British Treasury, as the amount of gold and other plunder he had taken in the Americas, and the trading he did in Asia, provided the Crown with over half of its income for that year, 1580. He was knighted, and later became a hero all over again when he was Vice-Admiral of the fleet that defeated the Spanish Armada, when it attempted to invade Britain.

Continuing Drake's tradition of exploration in the 18th century, though with perhaps a little less plundering and warfare, was Captain James Cook. He was born in 1728 in North Yorkshire, and his first job was in the little fishing village of Staithes. He first went to sea from the port of Whitby, ten miles away, though his first voyages were not very glamorous as he worked on colliers transporting coal from the coal mines of northeast England down to London.

From these humble beginnings Cook went on to acquire a great knowledge of navigation, astronomy, surveying and cartography, which he furthered when he served with the Royal Navy. Between 1763 and 1767 he produced the first large-scale maps of the coast of Newfoundland, and then he went to the Pacific Ocean in 1768 at the request of the Royal Society, to record the transit of Venus across the face of the Sun, a rare occurrence. Once this was completed he opened some sealed orders he had taken with him, for the second part of his voyage, and these asked him to search the South Pacific for any traces of the rumoured southern continent of Terra Australis. After mapping the New Zealand coast he sailed westward and his crew became the first Europeans to visit the east coast of Australia.

Cook made two more lengthy voyages. He explored and mapped the South Pacific and then sailed up the western coast of North America as far as Alaska, enabling that coastline to be shown in detail on world maps for the first time. Cook also became the first European to visit Hawaii, though sadly he later died there in 1779 during a dispute with local people.

The bravery and curiosity of early explorers like Captain Cook was one reason people were able to claim that 'Britannia rules the waves'. And the grand maritime story continued with Lord Nelson, the military hero who died at the Battle of Trafalgar. It continues into the 20th and 21st centuries. Sir Francis Chichester, born in the great seafaring county of Devon, became the first person to sail single-handed around the world on the west-east 'clipper route', at the same time claiming the fastest global circumnavigation, taking nine months and one day.

In 2005, Dame Ellen MacArthur, born in the landlocked county of Derbyshire, created a new world record for the fastest solo circumnavigation of the world, in just over 71 days. Britain's maritime prowess shows no signs of stopping.

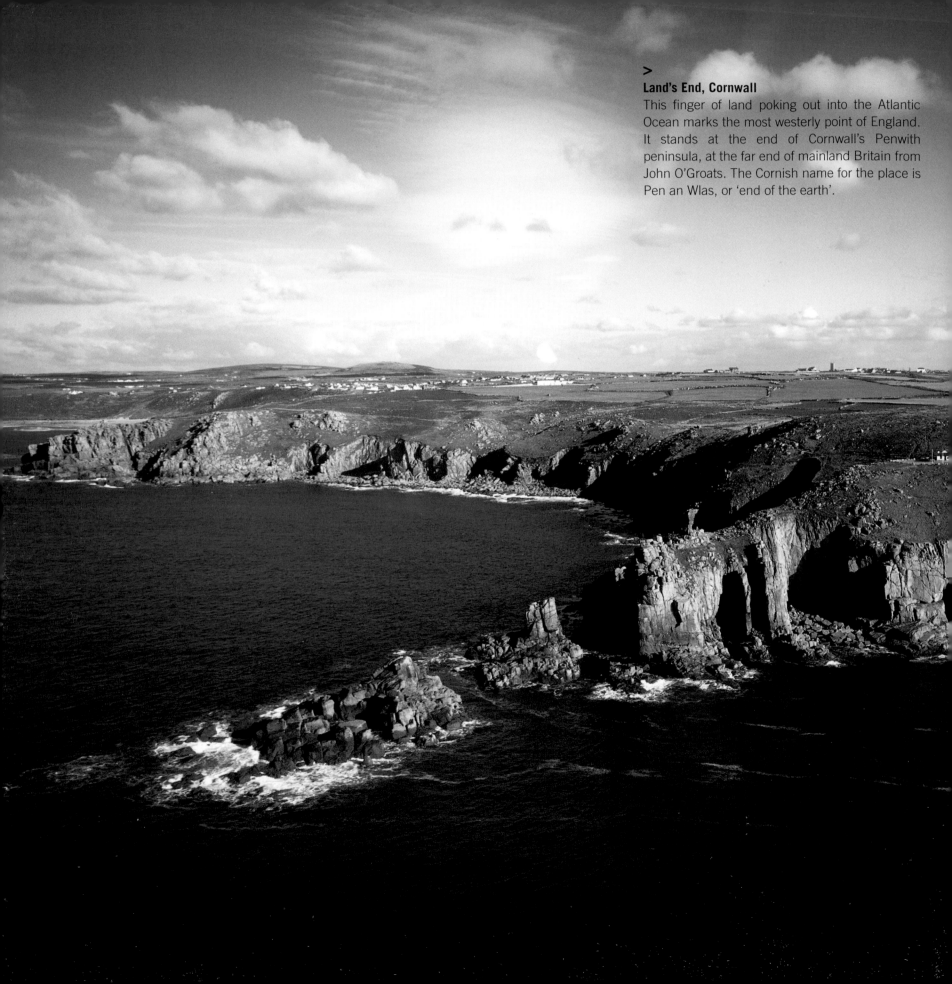

Land's End, Cornwall
This finger of land poking out into the Atlantic Ocean marks the most westerly point of England. It stands at the end of Cornwall's Penwith peninsula, at the far end of mainland Britain from John O'Groats. The Cornish name for the place is Pen an Wlas, or 'end of the earth'.

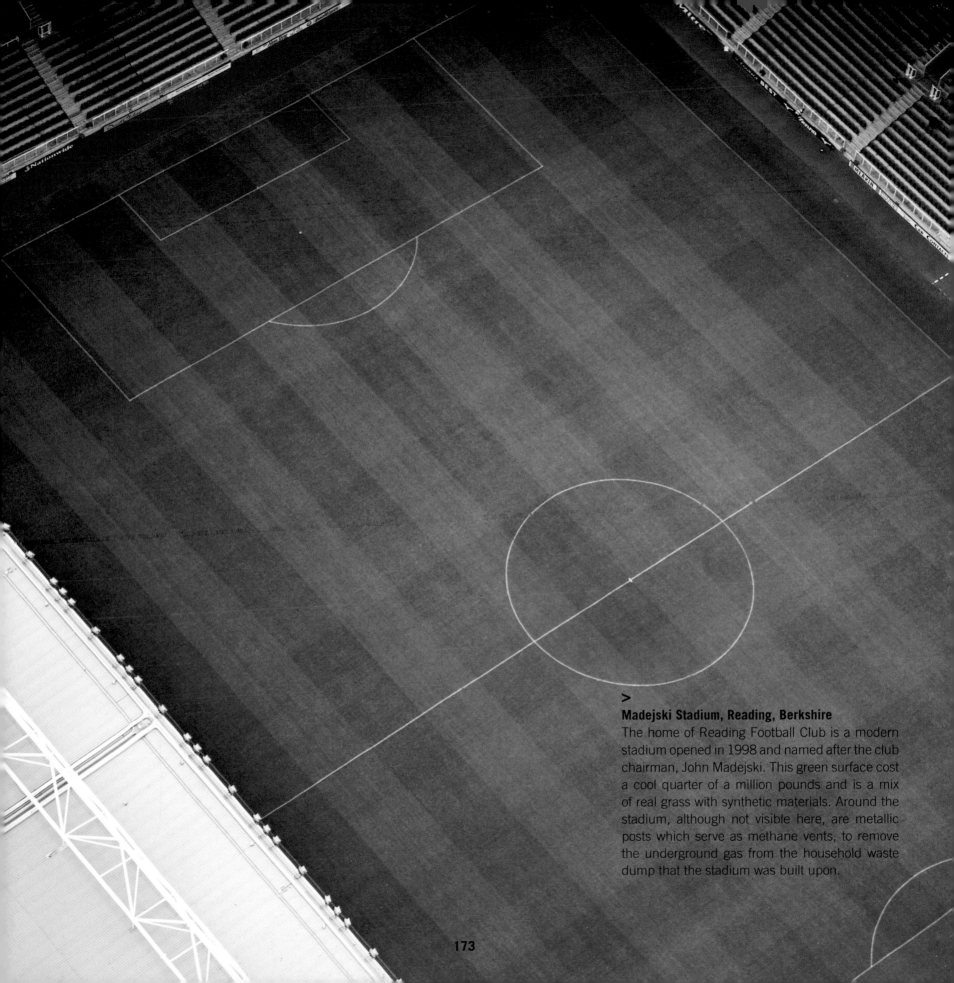

> **Madejski Stadium, Reading, Berkshire**
The home of Reading Football Club is a modern stadium opened in 1998 and named after the club chairman, John Madejski. This green surface cost a cool quarter of a million pounds and is a mix of real grass with synthetic materials. Around the stadium, although not visible here, are metallic posts which serve as methane vents, to remove the underground gas from the household waste dump that the stadium was built upon.

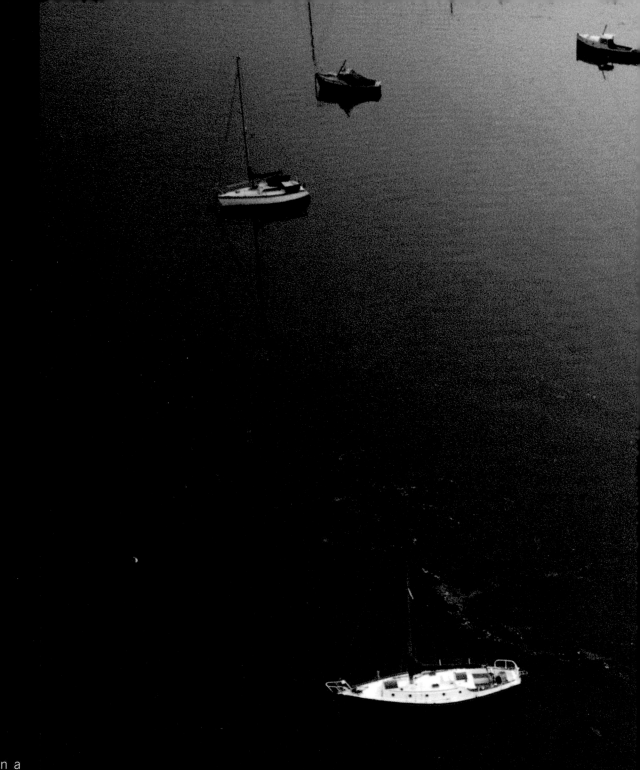

>
Medway Estuary, Kent
The Medway Estuary may look calm and, in a way, monotonous: nothing more than a few boats and a great expanse of water. However, like all estuaries it is teeming with wildlife, on its shores, in the water, and beneath the estuary bed. Even the water balance is unusual, with varying degrees of salinity, and the sheltered nature of part of the estuary provides a safe haven for fish to spawn and for young fish to grow.

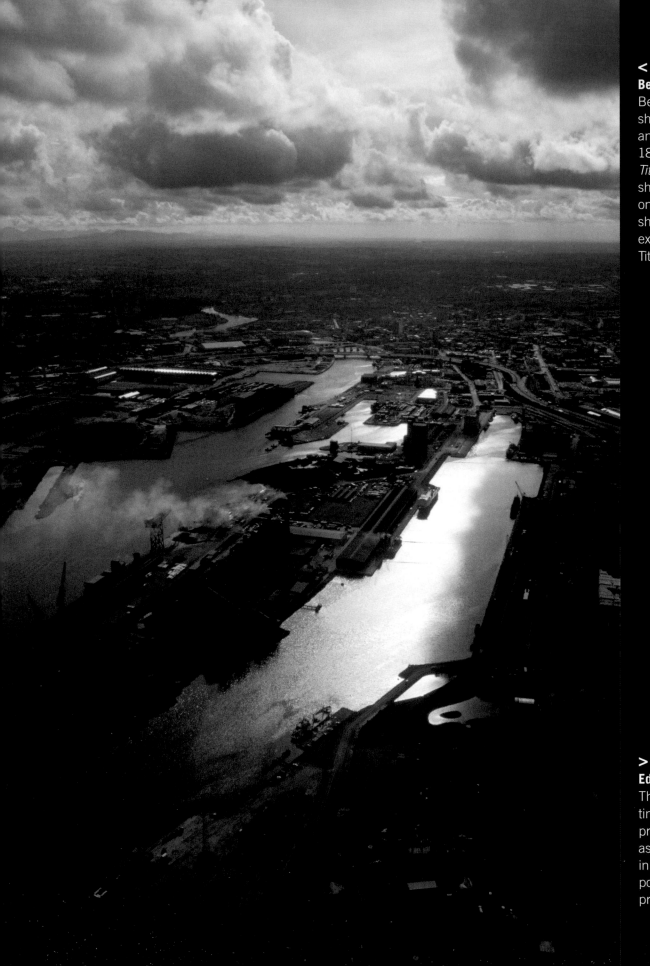

< LEFT
Belfast, County Antrim
Belfast has a long and proud tradition of shipbuilding, through names such as Harland and Wolff, a company which was founded in 1861. Their most famous ship was, alas, the *Titanic*, though what proved to be a monumental shipping disaster has been confronted head-on by modern Belfast and the area where the shipyards were located, Queen's Island, is being extensively developed and has been renamed the Titanic Quarter.

> OPPOSITE
Eden Project, Cornwall
This view of Cornwall's Eden Project is perfectly timed to catch the transition stage between its previous existence as a clay pit and its future as one of the most popular visitor attractions in Britain. The Eden Project brings millions of pounds a year into the Cornish economy, which is pretty impressive for one humble gravel pit.

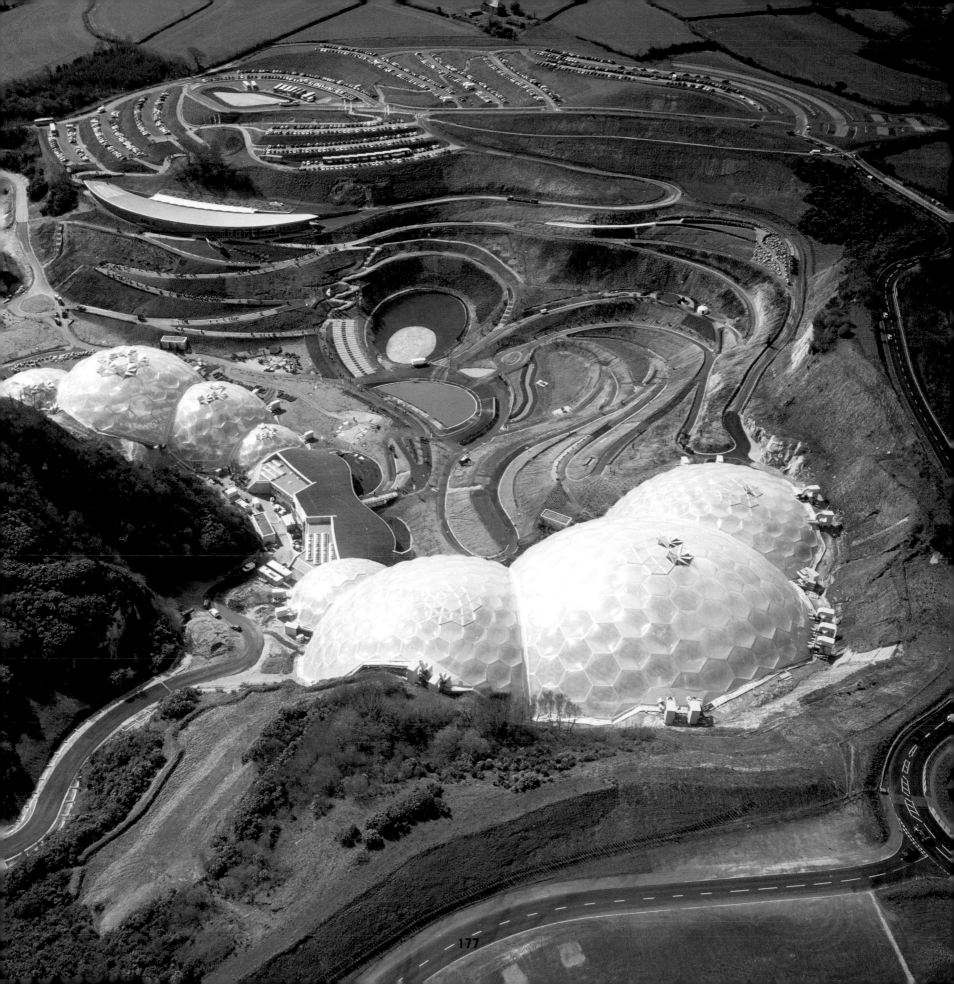

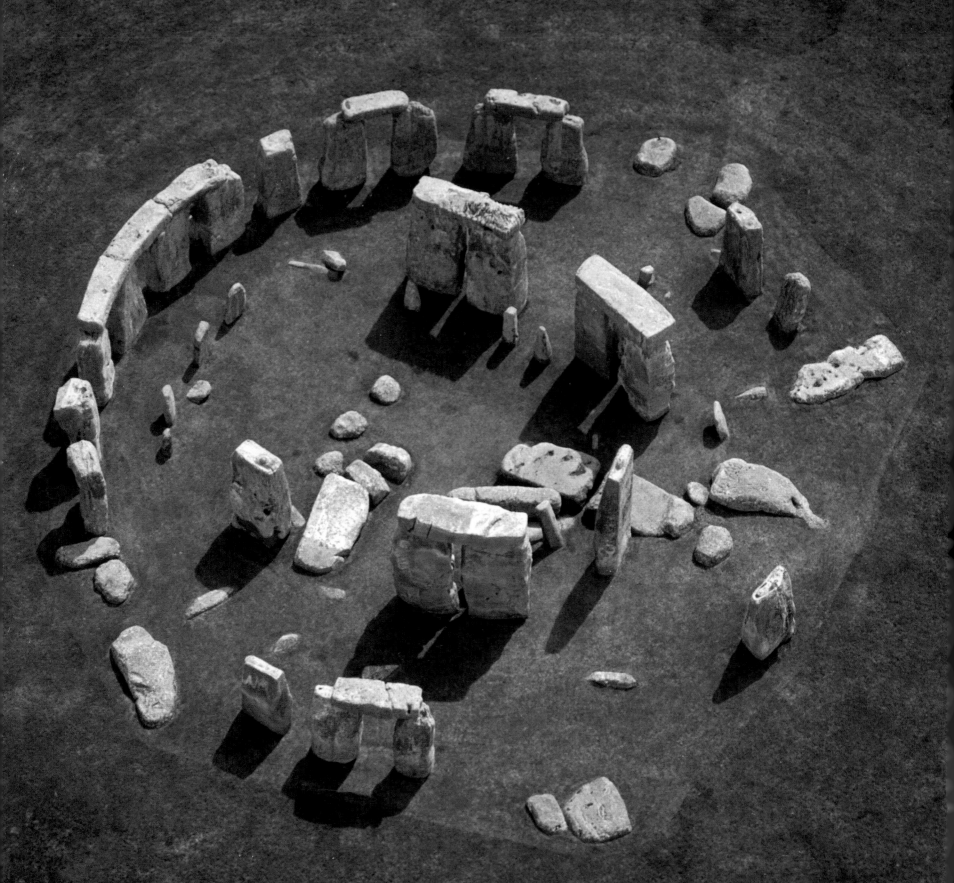

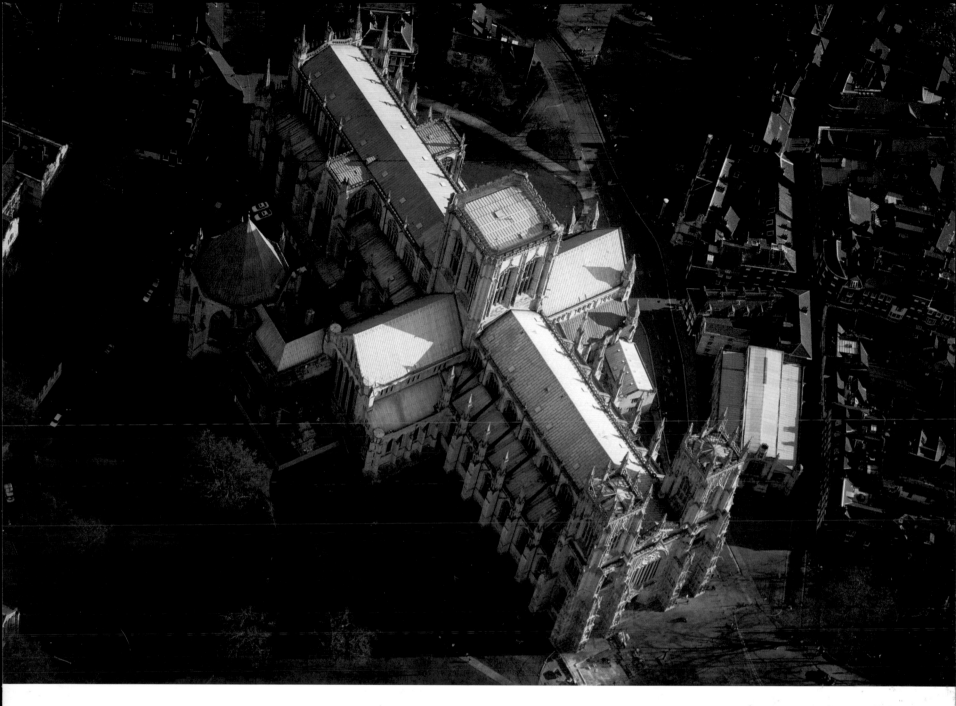

< OPPOSITE
Stonehenge, Wiltshire

For 5,000 years visitors have been coming to Stonehenge, but few are privileged enough to see this hawk's eye view, showing the layout and inviting more speculation as to the origins of the site. Why did people come here, so many thousands of years ago? Why did men labour for a few thousand years to build and maintain Stonehenge? How were the stones hauled and kept upright, and brought 245 miles (380km) from the Prescelli Mountains in South Wales? Perhaps the truth will always remain out of reach.

^ ABOVE
York Minster, Yorkshire

The Archbishop of York is second only to the Archbishop of Canterbury in the Church of England hierarchy, and York Minster is the largest Gothic cathedral in northern Europe. Its long history goes back to the 7th century, when a wooden church was built on the same site. There were several churches and changes until work on the present building began in 1220, and it was deliberately designed to rival Canterbury Cathedral.

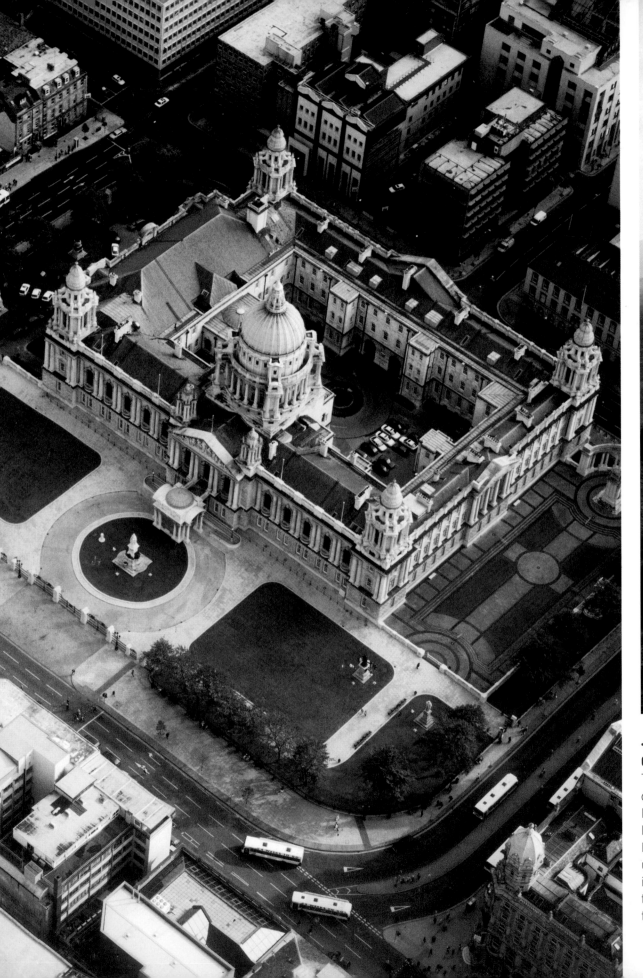

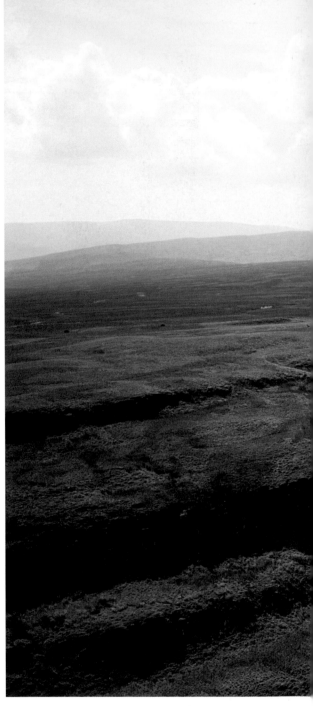

< **LEFT**
City Hall, Belfast
The impressive and imposing Belfast City Hall was deliberately built in this grand manner to reflect Belfast's new importance, having been made a city by Queen Victoria in 1888. Plans for the City Hall began immediately, although work didn't begin until 1898, and it was another eight years before it was finished. The interior is remarkable enough to justify regular guided tours for the public, even though it is still the working City Hall.

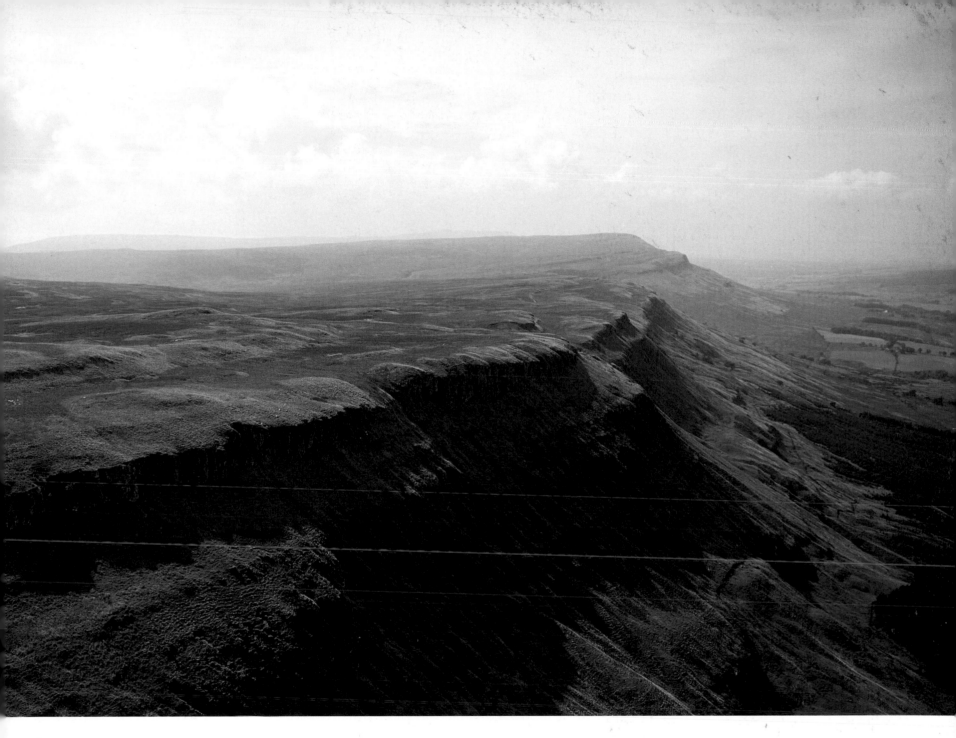

^ **ABOVE**

Gargunnock Hills, Stirling

The serene landscape of the Gargunnock Hills near Stirling gives no idea of the violent volcanic eruptions that created them some 340 million years ago. Nor does it suggest that they are only about thirty miles from the centre of Glasgow. The Gargunnock Hills today seem to belong to their own time, and their own space.

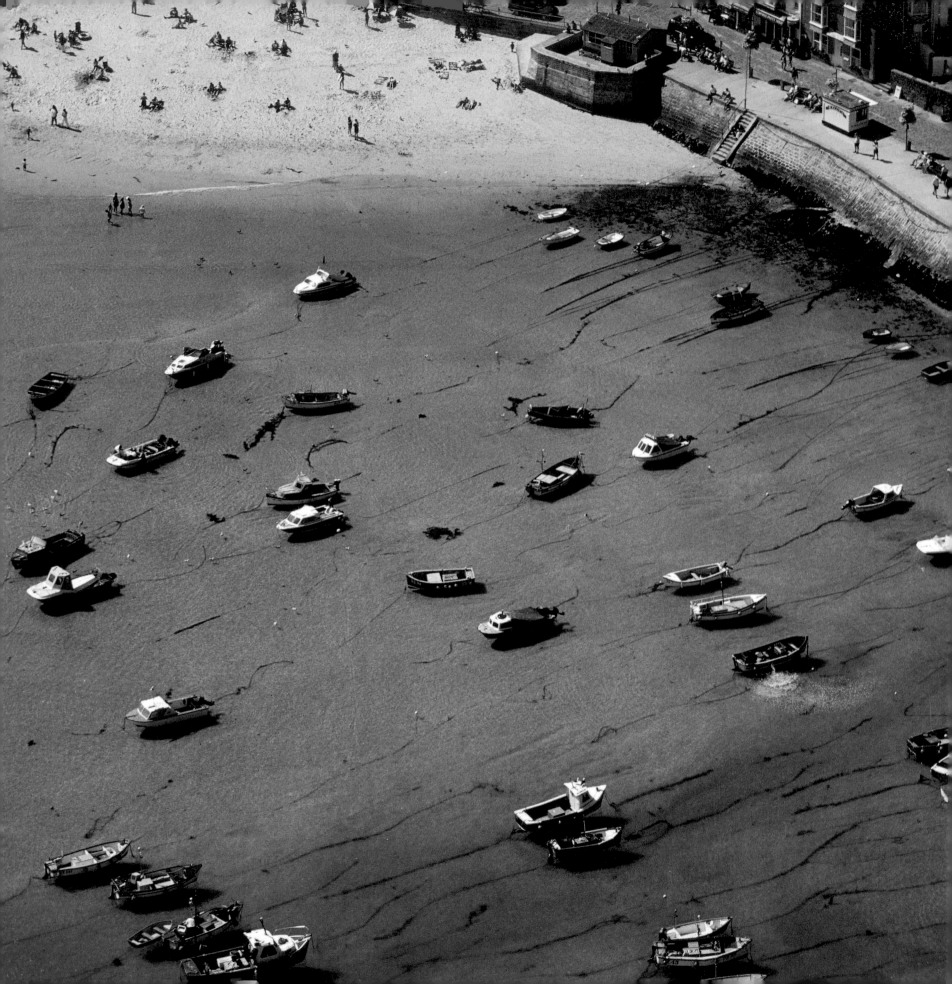

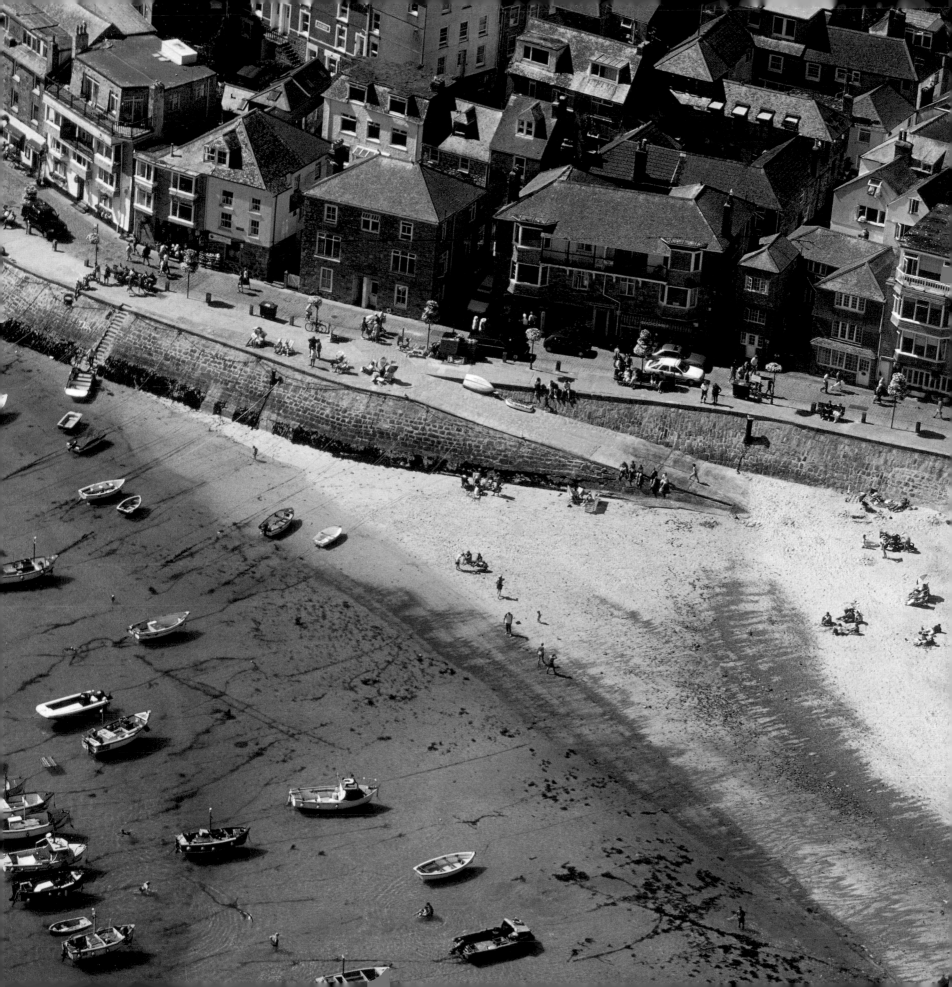

« PREVIOUS
St Ives, Cornwall

Little wonder that the pretty coastal town of St Ives in Cornwall has attracted so many artists over the years. From more recent names such as Barbara Hepworth, Patrick Heron, Bernard Leach and Ben Nicholson to earlier residents and visitors who include Sickert, Turner and Whistler. Today the town is still an intriguing mix of the bohemian artist and the mass tourist.

> RIGHT
Yorkshire Dales

The glacial valleys formed during the Ice Age have become the green and rolling Yorkshire Dales, one of Britain's National Parks. Famous dales like Wensleydale tend to overshadow the quieter dales like Arkengarthdale, whose harsh name harks back to Viking origins. It means Arken's enclosure in the valley, a dale simply being a valley.

> OPPOSITE
Wimbledon, London

The tennis courts at Wimbledon have evolved to their present state since The Championships were first held here in 1922. Today, from above, they look suitably theatrical, for the dramas played out here at the end of June every year.

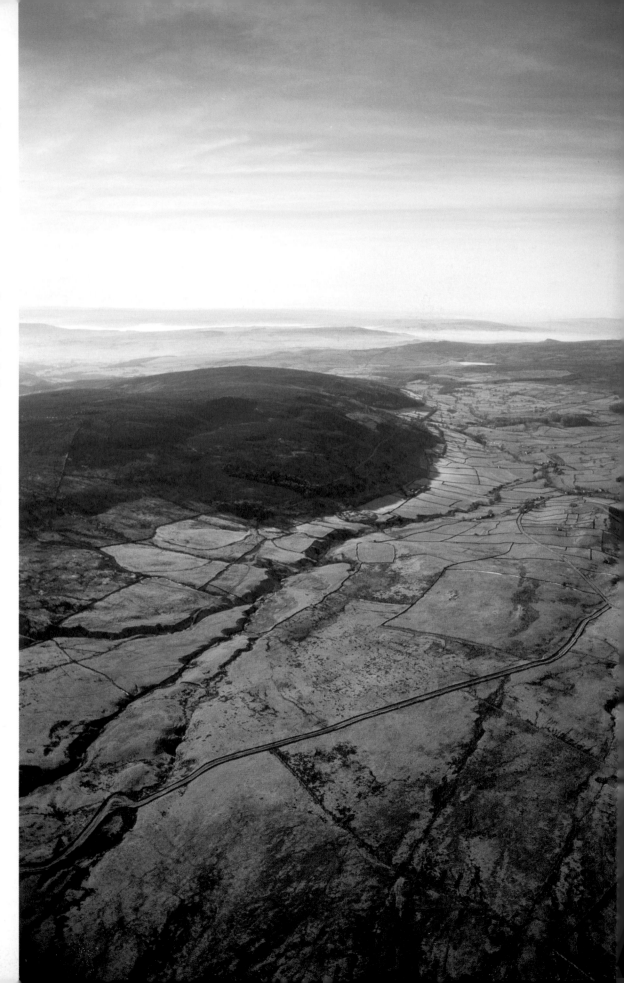

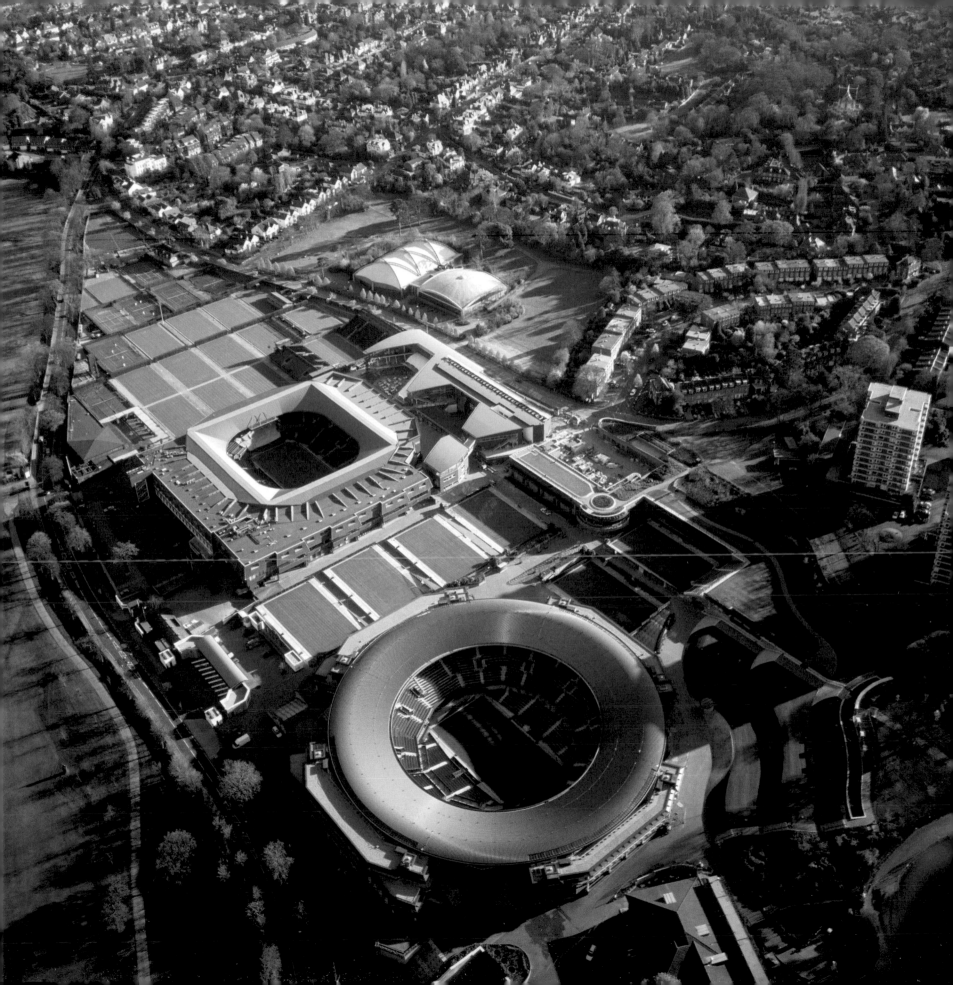

Polperro, Cornwall

Perfect Polperro would be one description of the Cornish fishing port on an English summer's day, and for several hundred years it was a perfect place for smugglers, bringing untaxed goods ashore off the rugged south Cornish coast. Parts of the South West Coastal Path, which goes by Polperro, originated through Customs and Excise officers patrolling up and down the coast in search of boats and hidden bays.

Edinburgh Castle

Like the Acropolis rock which dominates Athens, the rock on which Edinburgh Castle stands dominates the Scottish capital. Its significance is even better appreciated from the air than from on the ground, amid the thousands of daily visitors who swarm around it. Castle Rock has been inhabited since at least the 9th century BC, and here today visitors come to see such historic items as the Crown Jewels and the Stone of Destiny, the coronation stone of the Scottish monarchs.

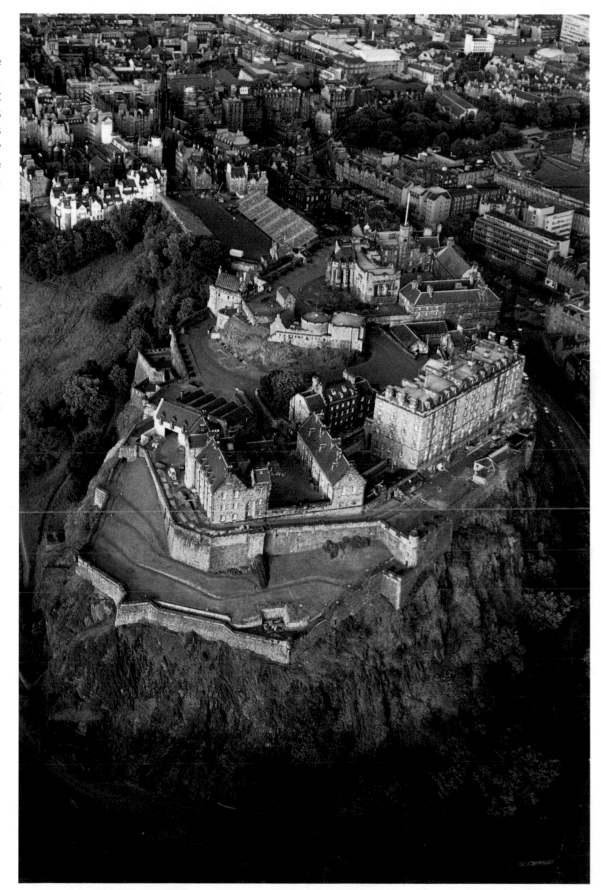

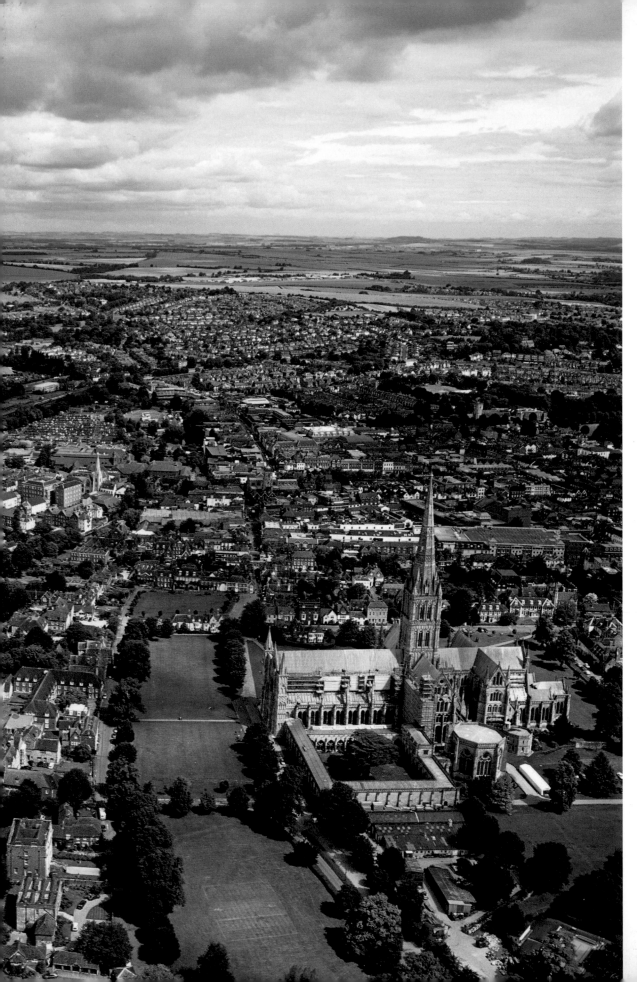

< **LEFT**
Salisbury, Wiltshire

Five rivers meet at Salisbury, making it an inevitable place for settlers to live. The first inhabitants have been traced back to the Iron Age, and later it was an important Roman town. It has also been a cathedral town since the 11th century, and it is easy to see from this perspective how the church dominates not just the town but the surrounding flat landscape.

> **OPPOSITE**
Cattle, Norfolk

Cows and their calves meet at the junction of four fields in the Norfolk countryside. The simple but clever arrangement of gates allows the farmer to get his herds from any one field into any of the other fields, by opening and closing the gates in different combinations.

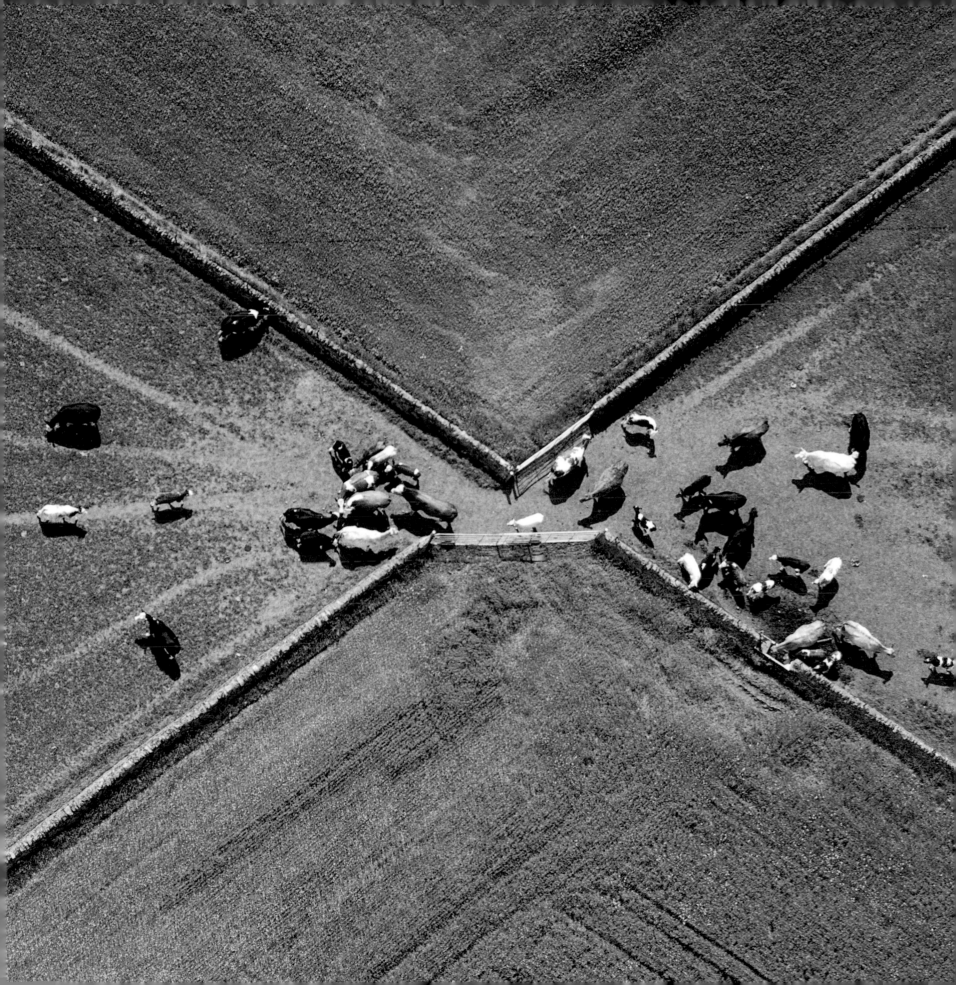

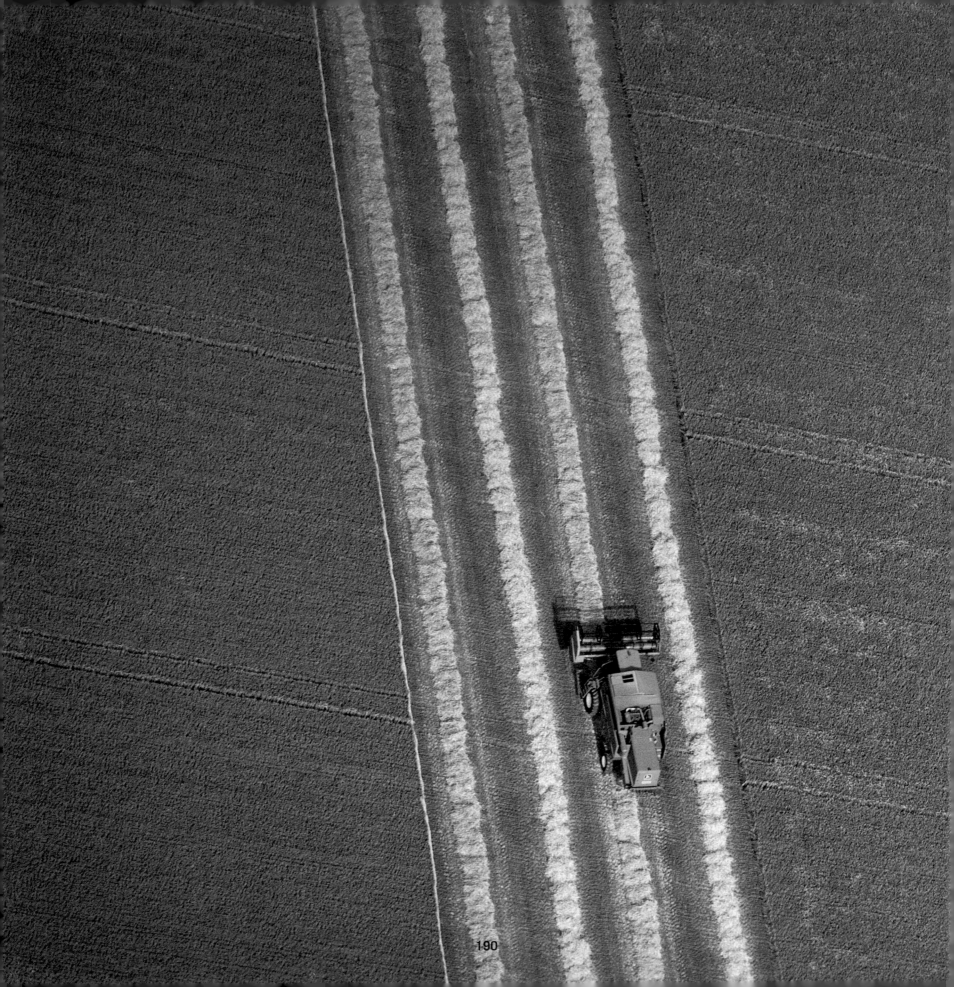

191

>
Combine harvester, Leicestershire
Agriculture, which literally means the cultivation of the fields, has existed for at least 12,000 years. Apart from machines like the combine harvester, which was invented in 1834, the work of tilling the land has changed very little. As the population grows, so too do the farms and the fields, and here in Leicestershire in the very heart of England, the job of feeding the nation remains that of one man, out working the land.

INDEX